HIEROGLYPHICS

The Writings of Ancient Egypt

MARIA CARMELA BETRÒ

HIEROGLYPHICS

The Writings of Ancient Egypt

ABBEVILLE PRESS PUBLISHERS
NEW YORK LONDON PARIS

The images in this volume are from the Mondadori Archive.

English edition:
Translated by S. Amanda George
Edited by Leslie J. Bockol
Cover designed by Molly Shields

First published in the United States of America in 1996 by Abbeville Press,
488 Madison Avenue, New York, N.Y. 10022.

Printed and bound in Spain by Artes Gráficas Toledo, S.A.
D.L.TO: 968-1996

First edition
10 9 8 7 6 5 4 3 2 1

ISBN 0–7892–0232–8

TABLE OF CONTENTS

Key to the Notes

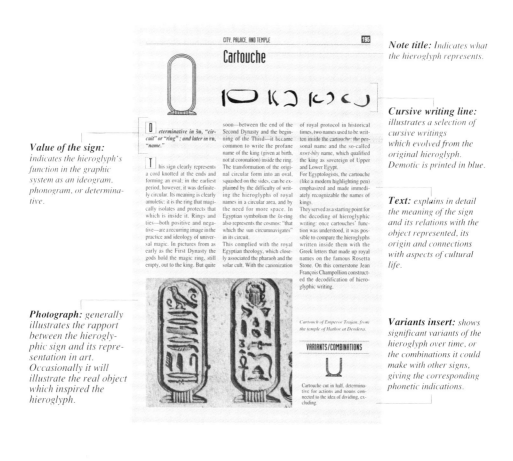

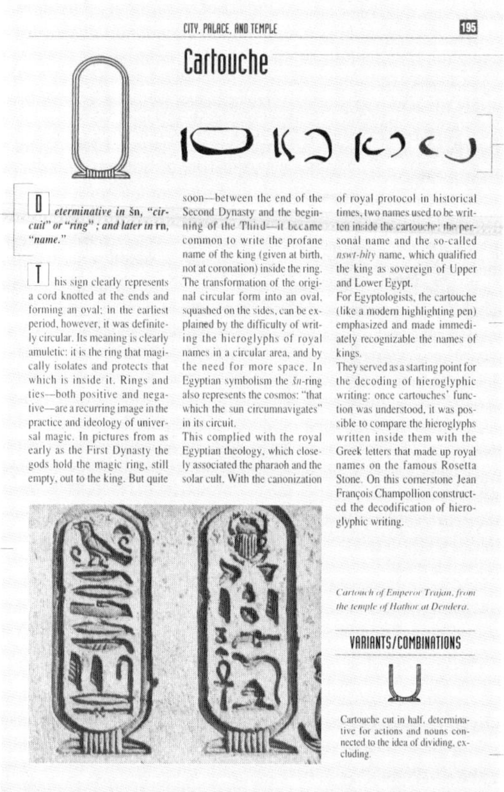

CITY, PALACE, AND TEMPLE 195

Cartouche

D ***eterminative in* šn*, "circuit" or "ring"; and later in* rn*, "name."***

T his sign clearly represents a cord knotted at the ends and forming an oval; in the earliest period, however, it was definitely circular. Its meaning is clearly amuletic: it is the ring that magically isolates and protects that which is inside it. Rings and ties—both positive and negative—are a recurring image in the practice and ideology of universal magic. In pictures from as early as the First Dynasty the gods hold the magic ring, still empty, out to the king. But quite soon—between the end of the Second Dynasty and the beginning of the Third—it became common to write the profane name of the king (given at birth, not at coronation) inside the ring. The transformation of the original circular form into an oval, squashed on the sides, can be explained by the difficulty of writing the hieroglyphs of royal names in a circular area, and by the need for more space. In Egyptian symbolism the *šn*-ring also represents the cosmos: "that which the sun circumnavigates" in its circuit.

This complied with the royal Egyptian theology, which closely associated the pharaoh and the solar cult. With the canonization of royal protocol in historical times, two names used to be written inside the cartouche: the personal name and the so-called *nswt-bity* name, which qualified the king as sovereign of Upper and Lower Egypt.

For Egyptologists, the cartouche (like a modern highlighting pen) emphasized and made immediately recognizable the names of kings.

They served as a starting point for the decoding of hieroglyphic writing: once cartouches' function was understood, it was possible to compare the hieroglyphs written inside them with the Greek letters that made up royal names on the famous Rosetta Stone. On this cornerstone Jean François Champollion constructed the decodification of hieroglyphic writing.

Cartouch of Emperor Trajan, from the temple of Hathor at Dendera.

VARIANTS/COMBINATIONS

Cartouche cut in half, determinative for actions and nouns connected to the idea of dividing, excluding.

Value of the sign: *indicates the hieroglyph's function in the graphic system as an ideogram, phonogram, or determinative.*

Photograph: *generally illustrates the rapport between the hieroglyphic sign and its representation in art. Occasionally it will illustrate the real object which inspired the hieroglyph.*

Note title: *Indicates what the hieroglyph represents.*

Cursive writing line: *illustrates a selection of cursive writings which evolved from the original hieroglyph. Demotic is printed in blue.*

Text: *explains in detail the meaning of the sign and its relations with the object represented, its origin and connections with aspects of cultural life.*

Variants insert: *shows significant variants of the hieroglyph over time, or the combinations it could make with other signs, giving the corresponding phonetic indications.*

This book concentrates its attention on hieroglyphs. The forms given in cursive—hieratic and demotic—for each sign are intended only as examples and do not cover the broad range of writings that appear in diverse epochs, schools, and types of documents. When possible, examples have been provided from the various epochs, starting with the oldest hieratic writing closest to the hieroglyph, and leading up to the later forms. Demotic writings (printed in blue) follow the hieratic on the page, even though they are frequently contemporary with or even older than the later hieratic variants. Variants of the demotic writings—at least one archaic and one later (usually Ptolemaic or from the early Roman period)—are generally given as well. When the hieratic and/or demotic presents the cursive form of the hieroglyph in combination with other signs, so that it is impossible to isolate it, the "tied" writing is preceded by the combination of hieroglyphic signs from which it is derived. Hieratic writings have been drawn from G. Möller's plates (3 vols., Leipzig 1909-12). Unfortunately, a similar source for demotic is still lacking, so the necessary research has been done by the author, using published demotic texts.

Preface

"A hieroglyphic inscription appears chaotic; nothing is in its place; everything is out of proportion; things opposed in nature are in immediate contact and produce monstrous alliances: nevertheless changeable rules, meditated combinations, a calculated and systematic method have undoubtedly guided the hand that drew this picture which seems so disorderly. These characters, so very diversified in their forms are, however, signs that record a regular series of ideas, express a fixed and continuous sense, and thus constitute real writing."

(J.F. Champollion,
Précis du système hiéroglyphique des anciens Egyptiens, II ed. 1828)

Jean François Champollion, the man who deciphered hieroglyphic writing, finally restored its true character with this statement, freeing it of allegory and symbolic apparatus. But he also accurately expressed the discomfort hieroglyphic texts may cause in those who are not accustomed to them.

This illustrated volume contains a global repertory of the culture of the Pharaohs in its notes on the hieroglyphs. The realistic signs of hieroglyphic writing are accompanied by the elegant calligraphy of hieratic and the hard-to-recognize stylizations of demotic, as well as by images drawn from paintings and bas-reliefs. Together, these provide an iconographic inventory of the world of the Nile Valley's ancient inhabitants.

Through the author's rich observations, the signs of "the sacred writing"—phonetic and ideogrammatic, phonograms and determinatives—have gained an undeniable attractiveness. In an ingenious and pleasant new manner, this book re-introduces that arid list which appears at the end of A.H. Gardiner's *Egyptian Grammar*, well-known to generations of Egyptology students.This new list can now serve as a useful tool for students, as well as for others interested in the culture and life of ancient Egypt.

The attractive anatomy of the hieroglyphic writing will also encourage appreciation of how the ancient Egyptians communicated through their complicated and conservative writing. Not only did they record every aspect of their political, legal, administrative, and religious culture, but also a literature vibrant with every sort of thought, sentiment, meditation, and eternal human aspiration. While this literature is distanced from us by centuries, it is accessible to the modern reader, if only in translation.

Edda Bresciani

A Microcosm in Stone

The hundreds of signs of which the hieroglyphic system is composed (the most commmonly used number about 700) were drawn from the reality which surrounded the Egyptian graphic code's anonymous inventors. Though they are stylized, the colorful sequences on the walls of monuments surviving from that ancient civilization recreate a world that has been lost or greatly modified in the thousands of intervening years. Birds strut or fly, though they have either become extinct or migrated to distant lands; objects familiar to those who lovingly inscribed and painted them keep the secrets of their use; men, women, and children dressed in exotic costume offer us their immobile profiles, or hurry towards unknown goals. A microcosm frozen in stone, these moments from thousands of years of history have been extracted from the ephemera of existence and fixed for us, like the footprints of a dinosaur in rock. Hieroglyphics offer a two-fold key to deciphering the distant world which this book proposes to illustrate. First, they are the graphic expression of the ancient Egyptian language. Since they were decoded they have provided access to Egypt's textual heritage, a many-sided mirror through which we can observe and try to understand that antique civilization. Second, they function as photographs of the environment and society of five thousand years ago. They are cultural fossils, charming traces of a world and a culture that is little by little being recomposed by Egyptology.

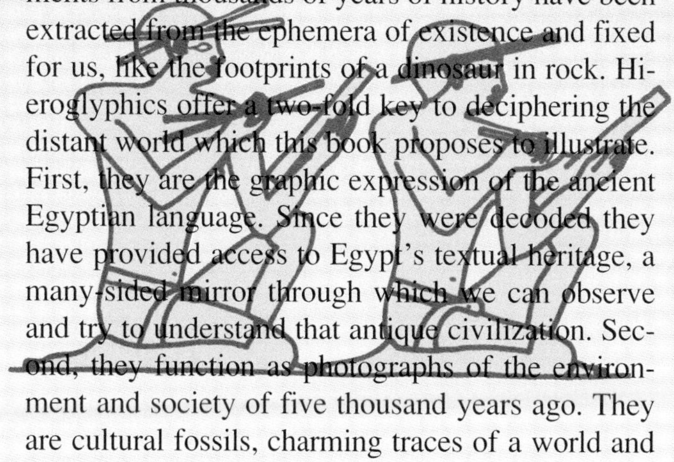

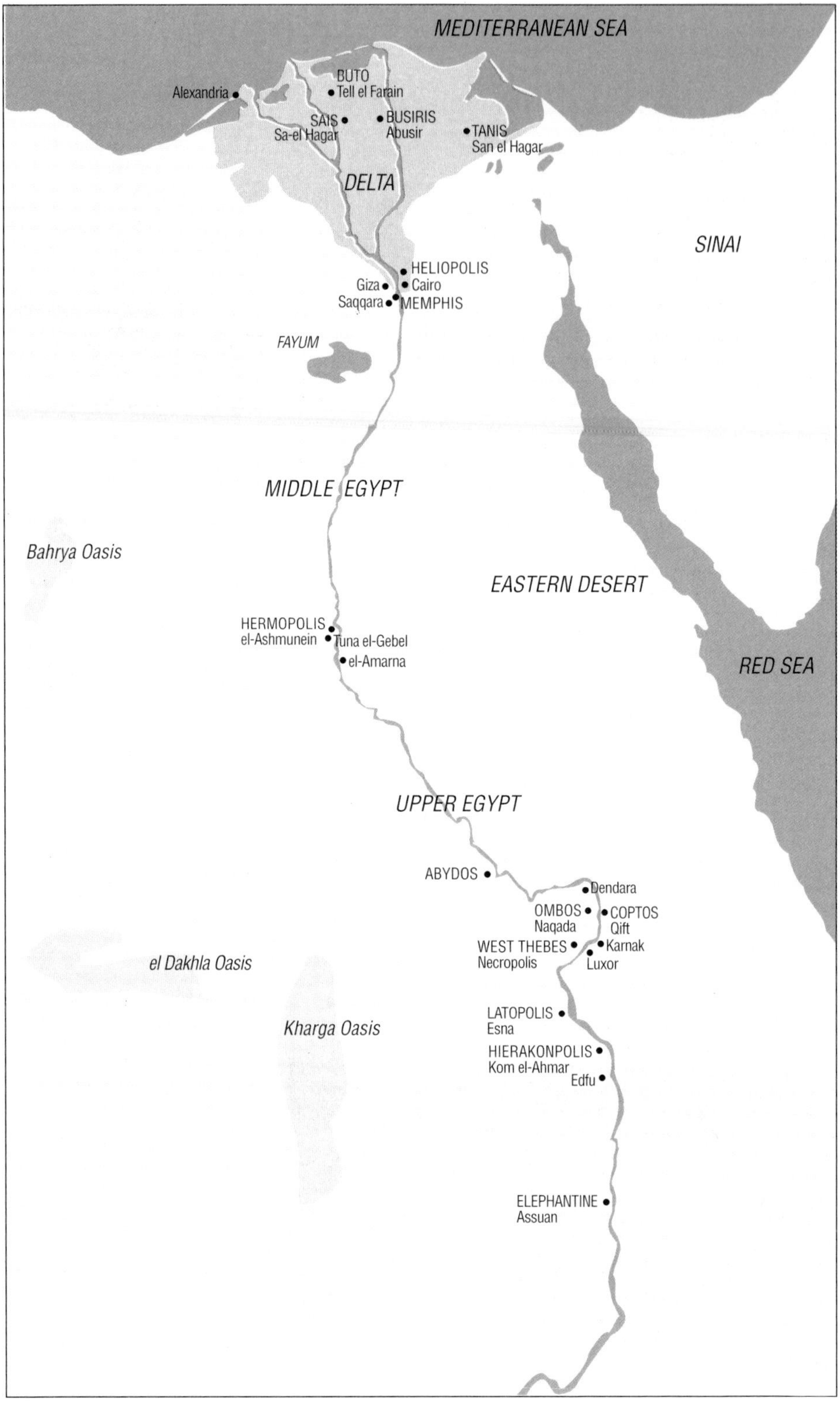
MEDITERRANEAN SEA
BUTO
Tell el Farain
Alexandria
SAIS
Sa-el Hagar
BUSIRIS
Abusir
TANIS
San el Hagar
DELTA
SINAI
HELIOPOLIS
Giza
Cairo
Saqqara
MEMPHIS
FAYUM
MIDDLE EGYPT
Bahrya Oasis
EASTERN DESERT
HERMOPOLIS
el-Ashmunein
Tuna el-Gebel
el-Amarna
RED SEA
UPPER EGYPT
ABYDOS
Dendara
OMBOS
Naqada
COPTOS
Qift
WEST THEBES
Necropolis
Karnak
Luxor
el Dakhla Oasis
LATOPOLIS
Esna
Kharga Oasis
HIERAKONPOLIS
Kom el-Ahmar
Edfu
ELEPHANTINE
Assuan

The Origins

Many millennia passed between the first appearance of wall paintings (c. 30,000 B.C.) and the first known instances of writing (c. 3,300 B.C., in the southern Mesopotamian civilization of Sumeria). Both express a similar need for communication, but the nature of the methods are fundamentally different. Drawings and signs describe objects, states of mind, and events; writing expresses the word and defines the spoken language. It was certainly a long and laborious process to reach that extreme form of abstraction in which the object or the action was no longer represented by a sign but instead was evoked by pure sound. The first Sumerian written evidence is still fundamentally pictographic. Only around 3,000 B.C. does the passage to phonetics become complete.

Writing appears in Egypt around this time (c. 3,150 B.C.), contemporary with the series of kings—Scorpion, Ka, and Narmer—who reigned over a united Egypt before the First Dynasty. These sovereigns are confused in the lists of kings under the general label of the original semi-divine kings, whose presence has been confirmed by archaeology. Although it is archaic and rudimentary, the Egyptian writing of this time differs from the Sumeric tablets in that it has all the characteristics of the mature hieroglyphic system. The already fixed code recapitulates a nearly complete panoply of alphabetic and multiconsonantal signs, as well as the other categories of graphemes: ideograms, and determinatives (classifying signs which have no phonetic value).

The Sumerian texts let us follow the first stuttering steps of a graphic system searching for its own identity. We can note the perfection and development of an idea originally conceived to satisfy the practical demands of arithmetic and commerce. Egyptian hieroglyphic writing, however, seems to break into history as a divine gift, ready for use. Perhaps the Egyptian sands still hide the texts that will one

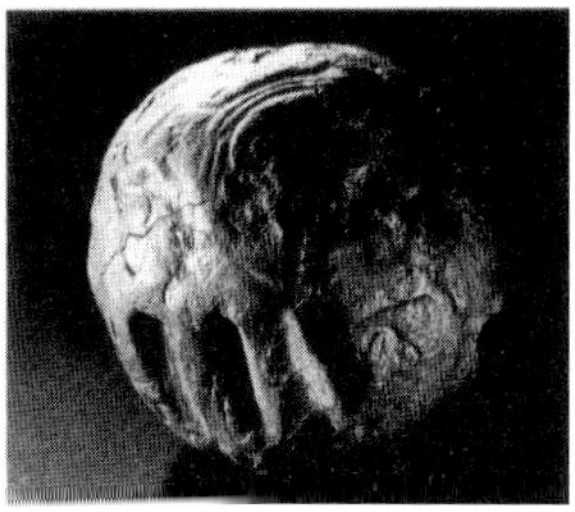

Above: *Sumerian Bulla with the tokens (calculi) that it contained. From Habuba Kabira, Syria, 3,200–3,100 B.C. Museum of Aleppo. It seems that the Sumerians developed the idea of writing from their custom of impressing the surface of these spherical terracotta containers with signs in the number and in the form of the tokens inside; tokens were symbolic representations of the number of objects exchanged in a commercial transaction.*

Left: *"Tokens" of a different shape, from Tell'Atij, Syria. Third millennium B.C. Museum of Deir-ez-Zor.*

Facing page: *Small map of Egypt with the names of the principal sites mentioned in the book.*

Above: *Fragment of a large wine amphora with the name of king Semerkhet clumsily inscribed; it is enclosed in a scalloped oval, which probably indicates the estate from which the wine came. From Abydos, First Dynasty. Paris, Louvre Museum.*

Above right: *This cuneiform tablet fragment from Uruk in Mesopotamia (now Warka, Iraq) carries one of the most ancient known texts. The repetition of columns of signs probably means that it is a fragment of an accounting record. Second half of the fourth millennium B.C. Baghdad, Iraq Museum.*

day allow us to trace the obscure evolution of this fascinating graphic code; or perhaps in those remote times perishable papyrus was already in use for the early experiments, intact rolls of papyrus were in fact found in a First Dynasty tomb at Saqqara. Archaeologists have uncovered much information about those formerly little-known epochs in the last few decades, Today's most credited theories about the birth of writing in Egypt will soon have to be re-examined.

Right: *Ivory tablet of King Den. From Abydos, First Dynasty. London, British Museum. Many ivory labels of this type were found in the burial places of the first kings. The recording of important events of the kingdom functioned as a dating system. In this example, ideograms, monoconsonant and multiconsonant signs are already present and used according to the classical rules.*

Based on current research, though, the precedence of Sumerian writing (however slight) and the fact that the first Egyptian written texts appear in a period rife with objects, styles, and motifs borrowed from the Mesopotamian and proto-Elamitic cultures suggests that the idea of the writing came from the same source. (The Elamites flourished in what is now Khuzistan.) This is no more than an assumption, however. From the outset, hieroglyphic writing seems to be deeply rooted in the Egyptian culture and reality and is substantially different in its structural principles from Sumerian writing.

The repertoire of hieroglyphic signs, the majority of which can already be found in archaic inscriptions, is itself derived from an indigenous tradition. The study of the oldest hieroglyphs are a gold mine of anthropological information about the more remote phases of the formation of Egyptian civilization, and frequently paleography and archaeology are mutually illuminating. It is possible that the anonymous scribes who defined the hieroglyphic code drew from the predynastic stylistic tradition, which had perfected elaborate canons of representation in the preceding centuries.

The American scholar Arnett (1982) has hypothesized that the stylized signs and ornamental motifs which decorate the predynastic ceramics constitute the elements of a rudimentary script—but enticing as it may be, this theory can not yet be proven.

But why would the Egyptians have decided to adopt a Mesopotamian invention? Many answers to this query have been offered, some of which are not fully satisfactory, while others are to be rejected out of hand. Earlier speculations included an invasion of Egypt from the east, which would have brought this new technique of writing along with real civilization. A more credible theory is that trade relations brought restless Sumerian entrepreneurs to the ports and countries of the ancient Orient, distributing their art, culture, and perhaps the concept or technique of writing along with their merchandise.

In either case, the growing new Egyptian state (formed in the second half of the fourth millennium B.C.) began to need a means of recording the complex activities of its public administration. Among the oldest examples of hieroglyphic inscriptions are names of royal properties, engraved in the bodies of large amphoras that contained the foodstuffs produced on these estates. On other vessels, the name of the sovereign and the contents of the vase are written.

Above: *This vase, decorated with the sign of a scorpion, probably contained wine or oil imported from Canaan—perhaps for the tomb of King Scorpion, if the sign in black ink on the belly of the vase is to be read as the name of the king. From the royal necropolis of Abydos. End of the predynastic period (3,150 B.C.). Paris, Louvre Museum.*

Below: *Red decoration on a light background is a distinctive mark of painted ceramics from the Gerzean period, ca. 3,300 B.C. New York, The Metropolitan Musem of Art.*

Hieroglyphic: The Writing of Kings and Gods

While administrative needs were crucial to the development of hieroglyphic writing, they were neither the only nor perhaps the first to use this powerful new technique.

Besides the engraved vases, the first labels, and the amphora covers of humble mud on which the warehouse-keepers' seals were impressed, the necropolises and sites of Upper Egypt have given us an impressive list of other contemporary objects. These consist of stone

This palette, which celebrated the victory of King Narmer over the north, has a style that is already "Pharaonic"—mixing ancient elements (such as the "oriental" motif of fantastic animals with long, sinuous, intertwined necks) with newer motifs (such as the image of a king grabbing an enemy by the hair, or the structuring of hieroglyphs and scenes in ordered sequential rows). From Hierakonpolis, Kom el-Ahmar, ca. 3,150-3,100 B.C. Cairo, Egyptian Museum.

votive palettes decorated with scenes from the royal repertory, for the most part relating to war and conquest, on which the earliest hieroglyphs appear. From the beginning, the beauty and pictographic nature of these signs gave them an expressive quality, even apart from their semantic context. This rendered them particularly appropriate to becoming the language through which the Pharaohs would choose to express their power to the world. Stimulated by the splendor of stone—the essence of monumental material—they were indeed the *medu-neceru*, the "divine words," as the Egyptians called their hieroglyphs, a term which is very similar to the much later Greek translation *ieroglupliikà*.

Furthermore, the Egyptian state was much morc than a bureaucratic organ occupied only with administration. Even at the beginning, the institution was thought by its very nature to be divine. As the state's means of communication, hieroglyphic immediately became a "sacred" script, initially used only by a small elect class who also possessed magical powers. The evocative power of these signs was such that they were considered to possess the property of life: the scribes took care, in the wall inscriptions of the Old Kingdom burial chambers in the pyramids or on sarcophagi, to render the signs harmless. To do this, they represent in a mutilated form those animals or men which might be inimical to the dead, or eliminated them. Even in later epochs, dangerous animals such as crocodiles or serpents were shown with a lance piercing the spine. On the other hand, the hieroglyphs representing desirable qualities, such as longevity, prosperity, or divine protection, were made into valuable and commonly used amulets.

Hieroglyphs, Registers, and Lists: the Coming of Order

The eruption of the hieroglyphic system onto the Egyptian scene accompanied the birth of a new artistic language, to which it was inextricably tied. Together they formed the semantic elements through which the ideology of the newly created state was expressed. In the severe and pure beauty of their stone, the decorated cosmetic palettes of the predynastic era show the fundamental characteristics of the two correlated systems. They demonstrate the courtliness of a graphic language born in a royal ambience and as an expression of royalty, with which is associated the monumentality of Egyptian art and writing. They also reveal a powerful impulse towards order and rigorous scansion of the elements, which the adoption of hieroglyphic writing brought into artistic representation, and into many aspects of cultural and social life as well.

With the first appearance of hieroglyphic signs on votive palettes, where they alternated with images, the elements of representation suddenly became arranged in regular horizontal rows: from then on this was the classic disposition of the scenes of ancient Egypt. The circular or spiral arrangements of the older tablets gave way to sequential

organization. The same order was carried over into mental and social organization: the need to classify reality—which the Egyptians demonstrate in the numerous word lists (called onomastics by Egyptologists) recapitulating the Egyptian experience of life—is accompanied by the interminable administrative tables, inventories, land and fiscal registers which we find in the papyri. These relics are tangible witnesses to the "bureaucratic mentality" that guided the country.
Hieroglyphic was, however, not just a code, made up of abstract signs arbitrarily associated with linguistic meanings. Unlike Sumerian or Chinese signs, hieroglyphic writing conserved its pictorial nature for the whole of its long history. This conditioned the structure of Egyptian thought and culture in a manner different from that of writing systems more distant from their pictographic origins. If it is true that writing restructures thought, it must also be true that writing systems that remain closely tied to the image will have restructured it in a different way than those that are alphabetic or syllabic. The strongly symbolic nature of Egyptian thought must certainly be considered in this light.
In a certain sense, the immediate expressivity of the hieroglyphic image, unlike the discrete neutrality of an abstract alphabetic code, frequently superimposed itself on the hieroglyph's own significance. Sometimes the image interacted with the meaning, sometimes obscuring it or providing a departure point for elaborate philosophical speculation.
The elaboration and enrichment of the graphic aspects of the single hieroglyphs and the continual exploration of the possibilities of writing became the constructive elements of philosophical-religious thought in ancient Egypt. Among the explorations in hieroglyphic writing were variants, new combinations of signs, and graphic puns—all the inexhaustible possibilities, in fact, offered by the two confluent aspects (graphic and phonetic) of a phonogram.

Above: *The circular movement within this image is typical of the phase before the appearance of writing. Predynastic Period (second half of the fourth millennium B.C.). Paris, Louvre Museum.*
Below: *This fragment , known as the "Libya Palette," is an ancient example of the horizontal arrangement which accompanied the introduction of hieroglyphics (the names of the fortified cities). From Abydos, late fourth millennium B.C. Cairo, Egyptian Museum.*

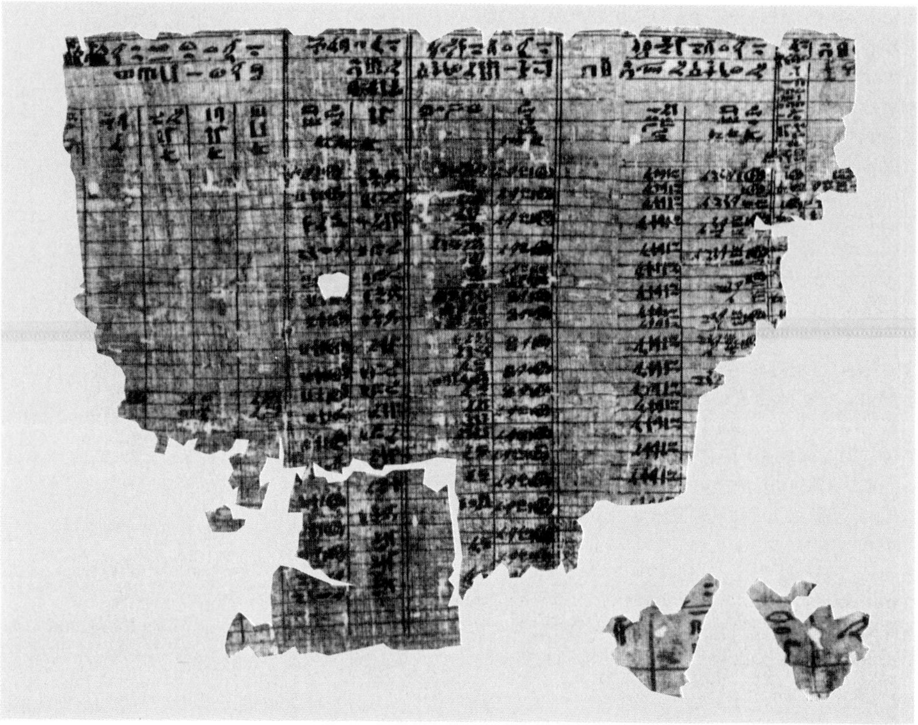

This fragment of a hieratic papyrus, from the archive of the funerary temple of Neferirkare at Abusir, recounts within a grid structure the services rendered by the temple's personnel over a period of thirty-five days. Fifth Dynasty. Paris, Louvre Museum

Writing as an Art

The constant relation between a hieroglyph and its value as an image explains the deep nature of its tie with art. Every hieroglyph may itself be a work of art, as often occurs in writing on monuments. Reciprocally, every artistic object from ancient Egypt should be read and decoded in its elements as a hieroglyphic whole, from which it frequently differs only in dimension.

Hieroglyphic writing is subject to the same rules as figurative representation in ancient Egypt. The little figures of men, animals, and objects which comprise the texts are represented as collections of parts seen from different points of view, alternately full-face, in profile, or in three-quarters profile. It is difficult to say if the texts are reduced-scale reproductions of the large scenes in temples and tombs, or whether these scenes are enlarged hieroglyphic compositions. The illustrations that accompany the notes in this volume are taken from ancient Egyptian artworks, and underline the close relationship between the codifying of the hieroglyph and the equally formalized artistic representation.

Text and image frequently interpenetrate: not rarely, especially in the Old Kingdom, a noble's portrait on a tomb wall functions as the determinative for his own name written nearby; the same occurs with statues, which are three-dimensional determinatives for the name written on the base. Some sculptures are truly three-dimensional hieroglyphs, gigantic stone rebuses. Even the disposition of the hieroglyphs is ornamental: like today's book designers with titles or other elements to be emphasized, ancient scribes could vary the size, spatial arrangement, or orientation of the signs to satisfy aesthetic concerns.

Above: *The versatility and beauty of hieroglyphic writing permitted it to adapt to all types of surfaces, creating charming decorative effects. Ushabti of the vizier Ptahmes, from Abydos. Eighteenth Dynasty. Cairo, Egyptian Museum.*

The Language

The language of the ancient Egyptians belongs to the so-called Hamitic-Semitic family, or as is preferred today, the Afro-Asiatic, which was distributed over a vast area between the Near East and North Africa. These two definitions are equally unsatisfactory; the exact position of Egyptian between Hamitic and Semitic is not easy to define. On one hand, its relation with North-African tongues, essentially Berber, appears much more vague and undefined than the rela-

Left: *Detail of a pilaster from the Sesostris I chapel at Karnak. Twelfth Dynasty. The complete protocol of the king, protected by a vulture and a falcon, give us an impressive example of the Egyptian stoneworkers' art, and of the particular relief style of the Middle Kingdom, with its clean and accentuated edges.*

Above: *Offerings carried by the sea-god in the Sahura temple at Abusir are graphically translated by the hieroglyph* hetep, *which pictures an offering table. Fifth Dynasty. Cairo, Egyptian Museum.*
Below: *In the burial chamber of Tuthmosis III, in the Valley of the Kings at Thebes, the walls of the tomb became a book, treated like a giant unrolled papyrus. Eighteenth Dynasty.*

tion it doubtlessly has with the Semitic language group. On the other hand many of its characteristics are extraneous to the latter group. It is possible that these characteristics came from North-African languages or dialects which have now disappeared entirely.
Hieroglyphic and its cursive forms, first hieratic and then demotic, do not record the presence of vowels. Because of this, it is very difficult to reconstruct the pronunciation of Egyptian and its dialectical varieties, up until the late phase of its evolution and, above all, before the adoption of the Greek alphabet in the first centuries A.D. It is also very difficult to distinguish the complex phenomena related to the changes in verb and noun forms during this period. Much work has been done and a great deal of valuable information has come from studies of Coptic—the later phase of the Egyptian language, which was transcribed into Greek and which obviously supplies the pronounciation only as it was after millennia of evolution. It is not yet possible to reconstruct with certainty the phonetic phenomena affecting the Egyptian language over the centuries, or through the dialect variants that spread over Egypt's broad territory.
Because of these uncertainties, Egyptologists who are transliterating from hieroglyphic customarily indicate the phonetic value for each hieroglyphic sign (without supplying any indication as to the possible presence and type of determinative), and avoid any dubious reconstructions of the real pronounciation of the words. A fictitious conventional pronounciation has been adopted: an e is inserted after every consonant except where the consonants *3* and ʿ occur; in these cases, a (pronounced ah) is inserted. The remaining special transliterations signs are as follows: *ỉ* is i (pronounced ee); *ḥ* is an emphatic h; *ḫ* corresponds to ch in the Scottish loch; *ẖ* is like ch in the German ich; *š* sounds like sh; *ṯ* is like c in Italian ciao; and *ḏ* is like dj.

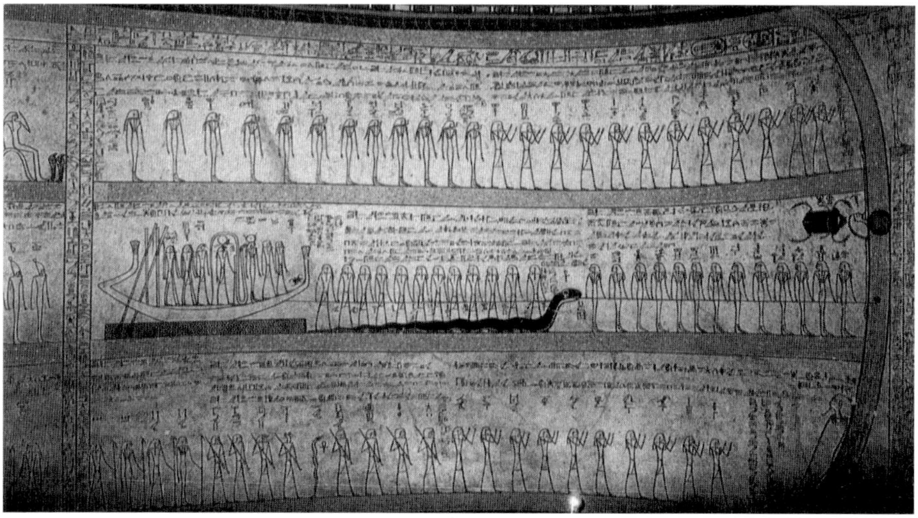

The Principles of Hieroglyphic Writing

For a long time, the European imagination relished fantastic interpretations of the enigmatic (and misleadingly expressive) signs of hieroglyphic writing. They saw a multi-faceted world of sometimes disquieting animals, of hieratic human figures, of objects of unknown function. But the key to this world had been lost in the dark night of the anti-pagan reaction in 391 A.D., when Emperor Theodosius ordered all the ancient Egyptian temples to be closed.
Despite his ruling, a few priests continued to study the arcane scripture: they were the last tenacious custodians of an indigenous tradition which was being slowly suffocated by time and by the needs of the Roman administration in Egypt. Since then, the Western attitude has wavered between extremes—a conviction that hieroglyphic writing really was the divine keeper of universal wisdom, or a scornful aversion.
Anyone attempting to investigate the significance of these signs from a rational approach encountered a dilemma with no apparent solution: there were too many characters to be an alphabet, but too few for them to be representative of concepts.
The explanation obviously lay somewhere between, as Champollion intelligently demonstrated, after the way had been smoothed by the discovery of the "Rosetta Stone." The system was a hybrid, combining ideograms with signs whose function was purely phonetic and completely independent of the image represented.

The eclectic and highly cultured Jesuit, Athanasius Kircher, was an important scholar of ancient Egypt during the Baroque age. Kircher was convinced of the symbolic importance of hieroglyphics, which in his opinion kept the secrets of "the original wisdom."
Reproduced here are two pages from his vast writings on ancient Egypt, one with the reproduction of two fragments of a water-clock and the other dedicated to the goddess Isis.

Above: *Portrait of Jean-François Champollion, painted by Léon Cogniet in 1831. Paris, Louvre Museum.*
Together with Ippolito Rosellini, Champollion guided the Franco-Tuscan expedition to Egypt in 1828, collecting and studying an enormous quantity of hieroglyphic texts, which they then published.

Right: *The famous Rosetta Stone furnished the key to decoding ancient Egyptian writing, since it provided three versions of the same text (in hieroglyphic, demotic, and Greek), from the Ptolemaic age (dated 196 B.C.). London, British Museum.*

Following page: *Neferetiabet's stele, from her* mastaba *at Giza, Fourth Dynasty. Paris, Louvre Museum.*
The detail gives us an example of the articulation of a hieroglyphic text.

The latter included true alphabetical signs (twenty-four in number) alongside signs of pluriconsonantic value (the most common numbering about eighty biliteral and a few triliteral). A special class of ideograms with no phonetic value served to classify words and to eliminate possible ambiguities.

A sign's inclusion in one category or another is neither rigid nor exclusive. A single hieroglyph may function as an ideogram (many scholars prefer to call them "logograms" but I use the more common traditional term), as a phonogram (with no apparent relation to the image evoked by the drawing), and as a determinative.

Note, however, that the Egyptians tended to use a single sign or ideogram for the words derived from a common root. The choice of an image appropriate to represent a whole family of words probably stemmed from the remote historic period in which the tradition of hieroglyphs began. Perhaps it indicated the category's most common object of the time, or the most prestigious, or simply the most immediately recognizable. John Ray (1986) suggests that this classification in terms of roots, whether conscious or not, could explain why the vowels are not noted in writing. This is typical of the hieroglyphic system (as well as Arabic and Hebrew): if vowels do not indicate dif-

Example of a hieroglyphic text

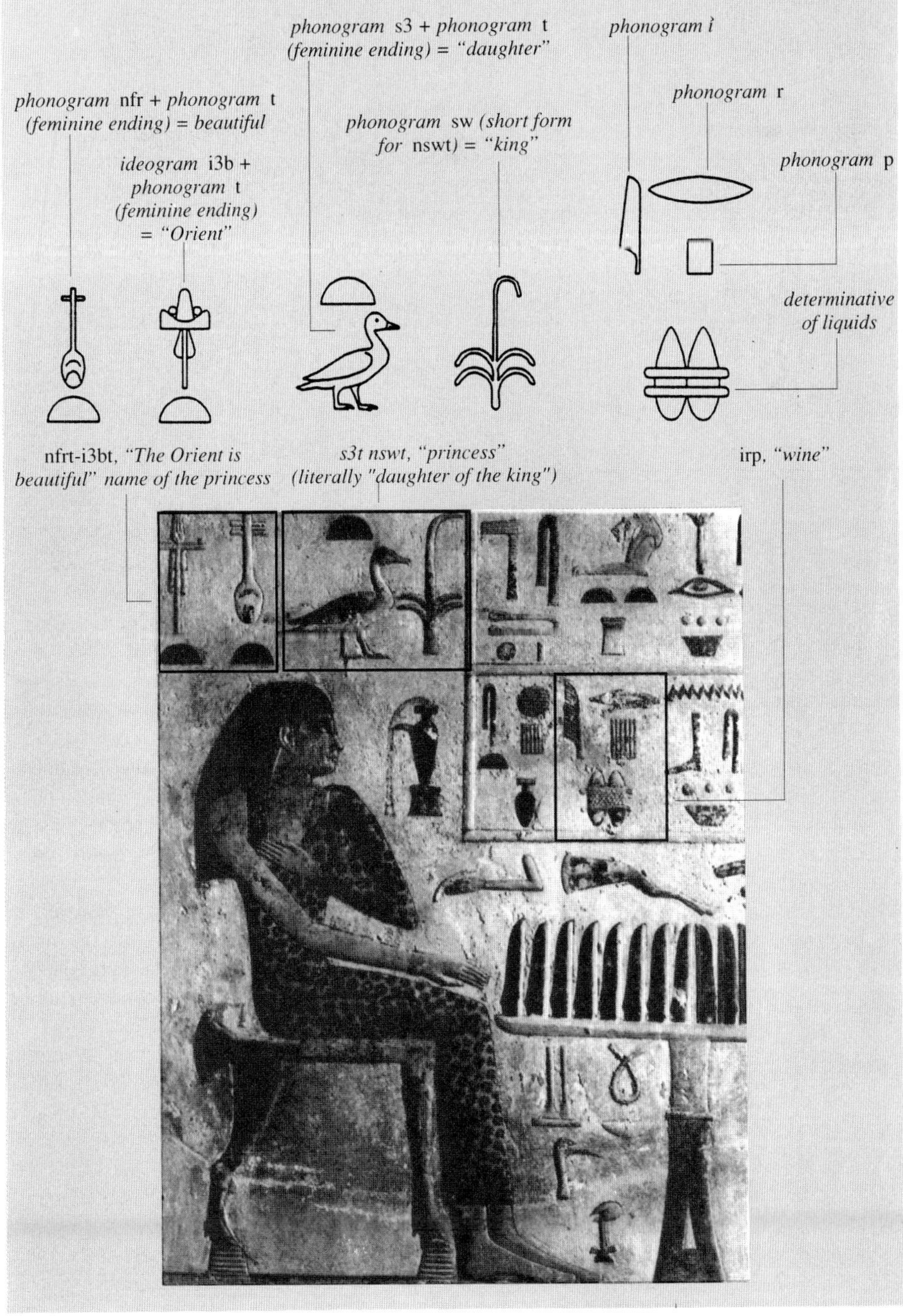
phonogram s3 + phonogram t (feminine ending) = "daughter"
phonogram ỉ
phonogram nfr + phonogram t (feminine ending) = beautiful
phonogram r
phonogram sw (short form for nswt) = "king"
ideogram i3b + phonogram t (feminine ending) = "Orient"
phonogram p
determinative of liquids
nfrt-i3bt, "The Orient is beautiful" name of the princess
s3t nswt, "princess" (literally "daughter of the king")
irp, "wine"

Above: *The names of foreign kings were transcribed by the Egyptians using purely alphabetical signs, as in the Greek name Alexandros on this fragment of a water-clock, transcribed in hieroglyphic* 3-r-k-s-*-n-d-r-s. *End of the fourth century B.C. Paris, Louvre Museum.*

Below: *The twenty-four signs of the Egyptian alphabet with their transcriptions.*

ferences in meaning, they would be irrelevant and thus ignored. This would also explain the need for a class of determinatives, in this case to indicate which of the various homographic words derived from a single root the writer intended. In the hieroglyphic *sy*, determinatives are a useful aid against possible ambiguities. In addition, they help in the scansion of sentences, allowing the reader to distinguish where any given word ends.

The system thus defined was still very imprecise and subject to misunderstandings. The Egyptians attempted to perfect it by inventing uniliteral or "alphabetic" signs. This development was not derived from Mesopotamian writing, and demonstrates the total autonomy of the development of the hieroglyphic system. These alphabetic signs were present from the beginning and were probably obtained by acrophony from the original ideograms. Their function was to offer support for the reading of single ideograms, to add certain grammatical elements to a root, and to allow the transcription of words difficult to render with images (such as prepositions and other grammatical constructions).

The twenty-four alphabetic signs allowed coverage of the entire phonetic range of the language. Even though they were widely used in some periods, the Egyptians never really exploited this intelligent invention because of the ideological characteristics of their writing, as described above. Perhaps it was no accident that these were used in transcribing foreign names (the fortunate starting point for Champollion's decoding), which were perhaps considered unworthy of the magic-evocative power of the more authentic graphic hieroglyphic tradition.

More than twenty-four hundred hieroglyphs have been found in Egyptian texts that date up until the Graeco-Roman era. The count rises to seven thousand if the many variants are included, especially those from the prolific Ptolemaic era. However, signs that recur in the texts, the language, and classic literature of Middle Egypt do not number more than seven hundred. These are indeed those to be found in Sir Alan Gardiner's canonic list for Egyptologists.

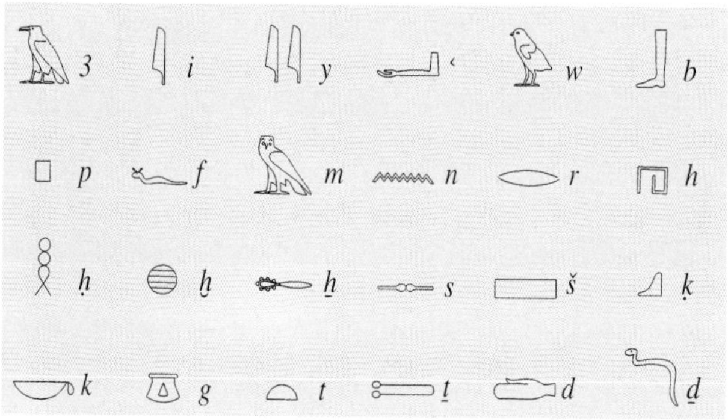

The Gardiner List

The hieroglyphs in this book are a selection drawn from the list of seven hundred signs made by the English Egyptologist Alan Gardiner, an essential point of reference for every student of ancient Egypt. Some signs, included below in the "Gods" section, have been drawn from other sources. The subdivision of this book into eight categories differs from the system adopted by Gardiner, who divided the hieroglyphs into twenty-six classes in order to offer a functional, more homogeneous view of the ancient Egyptian world as it appears in the mirror of its writing. The hieroglyphs from Gardiner's list which appear in this book are highlighted in blue and are accompanied by their page numbers in Gardiner's book, for easy identification and reference.

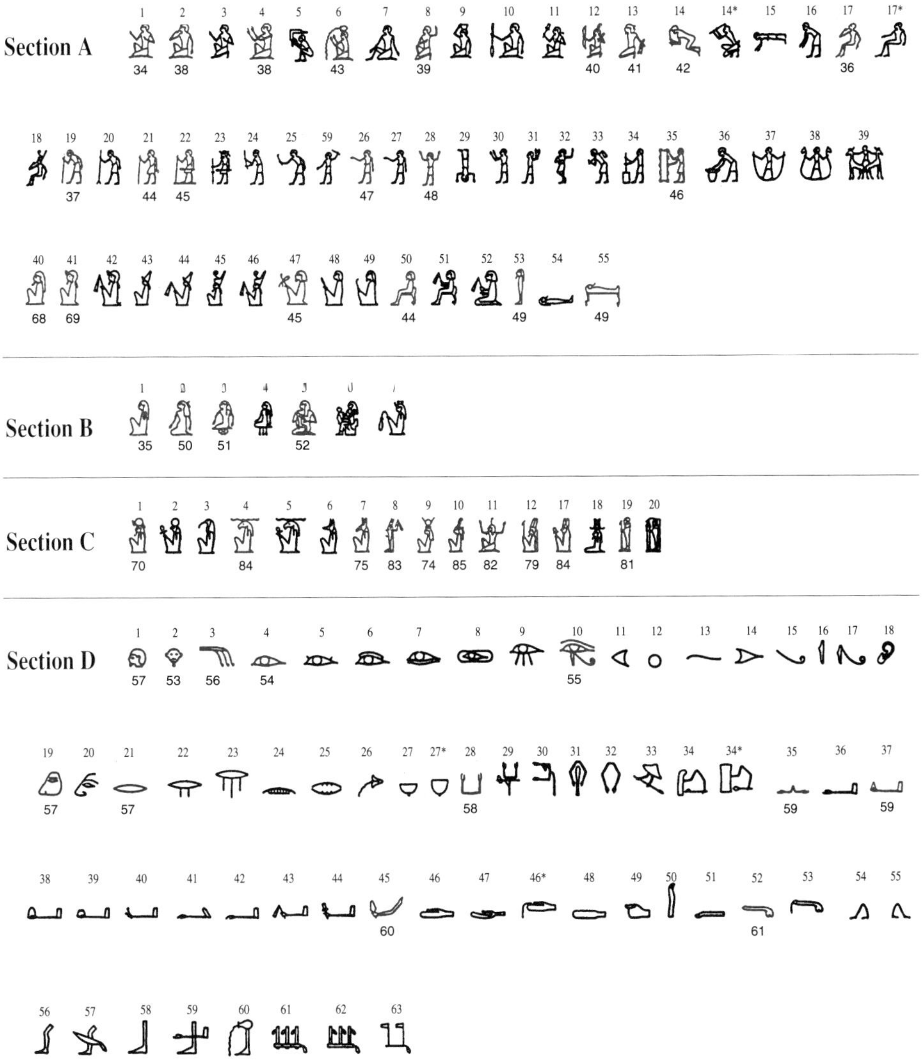

Section E

Section F

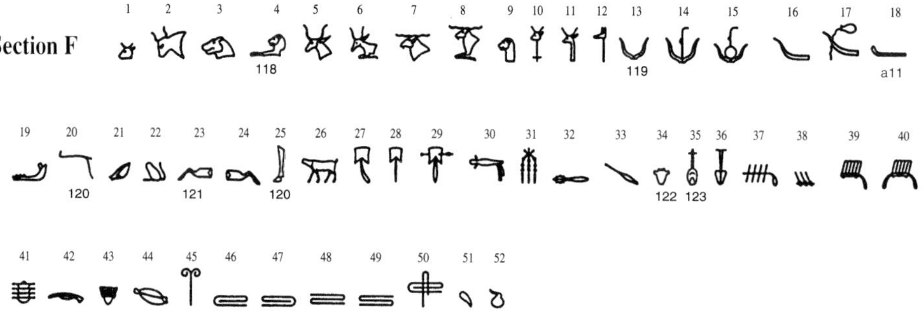

Section G

Section H

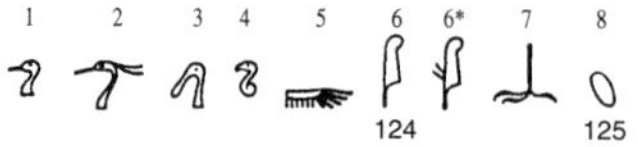

Section I

Section J

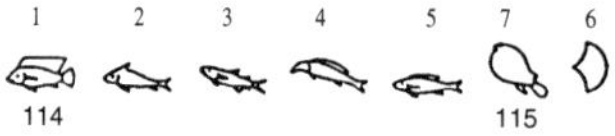

Section K

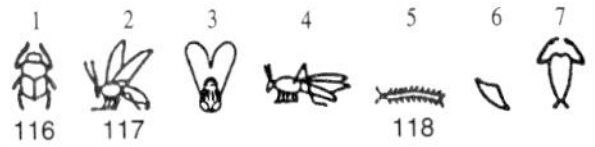
1 2 3 4 5 6 7
116 117 118

Section L

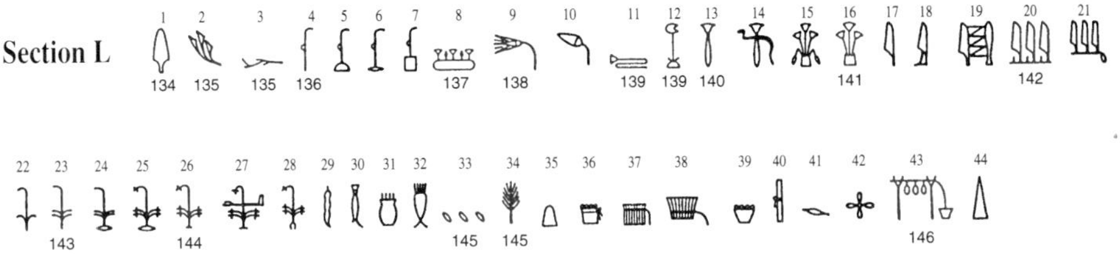
1 2 3 4 5 6 7 8 9 10 11 12 13 14 15 16 17 18 19 20 21
134 135 135 136 137 138 139 139 140 141 142
22 23 24 25 26 27 28 29 30 31 32 33 34 35 36 37 38 39 40 41 42 43 44
143 144 145 145 146

Section M

1 2 3 4 5 6 7 8 9 10 11 12 13 14 15 16 17 18
150 151 152 153 154 155 156 157
19 20 21 22 23 24 25 26 27 28 29 30 31 32 33 34 35 (35) 36 37 38
159 157 158 159 161 161 162 165 163 163 160 164
39 40 41 42
165

Section N

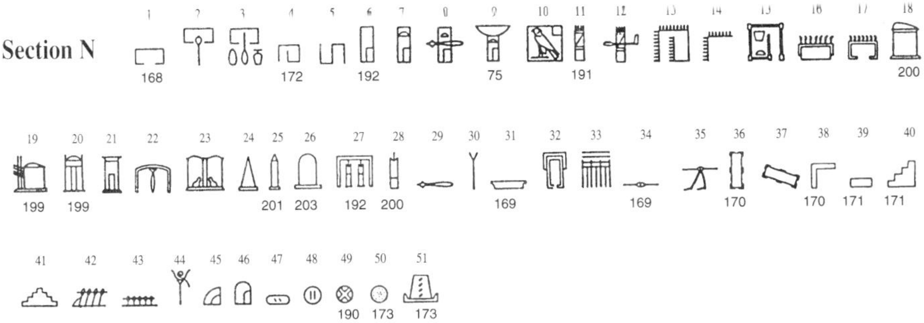
1 2 3 4 5 6 7 8 9 10 11 12 13 14 15 16 17 18
168 172 192 75 191 200
19 20 21 22 23 24 25 26 27 28 29 30 31 32 33 34 35 36 37 38 39 40
199 199 201 203 192 200 169 169 170 170 171 171
41 42 43 44 45 46 47 48 49 50 51
190 173 173

Section O

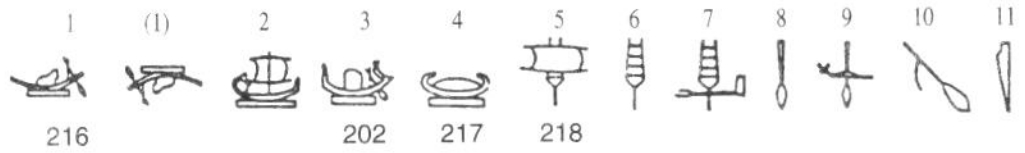
1 (1) 2 3 4 5 6 7 8 9 10 11
216 202 217 218

Section P

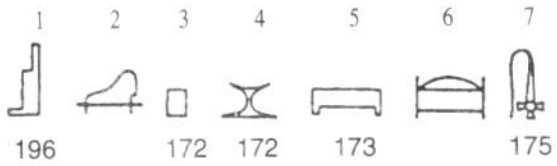
1 2 3 4 5 6 7
196 172 172 173 175

Section Q

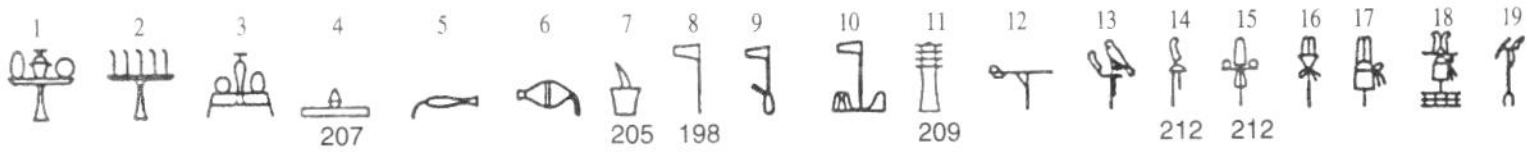
1 2 3 4 5 6 7 8 9 10 11 12 13 14 15 16 17 18 19
207 205 198 209 212 212

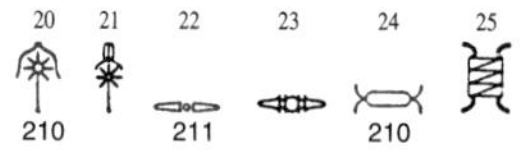

Section R

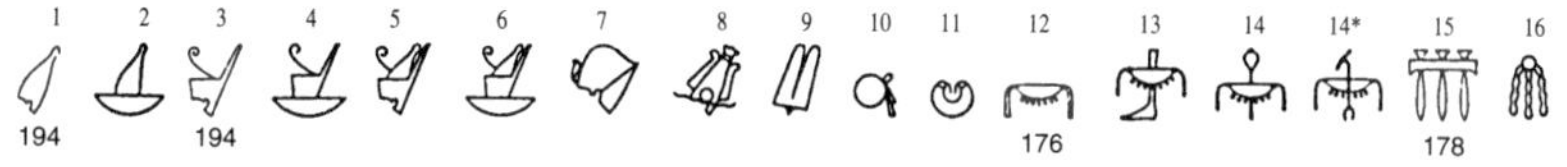

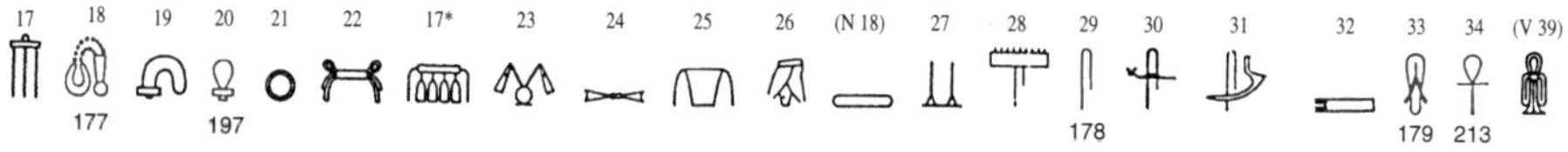

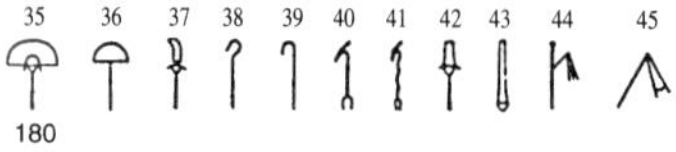

Section S

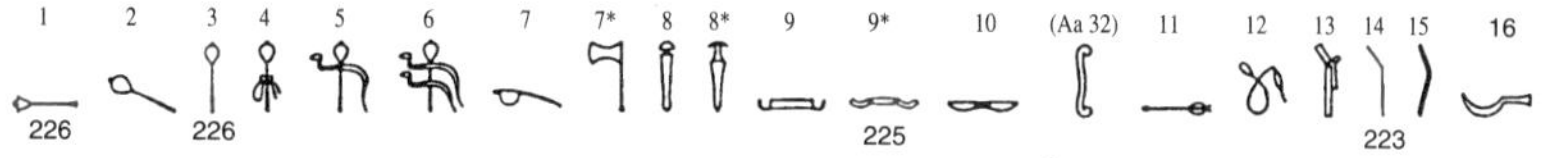

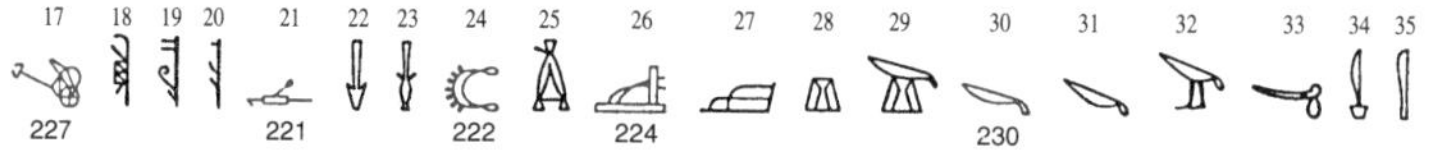

Section T

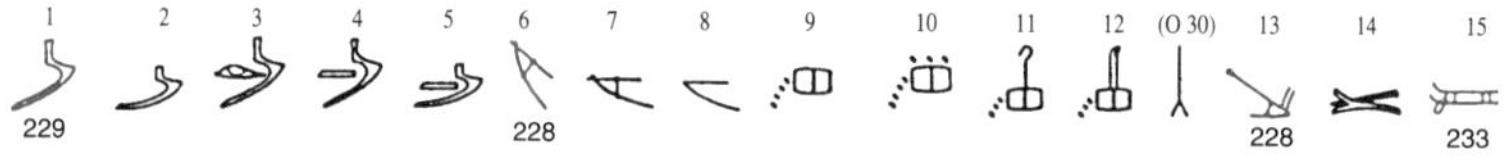

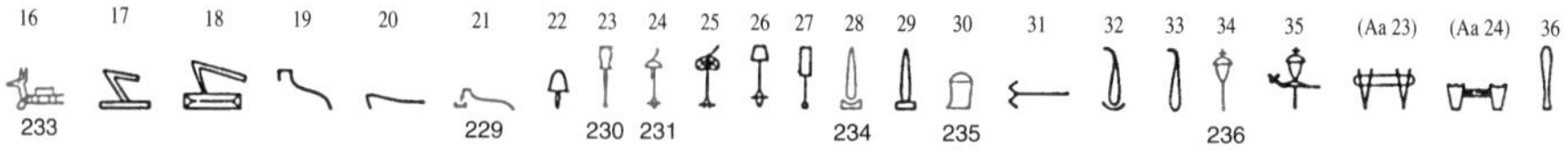

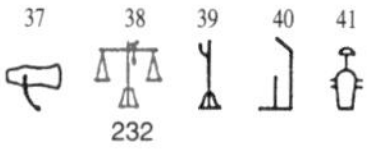

Section U

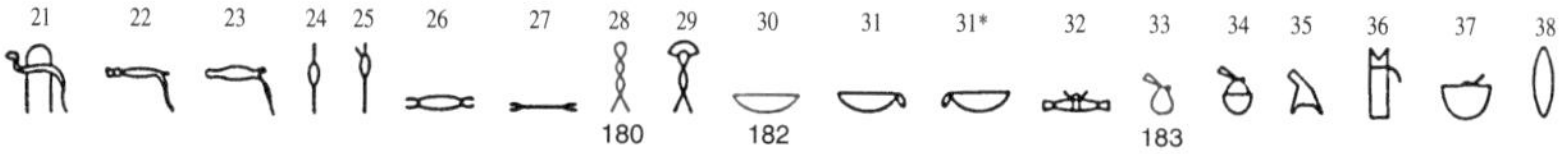

Section V

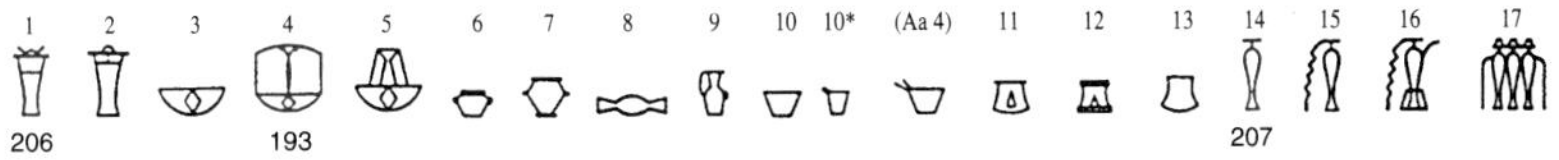

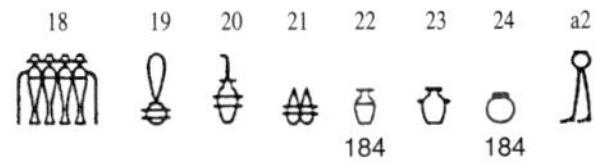

Section W

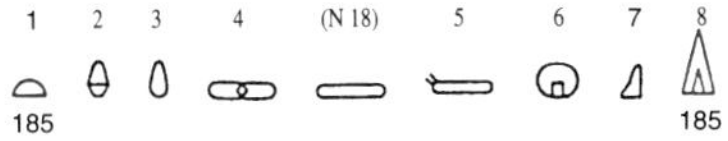

Section X

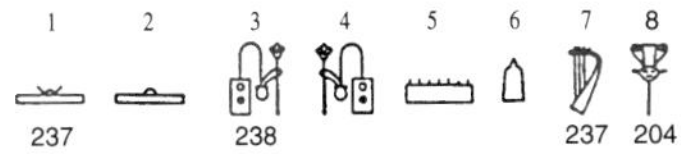

Section Y

Section Z

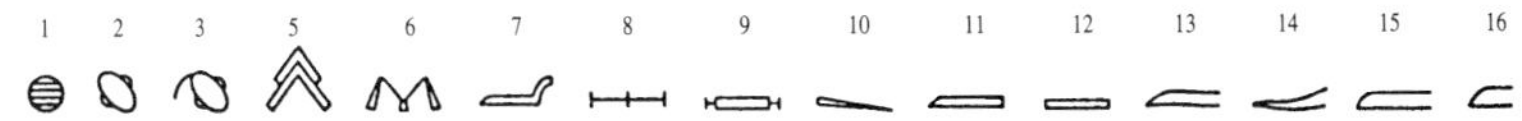

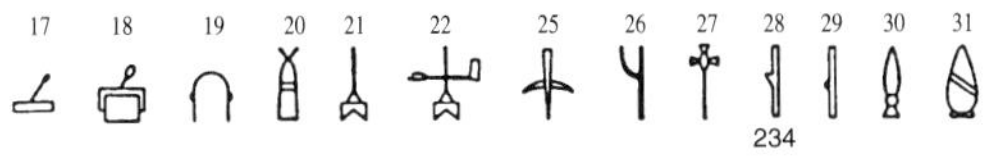

Signs from other lists

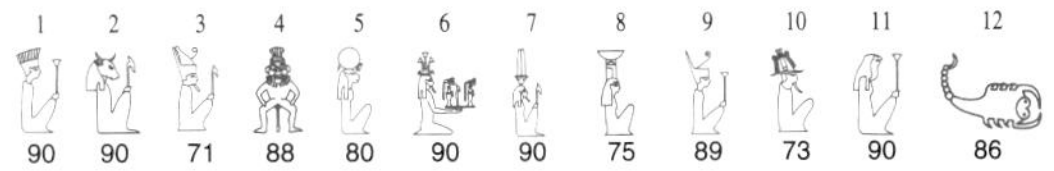

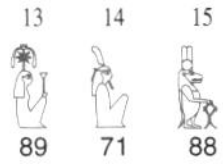

The Evolution of Hieroglyphic Writing

The system thus developed had a very long history: the last known hieroglyphic texts, found at Philae, date from the fourth century A.D. In the course of almost four millennia the system was subject to contrasting forces: the conservative tradition, which wanted the "divine writing" fixed forever as it had been created; and the innovative stimulus, determined by the need to update the graphic code and adapt it to different experiences and Egypt's new horizons. Another innovative influence was the intellectuals' speculative efforts regarding the powerful hieroglyphic symbols.

These conflicting tendencies resulted in a substantially open system, in which hieroglyphs (the cat, the chariot, the panoply of Asiatic arms, an exuberant crowd of Ptolemaic signs, and many others) were added without hesitation, while anachronistic images which no longer corresponded to the Egyptian reality nonetheless remained part of the lexicon. A significant example is the hieroglyph *sö*, the scribe's tablet, which until the end was proposed in a form which had certainly been abandoned in the middle of the Old Kingdom; other cases are pointed out in the notes.

In addition to changes in the original graphic tradition made because of changes in the reality it reflected, the signs underwent stylistic modifications. This usually allows us to distinguish Old Kingdom hieroglyphs, characterized by a greater adherence to reality, from the more synthetic examples of the classic era; the late period, in turn, is marked by a return to an archaic type of writing.

Below: *On the white limestone stele of Wepemneferet, the vivid colors and rich naturalistic details that describe the funerary offering leap out (the spots of the frog's back, the birds' feathers, the woven baskets). Fourth Dynasty. Berkeley, Lowie Museum of Anthropology, University of California.*

Facing page: *An example of the cold classical containment reached in hieroglyphic writing in the Nineteenth Dynasty. Temple of Seti I at Abydos, Nineteenth Dynasty.*

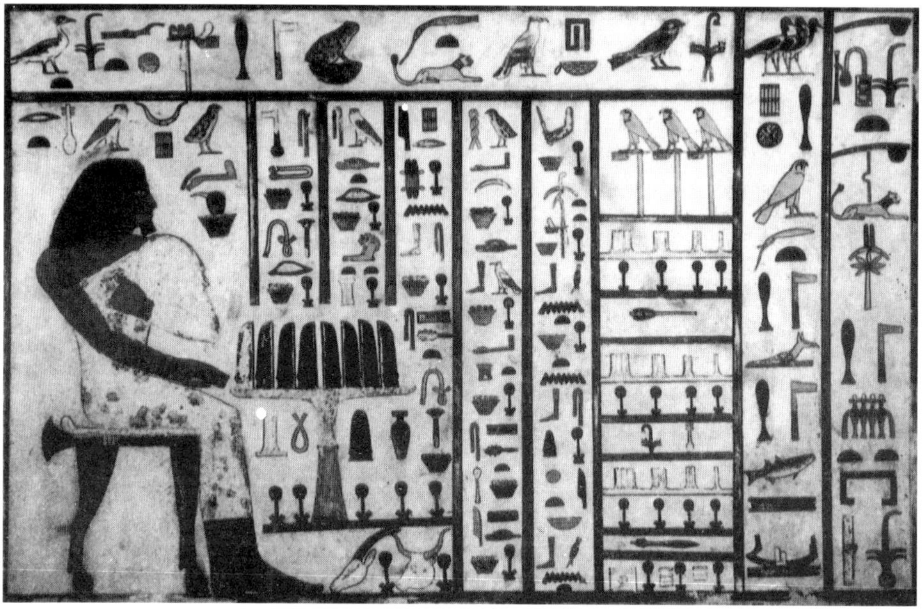

Cursive Writing

Hieroglyphic writing's ability to maintain its expressive pictorial nature until the very end was thanks to the fact that the scribes developed a cursive method of recording the language almost at the very beginning. Cursive was much more quickly written and more practical than the beautiful but laborious hieroglyphs.

Egyptologists call this writing "hieratic" (from the Greek *hieratikos*, "priestly"). In the Graeco-Roman era it was indeed a prerogative of the cultured class of priests who could read and transcribe ancient religious texts. But at its outset hieratic was developed for much more prosaic reasons: for state administration and accounting, and to record daily life. It kept this function until the Saitic Dynasties of the seventh century B.C., when the center of power returned to Lower Egypt. The scribal hieratic tradition developed at Thebes and in Upper Egypt then ceded its post to the cursive tradition of Lower Egypt, the script known as demotic ("popular writing").

Hieratic did not become extinct, however, but continued to co-exist with the other two forms of writing. It was used especially in literary and religious texts, spheres it shared with the demotic, which had become omnipresent.

A similar fate awaited the quick and elegant demotic, which was used to express one of the more supple and multifaceted phases of the Egyptian language. It co-existed for ages with first the Greek and then the Roman conquerors, but finally was overcome by the language of the rulers, giving way to the more modern Greek writing. Although the last demotic writing is found in the fifth century A.D., its end had al-

Below: *Relief of Sesostris I held by the god Ptah. From Karnak, Twelfth Dynasty. Cairo, Egyptian Museum.*

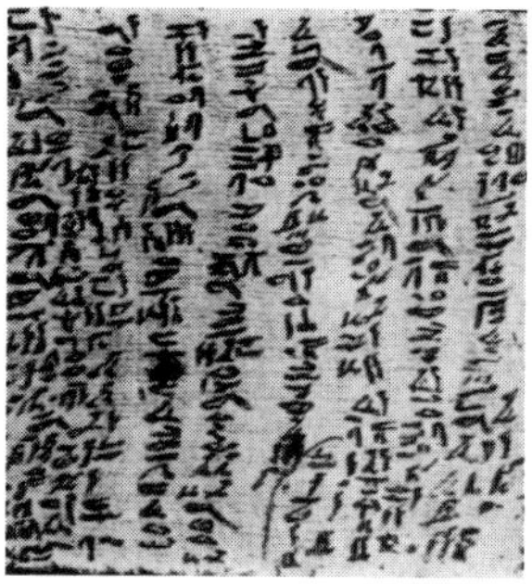

Above: *Hieratic text on linen from Saqqara. Datable to the Sixth Dynasty. Cairo, Egyptian Museum.*
The text, a letter written to a deceased man by his wife and son, probably placed in the tomb, is a good example of hieratic writing at the end of the Ancient Kingdom.

ready been determined between the second and third centuries A.D. The Greek alphabet, enriched by some special signs derived from demotic (in order to allow expression of sounds that were foreign to Greek phonetics), continued to give voice to the Egyptian language in the form of Coptic.

Semicursive hieroglyphic forms may be found very early, as seen in an inscription painted in ink on a predynastic vase of King Ka. But the first papyrus examples which can be considered hieratic do not appear before the Fifth Dynasty.

Brush and ink characterize this writing technique and determine the much more fluid and concise nature of its signs. The evolution of hieratic writing, and even more so of demotic, is much more pronounced than that of the hieroglyphic. Hieratic and demotic scribes tended to seek greater conciseness and abstraction, distancing themselves increasingly from the initial image until all traces were lost. The more frequently a hieroglyph was used, the more this process is accentuated. The development of hieroglyphic signs in hieratic and then demotic (illustrated above the discussion of each sign) shows that only rarely-used signs kept their original forms in the cursive.

A further consequence of cursive's tendency to simplify was the reduction of the number of signs used. Contrary to the variety of hieroglyphic signs used as ideograms and determinatives, hieratic (and even more so, demotic) thinned out the repertory; scribes preferred to use a more general category sign than a precisely individualized hieroglyphic representation whenever possible.

For example, many animal hieroglyphs not used commonly as phonograms were replaced by the sign for fur with a tail, which then became the normal determinative for names of animals and parts of animals. The majority of signs determinative of gods evolved the same way. Hieroglyphic preferred phonetic script for names of deities;

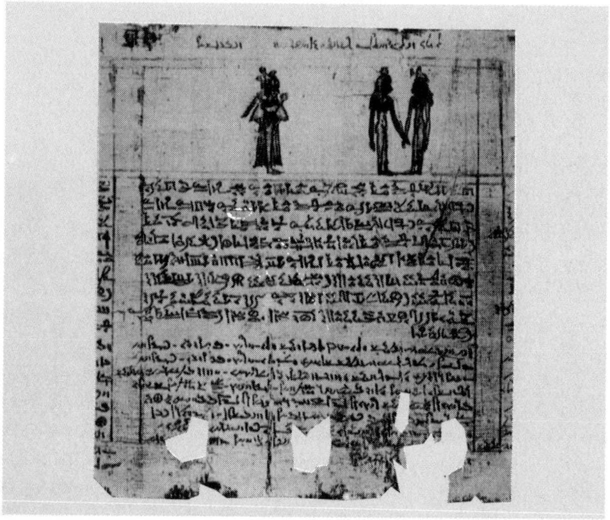

Right: *A sheet of the hieratic-demotic papyrus Rhind II, found in a Theban tomb.*
The funerary text, adorned with drawings, was written in hieratic (above) and demotic (below). End of the first century B.C. Edinburgh Museum.

Left: *Two large vase fragments with a ghost story in hieratic. From Thebes, Nineteenth–Twentieth Dynasty. Florence, Egyptian Museum.*
Together with other ostraka, these two large fragments use an elegant and ornate literary hieratic to narrate the fantastic story of the high priest Khonsuemheb and the ghost of a man who lived a thousand years before, an apparition which torments the priest until he finds and restores the man's ruined tomb.

hieratic and demotic confirmed and accentuated this tendency, supplanting specific single determinatives with the falcon on a standard-bearer, the ancient sign for god. Thus, cursive writing leaned toward synthesis, while hieroglyphic was more analytic.

The fact that hieratic and demotic cursive writings were more associated with daily affairs than hieroglyphic had been requires some discussion. To begin with, both forms of cursive show much greater change over time and space than hieroglyphic does, since different locales developed different cursive scribal traditions. Furthermore, all observations about variations in modern handwriting likewise apply to these ancient scripts. It is obvious that the difference between a text for personal use (a note jotted rapidly) and one meant for others will be significant.

The same may be said for the stylistic differences between a literary or religious text and an administrative account. The first may have been produced with the loving care and flowing writing of a scribe; the latter would certainly demonstrate a preference for abbreviations, ligatures, and other conveniences.

Even in hieroglyphic, naturally, there may be strong differences between a royal and a private text in terms of showing greater or lesser artistic quality and attention to detail. But rarely does this involve a real distortion of the sign. Indeed, when there is significant distortion in the hieroglyph, it is more correct to call the signs "hieratic writings" or "demotic writings." Keep this in mind while considering the various cursive scripts shown in this book; they are simply examples.

Below: *Fragment of a vase in the name of Ka, from the royal necropolis at Abydos, carrying an inscription in black ink with the name of the sovereign beside other signs (already of a semi-cursive nature) which probably note the contents of the vase, ca. 3,150-3,100 B.C. Paris, Louvre Museum.*

Chronological Table

This table records the succession of the principal dynasties. When the dates of two dynasties overlap, it means that there was a period of co-reign. When two or more dynasties coincide, it means that they were recognized in different parts of Egypt. The dates are taken from ancient lists, with a margin of error which may be as large as one hundred and fifty years for the beginning of the First Dynasty.

(fourth millennium B.C.)	Predynastic Period	
(c. 2,575–2,134 B.C.)	Protodynastic Period	*First Dynasty c. 2,920–2,770 B.C.*
		Second Dynasty c. 2,770–2,649 B.C.
		Third Dynasty c. 2,649–2,630 B.C.
(c. 2,134–2,040 B.C.)	Old Kingdom	*Fourth Dynasty c. 2,575–2,465 B.C.*
		Fifth Dynasty c. 2,465–2,323 B.C.
		Sixth Dynasty c. 2,323–2,150 B.C.
(c. 2,134–2,040 B.C.)	First Intermediate Period	*Ninth Dynasty c. 2,134–2,040 B.C.*
		Tenth-Eleventh Dynasty (Theban) c. 2,134–2,010 B.C.
(c. 2,040–1,640 B.C.)	Middle Kingdom	*Eleventh Dynasty c. 2,040–1,991 B.C.*
		Twelfth Dynasty c. 1,991–1,783 B.C.
		Thirteenth Dynasty c. 1,783–after 1,640 B.C.
		Fourteenth Dynasty (same time span)
(c. 1,640–1,532 B.C.)	Second Intermediate Period	*Fifteenth Dynasty c. 1,585–1,582 B.C.*
		Sixteenth Dynasty (same time span)
		Seventeenth Dynasty c. 1,640–1,550 B.C.
(c. 1,550–1,070 B.C.)	New Kingdom	*Eighteenth Dynasty c. 1,550–1,307 B.C.*
		Nineteenth Dynasty c. 1,307–1,196 B.C.
		Twentieth Dynasty c. 1,196–1,070 B.C.
(c. 712–332 B.C.)	Third Intermediate Period	*Twenty-first Dynasty c. 1,070–945 B.C.*
		Twenty-second Dynasty c. 945–712 B.C.
		Twenty-third Dynasty c. 828–712 B.C.
		Twenty-fourth Dynasty c. 724–712 B.C.
		Twenty-fifth Dynasty c. 770–750 B.C.
(c. 712–332 B.C.)	Late Period	*Twenty-fifth Dynasty c. 712–657 B.C.*
		Twenty-sixth Dynasty c. 664–525 B.C.
	(Persian domination)	*Twenty-seventh Dynasty c. 525–404*
		Twenty-eighth Dynasty c. 404–399 B.C.
		Twenty-ninth Dynasty c. 398–378 B.C.
		Thirtieth Dynasty c. 380–343 B.C.
	(Second Persian domination)	*Thirty-first Dynasty c. 343–332 B.C.*
(332 B.C–395 A.D.)	Graeco-Roman Period	

This table is based on one shown in the Atlas of Ancient Egypt *by John Baines and Jaromir Màlek.*

Mankind

Differences in age, sex, and social status each finds its place in this category of the hieroglyphic code. It includes men in diverse poses and pursuits; women, children, and the aged; and dignitaries, priests, and workers. Even ethnic and cultural diversities are represented—the Asian, as the well-known general symbol for foreigner; the nomad-shepherd, who with his minimal baggage—a handkerchief knotted around his things and hung on a stick—has a place; and, at the margins of social life, the prisoner or enemy, the perfect "other," hostile, negative, and therefore discredited. Those who translated into hieroglyphic code the varied world of human and social reality of the fourth millennium B.C. were certainly men: all the generic symbols are masculine. When woman appears—other than in the generic hieroglyph for female—it is only as mother and nourisher.

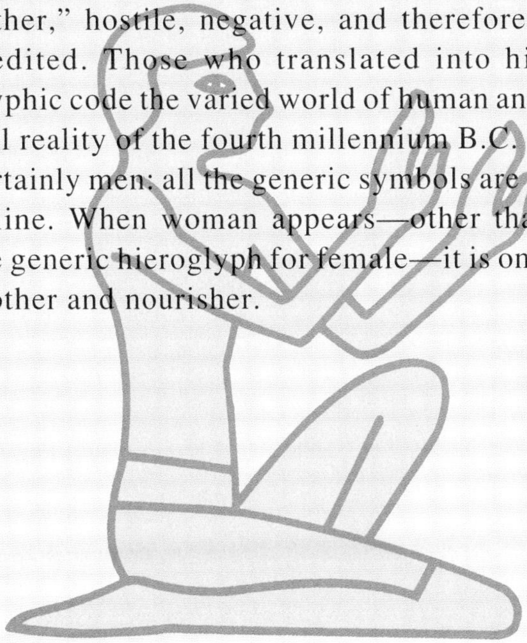

Man

Ideogram in* s, *"man." Determinative in words relating to man and his occupations. It may also be used as an ideogram or determinative in writing the personal pronoun of the first person singular.

When the Egyptian wishes to represent man in his entirety or to classify a word as being in the human and masculine orbit, he draws a man seated on the ground in the habitual posture that has come down to us in many paintings and reliefs: one leg with the knee raised, the other folded under the thigh, the foot flat on the earth, and all the weight of the body on the heel. More than any other, this position of repose, devoid of any suggestion of movement or action, expressed to Egyptian eyes the general nature and essence of the concept of man. Any other image would have transferred attention to the action or gesture, or to the contingent and transitory, ignoring the universal and eternal. According to Egyptian drawing conventions, man is shown in profile, with the torso frontal. This position reveals the most possible information, at once recognizable and a true essential portrait. For this reason the eye, which in profile would be scarcely represented, is shown from the front. This hieroglyph is the basis of a series of combinations that define other human actions or conditions. Almost always, the position of the arms is the fundamental discriminating factor.

Seated man singing. Saqqara, mastaba of Akhhotep, Fifth Dynasty.

VARIANTS/COMBINATIONS

A man and seated woman, placed above the signs for the plural, indicates the collective nominative, referring to human subjects like *rmṯw*, "people," ethnic groups, etc.

Woman

Determinative in words associated with woman and the female sphere in general. Starting with the New Kingdom, it is used for the feminine in place of the suffix for the first person singular, ỉ.

Tightly wrapped in a dress or cloak that covers her feet, the seated woman is the female equivalent of the hieroglyph of the seated man.

In a way comparable to the hieroglyph for the male, this sign indicates the female sphere and determines women's proper names. It is characterized by the woman's long wig that falls along the back and on the breast, which is sometimes suggested. The composed and reserved attitude gives an image of the woman as rather chaste and modest, which is somewhat belied by sculpture and paintings, where from the earliest times the clothes bind and frequently reveal more than they conceal. The later refinements of fabrics in the New Kingdom-the light and transparent white linen of the long tunics-do not avoid suggesting the slim silhouettes underneath, which in all eras of Egyptian civilization mark the aesthetically ideal woman. Art, literature, and legal and economic documents all show a degree of freedom and a cultural position of women that was virtually unparalleled in the ancient world, and one that is amply demonstrated by Egyptological studies. Nevertheless, the message in this hieroglyph—those arms disconcertingly hidden by the dress—implies a deeper and often ignored truth about the condition of woman in ancient Egypt, that was nonetheless tied to an ideal of submission and remissiveness. That this hieroglyph is comparatively less diffuse than its male counterpart reminds us that in general the women of ancient Egypt spoke through their male relatives—husbands, fathers, or sons. However honored, they were guests in their tombs, subjects of scenes ordered by prevalently male patrons. In her own funerary temple, Queen Hatshepsut, a "usurper" of a royal authority traditionally held by a man, rejected her own femininity in adopting masculine iconography. The art and writing reveal a primarily masculine elite, providing more man's ideal image than what must have been a conflicted reality. Unlike the variety of hieroglyphs that illustrate the world of male occupations, the activities of women are only one: motherhood.

Women seated at a banquet. Thebes, tomb of Djehuty (no. 45), Eighteenth Dynasty.

Child

***Determinative in words related to childhood; often used as abbreviation for* ẖrd, *"child." From* nn, *synonym of* ẖrd, *phonetic value* nn.**

As in a "mutilated" hieroglyph, this sign seems to emphasize more the missing mother, invisible but still holding the child in her lap, suggesting the Egyptian concept of total dependency and a near-symbiosis with the mother. We know that children were breast-fed until age three, and scenes of daily life in tombs and temples emphasize a child's constant intimacy with the mother. It is physically underlined: if a child is not well tied on the mother's back with shawls (or in a sort of basket, as in the case of a Nubian woman in the Theban tomb of Huy), he is always nearby, holding the mother's hand, tugging on her clothes, or grabbing her legs in an attempt to be picked up.
The child in the hieroglyph is in the same pose as children in thousands of small sculptures and other images from ancient Egypt. The mother, whether common woman, goddess, or queen, holds him in her lap. Even though the proportions are altered and abnormally attenuated for the clarity of the hieroglyph, which probably also influenced artistic representations, it is clear that the child is very young. One hand hangs, while the other is at the mouth, as if sucking his thumb.
In more detailed examples, the so-called "side-lock of youth" is clearly visible: this hair style, for both boys and girls, called for the head to be shaved except for a broad braid at the side, which curled upwards.
They are nude, as in nearly all the scenes depicting real life. This could be a conventional image of infancy or a result of the hot Egyptian climate.

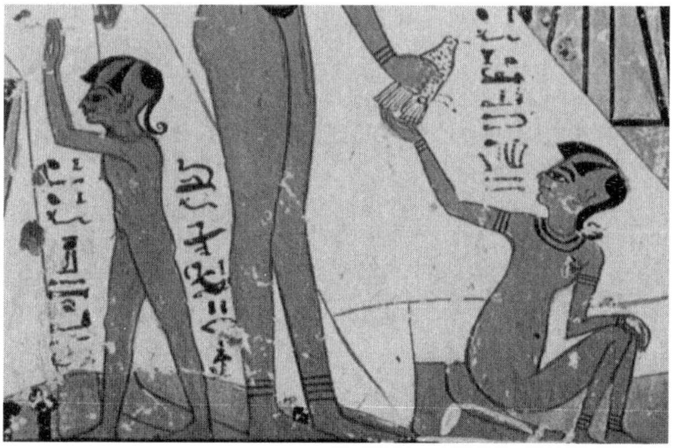

Scenes of family life: children, with the typical side-lock, at their mother's feet. Deir el Medinah, tomb of Anhurkau (no. 39), Twentieth Dynasty.

VARIANTS/COMBINATIONS

The child bearing the crown of Lower Egypt is determinative of everything pertaining to royal princes. One might recall that when Memphis, in Lower Egypt, was not the capital, it was still the traditional seat of princely education.

Old Man

***Ideogram or determinative in* ỉ3w*, "old man," and in* smsw*, "the greater (= older)"; determinative in words connected with old age. From the rare verb* ỉ3k*, "to be old": phonetic value* ỉk.**

The bent-over body and supporting cane are the features of this hieroglyph of old age. Weakness and deterioration of mental and physical faculties are the other sad aspects of old age, as lamented by the wise man Ptahhotep, vizier of King Isesi of the Fifth Dynasty, in the impressive description in his *Instruction*. Sometimes more detailed examples of the sign show other characteristics of advanced age: balding foreheads and an orange color to the skin, which for the Egyptians indicated pallid skin no longer exposed to the sun, as opposed to the red-brown color of virile bodies.
The Egyptians did not like to represent old age and only in some instances does reality break through the idealized representations of mankind, which is always in the image of splendid and vigorous youth. Thus, besides the baldness and pallor, old age is shown by the spider's web of wrinkles on the face, by thin and flaccid bodies, and by a long beard. The realism of these portraits reveals social status: if wrinkles are common to all, obesity besets the well off, while emaciated bodies and gaunt faces afflict old farmers. Even the beard and baldness seem to be attributes of rural men; city dwellers shave carefully and wear wigs.

An old cowherd.
Meir, tomb of Ukhhotep,
Twelfth Dynasty.

Man with His Hand to His Mouth

Determinative in words relating to the mouth's activities (eating, drinking, speaking, keeping silence, recounting, etc.) and, by extension, to intellectual activity in general (thinking, feeling, loving).

The movement of the arms differentiates this sign from the more generic seated man, though otherwise the position is identical. In place of the two fisted hands held near the breast, here one hangs at the side while the other is lifted toward the mouth. The oldest inscriptions show that originally there were two distinct determinatives, one for actions associated with eating, identical to the image here, and the other for intellectual actions—primarily speaking—in which the raised hand does not touch the mouth but is shown palm facing outward. Many examples show that this was often the determinative of exclamations; the gesture clearly suggests oratory. At the end of the Old Kingdom, in the First Intermediate Period, texts show confusion between this hieroglyph and that of the seated man. To avoid this, the sign of the man with his hand to his mouth was substituted by the image of a standing man in the same pose.

Man in Adoration

Determinative in words expressing adoration of the gods.

This is man praying to the gods, seated with one knee raised and his arms lifted up, hands palm outward, toward the object of prayer. The Egyptians defined the activity illustrated by this position as *dw3*, "adore," or *rdỉt ỉ3w*, "give praises." As in the gestures of greetings, the presentation of the open palm is a manifestation of helplessness and humility. Dedicators of stele or effigies of the deceased in his tomb are frequently represented in this position (or in the erect version), to illustrate the hymn to the gods. The god himself, an invisible but imposing presence, is almost never shown in these cases, but is clearly implied by the gesture of adoration. This representation of prayer appears in scenes at the end of the

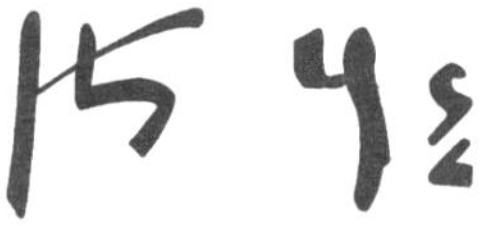

Old Kingdom: in general the king is shown thus saluting the gods, but it is the same attitude given to foreign princes sudordinate to the pharaoh. Often the pose is taken also by prisoners in front of the king, but this is the more typical gesture of surrender.

Man Striking His Chest

Determinative in the word **hnw**, ***"jubilation."***

This is an extremely ancient ceremonial gesture that could express jubilation and sometimes lamentation. The hieroglyph is of a man, generally in the seated position with one raised knee, but with the foot of the raised leg flat to the ground; he holds one arm to his breast with the fist closed and raises the other fist high. The fact that in some cases it is interchangeable with a similar gesture, in which both fists are held to the chest, leads one to think that the gesture was part of a sequence of movements and that this represented the act of beating the breast, alternating the strokes of the two fists. This is then an example of the original pre-instrumental form of music known as the "corporal." An ecstatic form of acclamation and greeting, this accompanied the appearances of the king before the court, just as it did on the horizon of the heavenly model, the sun god. On an earthly plane, the prominent figures of the kingdom—the priests and court functionaries—executed this gesture; on the cosmic level, it was the prerogative of the otherworldly cortège that greeted the sun with hymns at dawn and sunset.

In particular, this expression is associated with a series of divine figures, whose nature is not entirely clear, known as "spirits (*ba*) of Pe and Nekhen." Their traditional iconography constantly associates them with the jubilation-*henu* gesture. They are each in the form of a man, but one with a falcon's head, the other a jackal's. They are fixed elements in coronation scenes and in those illustrating the divine birth of the king. In Egyptian mythology these beings, tied to the mythic capitals of pre-unification Egypt (Pe = Buto, in the Delta; Nekhen = Hierakonpolis, in Upper Egypt), seem to have represented the theory of semi-divine kings that preceded (according to the historic reconstruction in Egypt's own annals) the first king of united Egypt. But another interpretation prefers to see very ancient gods in these two localities; they then became obscure and were absorbed into later cults. Their insertion in the solar theology, and the need to render them consistent with the organic spatial structure of that philosophy, brought about their association with other groups of spirits, which in turn were connected to other cities of ancient Egypt and to the cardinal compass points.

In scenes describing the sun god's arrival in the underworld at sunset, other gods, labeled the "occidentals," frequently substitute the spirits of Pe and Nekhen, and they too are fixed in this primordial welcoming gesture.

The Occidental gods shown in the henu *gesture. Deir el Medinah, tomb of Inherka, Twentieth Dynasty.*

Archer

Ideogram or determinative in* mš, *"army," and associated words.

The archer was, for the Egyptian, the image of the soldier par excellence, just as the bow was the symbol of the people at war. "The Nine Bows" was from earliest times the expression for the enemies of Egypt, in memory of the nine primitive peoples under the domination of the first kings. The archer wears a simple loincloth that does not impede movement; he holds his bow in one hand and a group of arrows in the other in the oldest examples, the quiver in later versions; the head is often bound by a band into which a feather is inserted (a very common ritual symbol and symbol of the state of war), or else a large pin (or bone?). The body is in tension, wide awake, ready to move. This is not the usual seated position; the leg with its foot on the ground is pointed against the earth, the weight is not on it, but balanced tensely on all the muscles. Often the variants from the First Intermediate Period, which was notoriously ravaged by bloody civil wars, show the archer in the act of drawing his bow. This was the era that has given us, in the tombs of its noble warriors, the wooden miniature armies, orderly and silent for their lord in the other world as they were in life. The images and texts often suggest Nubian origin, indicated by dark skin and slightly exotic clothing—the broad belts ending in fringe or animal tails or ornaments in their curly hair. Until the first professional armies were created in the New Kingdom, the period of Egyptian imperialistic expansion, the only permanent and specialized troops were mercenaries, frequently Africans. The New Kingdom, and the domination of the Asiatic Hyksos that preceded it, brought the first great innovations in the technology of arms and organization of armies; then came the first appearance in Egypt of the composite bow and the war cart. Soldiering became a profession, and was frequently the object of literary satire composed by the scribes (who talked meanly of the hard training, forced marches, brackish drinking water, and abductions of female prisoners), but it became attractive for its rich booty, the gold of the military decorations, and the small lots of property that awaited the returning veterans.

Wooden models of archers.
Asyut, tomb of Mesehti,
Eleventh Dynasty.
Cairo, Egyptian Museum.

Prisoner

Determinative in words referring to adversaries:* ḫfty, *"enemy";* sbỉ, *"rebel," etc. In the late period it was used also as an abbreviation of these.

According to the rigorous logic of Egyptian defensive magic thought, the enemy—and often the foreigner, as potential adversary—may only be represented in a harmless position: already vanquished and constrained to impotence by an uncomfortable and humiliating immobility. Occasionally fuller representations of the hieroglyph show the arms fixed to a forked stick stuck in the earth, the execution stake to which prisoners were tied for burning. The same stylized representation, more or less realistic and rich in appropriate folkloric details, was used with exorcistic intent in the rows of foreign peoples that decorated the bases of the thrones, royal statues, pavements in palace rooms, arms, and—even more incisively—-the soles of sandals.

A variant of the hieroglyph of the man with his hands tied behind his back can frequently be found on monuments, primarily in the lower areas of the decorations: this encloses in the body the so-called "fortified name-rings," closed ovals that surround the names of the forts and foreign countries conquered by the reigning Pharaoh.

In the more precise examples like the splendid reliefs decorating the columns of the hypostyle hall in the temple of Amenophis III at Soleb, in Sudan—the physiognomic characteristics of the prisoners are represented with ethnological care.

In crude three-dimensional clay form the hieroglyph also found a public use in magic rituals against the enemies of the Egyptian state. Numerous little statues of "prisoners" have been found buried at Saqqara, necropolis of ancient Memphis, and even at Mirgissa in Sudan. The texts inscribed on these identify various enemy sovereign of the time: "Aktui, king of Shaat (Nubian region), born of Rehai and for Setikekhi, besides all those allies striken (= the subjects)." There is no doubt that certain death attended the enemy who was the subject of such a ritual.

Foreign prisoners of war shown on the golden war cart of Tutankhamen. Eighteenth Dynasty. Cairo, Egyptian Museum.

Dying Man

Determinative in mwt, "to die" (and related words), and in* ḫfty, *"enemy."

This is the only hieroglyph that opens a crack in the repugnance that the Egyptians had for death, and particularly for violent death. The man in this sign is in an untidy position, is perhaps falling, fallen, with his legs folded back toward his chest. What in later examples seems to be a weapon, probably an ax—and the Egyptians themselves made this mistake—was in earlier versions a stream of blood coming from the wound on his head. As early as the Twentieth Dynasty, texts show a variant with an ax stuck in the head of the man.

The intellectuals of the late period puzzled about this sign and deduced that it represented suicide (papyrus Jumilhac, XVI, 20). It represents traumatic death and therefore, for the ancient Egyptians, unnatural and outside of the harmonious order that governs life and the cosmos.

That it could also serve to determine the word "enemy" *(ḫfty)* is easily explained by the usual inclination for execratory magic: the enemy determined by such a sign was already a dead man. But that the Egyptians, so reluctant to represent the physiological fact of their own death—always ready to skip the abhorred moment in favor of mummifying, funerals, and life in the afterworld—should have opted to use this hieroglyph to show the moment of death sheds light on how they conceived of it as a violent and "unnatural" event.

When the ancient Egyptian describes death, it is seen as the inverse of life: "Honey is sweet for the living and bitter for the dead" is a magic formula; innumerable formulas try to avoid the danger of walking head-down, drinking one's own urine and eating one's excrement.

This is the other side of the coin of a culture that, though nullifying the moment of death, has anyway tenaciously and continuously attempted to reintegrate it in its concept of life as cyclical eternity, a culture with poets that sang: "Death is before me today as the perfume of myrrh, like sitting under the sail on a windy day," and, "No one does not join us here [in the afterworld]. That which one does on earth is like a dream; but one says 'Welcome!' to those who reach the West."

Dying and dead in battle on the "Battlefield Palette." End of fourth millennium B.C. Oxford, Ashmolean Museum.

Priest

Ideogram in* w'b, *"pure"; also designates a priestly class.

The notion of purity and purification essentially pertained to the religious sphere: the man bathed by the water flowing from a ritual vase is shown in the position of adoration; as in a rebus, the hieroglyph signifies the juxtaposition of the prayer and water that washes away all dirt, the ideal condition of purity and hygiene that is the principal quality of the priest. "Pure" or "purified" was the Egyptian term for the adepts of the cult; purity was the common denominator of the highest and the most lowly within the great variety of priestly subcategories.

This fundamental condition, both physical and spiritual, began with an ablution, which freed the officiating priest from all contamination; but aspersions of temple holy water were frequent, often using the clear cold water from the lakes or the holy basins present in every temple.

The scrupulous rules of cleanliness and purity for the servants of god impressed Herodotus greatly when the Greek historian visited Egypt in the fifth century B.C. The priests washed frequently, and shaved the whole body, and dressed only in linen, avoiding wool because it was the product of a living being.

They respected local taboos, and in the period of officiating, abstained from sexual activity. But the only pure state that allowed them to come in contact with the god and serve him was not just the result of a series of concrete rules and prescriptions, as Porphirius (*De Abst.*, 4, 6–8) recounts: "Contemplation and reflection gave them the necessary ascetic qualities."

The priest Niaiy and his wife receive the purifying water poured by the goddess of the sycamore. Limestone relief from Saqqara, Eighteenth–Nineteenth Dynasty. Hanover, Kester Museum.

VARIANTS/COMBINATIONS

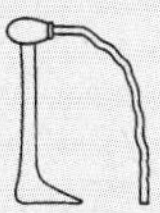

This sign, with an identical phonetic value *w'b*, combines the image of purifying water with the phoneme *b*.

Dignitary

Ideogram or determinative in* sr, *"dignitary" or "magistrate," and determinative in the words for high functionaries and courtesans. It was often mistaken for the hieroglyph for old man.

The pose is erect, the movement magisterial, the symbols of rank (the long staff in one hand, the handkerchief or sometimes a scepter in the other) denote the position of power occupied by the *sr*, or whomever may have been able to appropriate the hieroglyph as determinative of his title. Egyptian script adopted this representation of power very early: the sign was first used for the king himself in the ivory tablets of the protodynastic, but its use was then extended to cover other dignitaries close to the king and his circle. The erect posture was intended to impose and instill respect and fear, the procession to suggest activity. The *sr* was a power exercising his functions, important and prestigious, whose effects would move down the hierarchical steps and touch the lives of the greater Egyptian population.

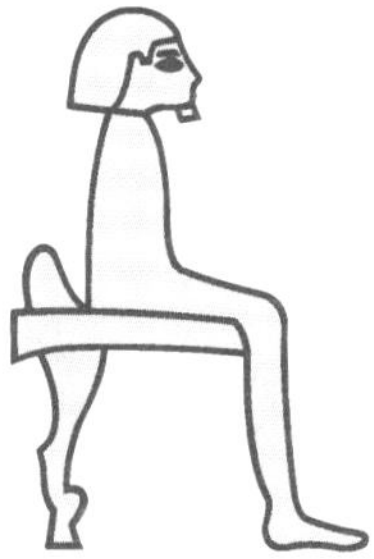

Seated Dignitary

Ideogram in* šps, *"noble being, revered" and similar words.

If the erect strutting male figure was the eloquent image of the authority of a functionary, the seated counterpart evokes the hedonistic side of a noble's life: the first illustrates rights and duties, the second, the pleasures. The word *šps* in effect covers a range of meanings, from the title of a "dignitary," to the notion of "venerable revered," to "precious"; *špswt* are also "riches." This is the typical image of a noble presiding at banquets or receiving an offering: in ceremonial dress, he sits erect on a sumptuous chair with a lion's or bull's legs, according to the epoch and fashion. In the hieroglyph the man's legs are one with those of the chair. Because his arms are not indicated, the body seems to be wrapped in a cape (in older images of funeral banquets the noble is frequently dressed in a long tunic and wrapped in feline fur). The short beard may or may not be drawn.

Statue of a Nobleman

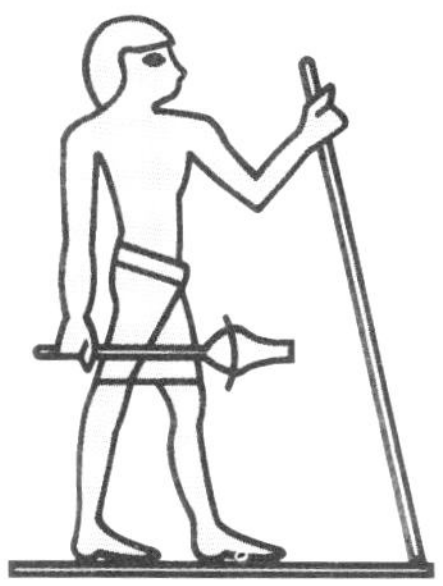

D*eterminative in nouns meaning "statue":* **twt, ẖnt** (y), *etc.*

Having a statue of oneself made was not a question of narcissism or love of art for the ancient Egyptian, but one of ritual and deep religious meaning. *twt* was etymologically "that which is similar," that reproduces one's likeness, but also, thanks to animatory rites, one's own personality. The statue was a real substitute and thus had a precise place in the tomb.
The ritual in which the "soul" of the owner was conferred on the statue, known as the Ritual of the Opening of the Mouth, was the same with which the lector-priest vivified the mummy. The statue in the hieroglyph was one of the best-loved images of the human figure in ancient Egypt: the nobleman is shown erect and walking, with the marks of his rank in hand, the staff and sceptre *ʿbʿ*, already chosen as the outstanding traits for the characterizing of his power and authority. The presence of the pedestal distinguishes this as a sculpture and not the dignitary himself.

Cowherd

I*deogram for* **mniw**, *"cowherd,"* **s3w**, *"guard." From the First Intermediate Period ideogram or determinative in* **iry**, *"concerning, belonging to."*

As examples from the Old Kingdom show clearly, the man dressed in a long cape holds a staff around which is wound a cattle goad. In rural scenes shepherds frequently hold not only a whip and a staff in one hand, but also a puzzling object which seems to correspond to that drawn around the staff in the hieroglyph. It is a ring of rope from which hang strips of leather (others have thought of thorns), a cat-o'-nine-tails to goad recalcitrant animals. Sometimes the man is shown with a beard, like the foreigner, and frequently the sign is mistaken for the similar one of the Asian holding a staff.
There is a very similar sign, the man beardless and with a puzzling object in hand, which was for a long time considered an autonomous hieroglyph of phonetic value *iry*, but it is a variant of the former.

Mason

Ideogram or determinative in ḳd, “to construct.”

The Egyptians built in brick and stone, the brick being of sun-dried clay. While the malleable clay was preferred for the living, whether it was a farmer's modest house or a splendid royal palace, stone was generally reserved for sacred buildings: gods and the dead were given buildings meant to last.
It is not easy to say whether the wall the man in the hieroglyph *ḳd* is working on is of stone or brick; it is likely the latter. Brick architecture preceded stone by hundreds of years and is well documented in the pre-dynastic era.

The verb *ḳd* designates the activity of the mason as well as that of the potter: its real meaning is “to model,” and the material is the same in both cases. Only the determinative differentiates them semantically: the mason at work for “construct” and the wheel or potter for “model.”
The oldest examples of the hieroglyph show some differences in the wall: sometimes it is somewhat oval; in other cases it is a simple rectangle of variable dimensions.
The activities of the mason are described in a lively sequence of scenes in the tomb of Rekhmira, on the western bands of the Nile facing Luxor. First came the preparation of the materials, mixing Nile mud with water, chopped straw, and dung; it was poured into rectangular wooden forms and left to dry in the sun; the bricks thus made were carried to the construction site and, if necessary, brick ramps were constructed to allow the erection of large public buildings. The usual procedure was to lay bricks in alternating lengthwise and crosswise rows. There were thick layers of mortar between the rows. The work of the mason also came under the satirists' fire. *The Instruction of Kheti* states: “I tell you also of that mason who builds walls: the whip hurts him; even though he is exposed to the wind, he works unclothed; his loincloth is a twisted rope with a cord hanging down the back; his arms are broken with fatigue, and after having mixed all kinds of muck, he eats his bread with those hands.”

Masons at work.
West Thebes
(Sheikh Abd el-Qurna),
Tomb of Rekhmira (no. 100),
Eighteenth Dynasty.

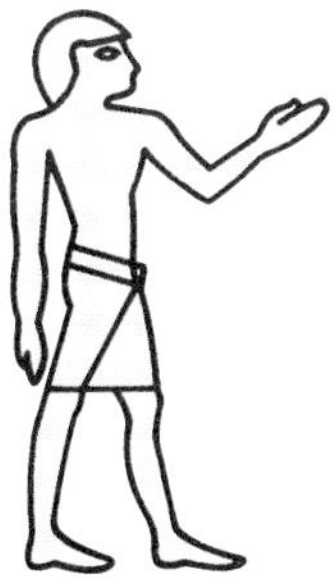

Supplicate

Determinative in verbs meaning "to call," "to invoke": nỉs, ḍwi, ʿš. Abbreviation for ʿš in the title sḏm-ʿš, "servant" (literally, "he who listens to the call").

One arm hangs along the side, the other is streched forward with the palm turned upward: this is the gesture that expresses invocation. In body language the palm turned upward and slightly cupped is almost universally indicative of asking; the outstretched and slightly bent arm emphasizes the hand's meaning and minimizes any suspicion of aggression by avoiding all rigidity in the posture. It belongs to the gestures that accompany speech, is a declamatory gesture, and it should be noted that the Egyptian *ʿš* (one of the verbs determined by a hieroglyph) signified also "to read" and "to recite [by memory] a text."
The interjection *ỉ*, which generally introduced the vocative, is also determinative of the same sign. In scenes representing oracular interrogation of the god on his processional litter, this is the position assumed by the priest intermediating between god and the supplicant, the person authorized, due to his purity and sacredness, to "speak" with god and present the supplicant's request. And, again, the verb that expressed the request of the oracle is *ʿš*. These scenes show the various differences in the attitude of the inter mediaries, which are sometimes reflected in variants in the hieroglyph: the arm may be more or less flexed, and if more, the palm may be turned outward instead of upward.
The same position, with an analogous meaning, was maintained by all the priests who carried the holy litter; they assumed the gesture of invocation to the appropriate god by raising the arm that was not resting on the litter.

Priest bent in the supplicant's gesture while in procession. Limestone block from the temple of Deir el Medinah, Twentieth Dynasty. Cairo, Egyptian Museum.

Man with Arms Raised

***Determinative in words associated with the idea of height or raising* (ḳ3i, *"to be tall,"* sw3ʿš, *"to exalt"*) *and to the espression of joy and triumph* (ḥʿi).**

The gesture represented by the hieroglyph is multisemantic: the upraised arms certainly convey the idea of height by indicating a level above one's own head and in an imprecise spot toward heaven; at the same time, it is not foreign to our own expressions of great joy and, in particular, of the upraised arms of victory; it conjures almost immediately the image of a typical football player, having just made a touchdown. These were the meanings transmitted by the hieroglyph and the two probably are connected by the common emotional experience that unites the feelings of joy and the lightness of upward yearning. When the gesture is represented in scenes of daily life, it recurs in a series of contexts that are apparently not associated among themselves, but in truth are connected to the one idea of triumph: we find it above all in scenes in which an important personage or faithful subject is recompensed by the Pharaoh for his services and receives the so-called "golden reward," whereby praising servants anoint him with precious ointments; the person so honored is in fact figured in the position of the hieroglyph, arms raised and palms turned upward.

It recurs also in scenes in which the supplicant, having solicited the oracular judgment of the god in order to settle a difficult legal question, has received a favorable verdict. And finally, it appears in scenes in which the deceased, having undergone the divine judgment and the weighing of his heart, is proclaimed by the gods to be just and admitted to the company of the blessed.

A different, though apparently similar gesture, is connected to the expression of pain and grief, in the determination of the verb *ḥ3i*, "carry out the funeral lamentations, to grieve." It is rarely seen, and it must have been overshadowed by the use of this hieroglyph.

General Horemheb in the triumphal gesture. From his tomb at Saqqara, Eighteenth Dynasty. Leiden, Rijksmuseum van Oudheden.

Mummy

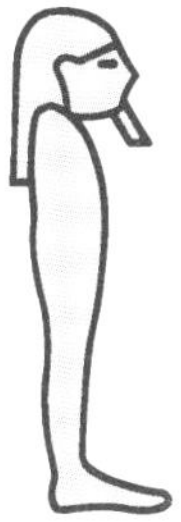

***Determinative in* wỉ, *"mummy,"* twt, *"statue," and in all nouns connected to the notion of form, aspect* (kỉ), *and metamorphoses* (ḫprw).**

This hieroglyph is relatively late: it does not appear before the Twelfth Dynasty, even though, as is known, mummification was practiced much earlier. The mummy is shown standing, the body bound by long strips of linen; on the head is the usual cartonnage, cloth, or plaster mask complete with wig and beard. The similarity between this hieroglyph and the little funerary statues known as *ushabti*, which were placed in the tomb with the deceased as a kind of substitute that would carry out unpleasant tasks for him in the afterworld, is remarkable. Perhaps there is nothing that suggests to us immobility more than a mummy does. Yet for the ancient Egyptian the mummy represented a phase in the evolutionary sequence, a stage in the metamorphic chain through which every being, whether dead man or god, passed. Every form, every exterior aspect is only a transitory moment, caught up in the gears of the eternal cosmic cycle: this is the message transmitted by the hieroglyph.

Mummy on the Funeral Bed

Determinative of the verb* sḏr, *"recline," "sleep," and in nouns connected to the notion of death.

Sleep and death are closely related and are both disquieting experiences, so it is not surprising that the Egyptians casually alternated the image of the sleeping man and the mummy in this hieroglyph. The same sign could serve to determinate the verb *sḏr,* "sleep," as well as *ḥpt,* "death, die," or *ḫꜥt,* "cadaver."
Like the dead entering into the underworld, the man entering the mysterious reign of dreams needed special protection: images of protective gods, such as the grotesque and benevolent dwarf Bes, adorned the walls of bedrooms and headrests. The night belonged to the obscure world of chaos, when genii and bad spirits traveled under the protection of dark to attack mankind. After the Old Kingdom, the figure of the sleeping man disappeared, ceding his place to the mummy. For the rest, the funerary bed with its leonine feet was none other than a depiction of beds in common use.

Pregnant Woman

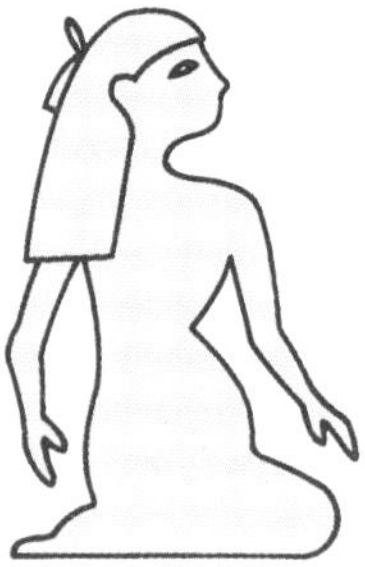

Determinative in* ìwr, *"to conceive," and* bk3, *"to be pregnant."

As always the woman is squatting on the earth; the change in the thin silhouette and the arms hanging down and away from the body, suggesting encumbering weight, indicate pregnancy. The Egyptians were cognizant of the connection between sexual relations and conception, and medical papyri made mention of favoring or avoiding pregnancy. The Ebers papyrus prescribes a contraceptive method whose effects may last from one to three years, based on acacia, dates, and a type of squash (used only pharmaceutically), all to be ground up in honey. When the numerous recipes and prescriptive methods of contraception failed, one called on the gods; to avoid pregnancy, one resorted to abortion. The medical texts also carry a series of methods to determine if a woman is pregnant, mixing rational observation of symptoms (pulse rate, color of the skin and eyes, tendency toward nausea and vomiting, etc.) with other methods tied to the magical realm. As to the embryo, it does not seem that the Egyptians gave much credit to the woman's participation in its formation; in the later period, it was thought that the sperm was responsible for the formation of the bones and the woman for that of the flesh. There are numerous grotesque containers with enlarged abdomens and pendulous breasts that contained the ointments with which pregnant women massaged their bellies to help the elasticity of their skin and, as they believed, to benefit the child. The gestation period was considered to be about ten lunar months; but fabulous Egyptian tales tell that the more powerful wizards could foretell the exact day and hour of birth.

Small grotesque ointment vase in the form of a pregnant woman. Abydos, Eighteenth Dynasty. Cairo, Egyptian Museum.

Woman Who Gives Birth

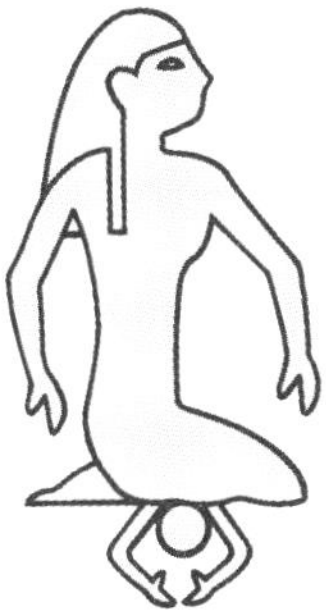

Ideogram or determinative in* msi, *"to give birth," and similar words.

In ancient Egypt, according to a practice still used in some cultures, women gave birth while crouching over bricks, called "birth bricks," that were personified in the goddess Meskhenet and invoked by the appropriate hymns during labor. The bricks are not visible in the hieroglyph, but the position favoring the child's exit is clear, as the little head and arms are shown below the mother-making explicit the meaning of the sign. Delivery and birth were considered special moments and were surrounded by an aura of sacredness, thus they required a particular separate space: in more humble dwellings it could have been a room dedicated temporarily, but paintings show that sometimes a structure was built, a pavilion of cane, papyri, and reed mats, probably erected in the garden or on the roof, and in which the delivery and the following fourteen-day ritual isolation took place. In these paintings the mothers wear their hair in a special way, collected in two large clusters at the side of the head with a sort of cone tied on top: perhaps the tightly tied hair was released during labor to accelerate the birth by means of sympathetic magic. In the birth description in one of the fabulous tales in the Westcar papyrus, the gods Isis, Nephtis, and the frog goddess Heqet assist the delivering mother, pretending to be doctors and presenting themselves at the door in the form of "dancing girls"—perhaps this is in reference to a ritual which is still unknown to us. Naturally, magic formulas and chants, various amulets and prayers to the gods who protected deliveries (the hippopotamus goddess Toeris, the dwarf Bes, as well as Meskhenet and Heqet) were called upon to ease the birth. But not always did each proceed in the best way.

In a room in the royal tomb of Tell el-Amarna is to be found the representation of the death during delivery of Princess Meketaton, second daughter of Pharaoh Akhenaton and of Nefertiti: the princess lies on the bed surrounded by the family in the posture of grief, while a woman carries away the newborn child, alive and kicking.

Woman delivering on the delivery chair, assisted by the two goddesses. Sculptor's model from Dendera, Greco-Roman era. Cairo, Egyptian Museum.

VARIANTS/COMBINATIONS

The variant substitutes fenek skins (phonetic value: *ms*) for the child's head.

Breast-feeding Woman

Determinative in* mnʿt, *"wet nurse."

The sign shows a mother, seated on the ground, who gives her breast to the child. Images in relief, painted, and in full round confirm that this was the usual position for breastfeeding; the more hieratic variant in which the woman is seated on a chair gave its traits to the very common iconography of the *dea lactans*, which was then transmitted also to Christian art. Normally, Egyptian mothers breast-fed their children for a long period: texts tell us that the prescribed time was three years, and that the norm did not change for thousands of years. Still in the third century B.C. a demotic wet-nurse contract reads as follows: "I come into your [= the father's] house, to be your wet nurse, [guarantee that] the milk in both breasts is good, in order to feed the newborn Petesuchos, your son. I will nourish him, feed him, and keep him from all harm or accident that a wet nurse might cause . . . until three years have passed." (Cairo papyrus, inv. 30604). It was believed that breastfeeding was contraceptive and that sexual relations during breastfeeding could damage the quality of the milk or make it dry up. The contract cited above has a clause for this case, in that it calls for a heavy fine should the wet nurse's breasts go dry. Wet nurses were used when the mother either did not have sufficient milk, or when she had died in childbirth.

Breastfeeding women wore amulets in the form of the waxing moon, as it was believed to increase the flow of milk. Mothers' milk—and particularly that of the mother of a boy—was considered to be a highly effective medical and magic cure. With this scope in mind, it was conserved in special anthropomorphically shaped containers that generally represented a crouching woman with a child in her lap or at her breast.

Small copper statue of a mother breast-feeding. Twelfth Dynasty. New York, Brooklyn Museum.

VARIANT/COMBINATIONS

Determinative in *rnn*, "nourish."

Head

Ideogram in* tp*, "head," sometimes to be read* ḏ3ḏ3*, with the same meaning; determinative in similar words and in verbs related to actions which implied movement of the head.

The head is in profile, bearded and wearing a wig of varying style depending on the era: in the Old Kingdom, for example, it was longer. When in profile, all the essential characteristics of the head could be shown, and it was differentiated from the hieroglyph that indicated the face. Even though the hieroglyph renders a perfect image of a head, none of the traits that form the graphic code correspond to the norms of reality: the eye, as we have already noted, was shown frontally, so as not to lose any part of this most precious element; the oversized ear was generally depicted at the center of the head, also frontal and flattened; and in the less stylized versions, the nose assumed proportions that were too large even for African physiognomy. Each element was really drawn as a single hieroglyphic sign in order to render this encompassing sign very clear and legible.

Face

Ideogram in* ḥr*, "face," from which it takes its phonetic value* ḥr*, and connected words.

This is one of the few hieroglyphs that appear in the frontal view: this point of view is in fact the most meaningful characteristic of this sign, from which the preposition *ḥr*, "in front of," or the adjective *ḥry*, "that which is in front, or over," derive. The image that it gives us of the human face is evocative and unequivocal; but not at all naturalistic. All its elements are exaggerated: the snub nose is flat and broad; the ears are the same as in the hieroglyph of the head, but here seem glued on afterward, so that they stick out; finally, the mouth, overly large and drawn with a single outline, as is the hieroglyph of the mouth itself.
The effect of the whole is almost brutal, but at the same time explicit. A curious detail is the chromatic convention used in this hieroglyph: while the skin color in the sign for head is the normal pink or red-brown, the color of the face is an intense golden yellow.

Eye

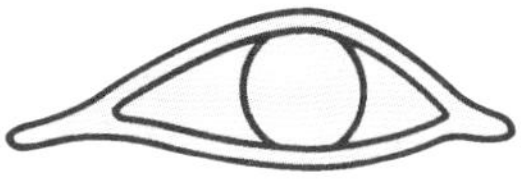

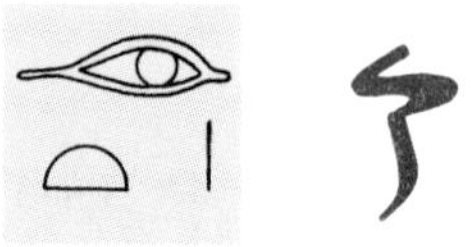

Ideogram in* ỉrt, *"eye," from which, phonetically,* ỉr. *Determinative in words relative to the act of seeing and to the organ of vision.

The drawing of the eye is quite elongated, as if the hieroglyph had transposed its rotundity onto the plane, and gained an "ironed-out" aspect. The surroundings and the iris are generally colored black, while the corners are red. The eye is the organ of perception, and at the same time expresses personality and sentiment; thus it occupied a significant role in Egyptian thought. It was the discriminating factor between seeing and not, between light and darkness, and it was considered a precious and religiously significant organ.

The eye could give off magnetic fluids, and the uraeus, the cobra which rises from the king's crown, was the metaphoric expression of this power to turn away malicious forces.

This belief in the power emanating from eyes explains their apotropaic use: eyes were represented on stele and on sarcophagi to give the power of their fluids to the deceased, and at the same time give the possibility of seeing out in defense.

On the other hand, belief in the evil eye was widespread: "the bad eye," as they called it. The eye's magic aura was amply developed on mythologic and religious planes: the solar disc (and, secondarily, the moon) was the eye of the supreme god; from his tears (*rmwt*) man had come (*rmṯ*), just as the most valuable aromas and ointments originated in his secretions. Various myths and a very beautiful saga center around the eye of the sun god Re. The saga tells how the eye, in its female personification of the divine (the goddess Tefnut, who is assimilated to many other goddesses), enraged with Re, took refuge in the distant African country of Kush and how the baboon-headed god Thot succeeded in bringing her back to Egypt.

Originally this was probably an astronomic myth, connected to the winter solstice, which became stratified with time and incorporated different versions. Its final version comes to us in a long demotic papyrus of the third century A.D.

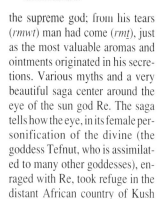

Detail of the eyes from a portrait head of Queen Hatshepsut. From Deir el Bahri, Eighteenth Dynasty. Cairo, Egyptian Museum.

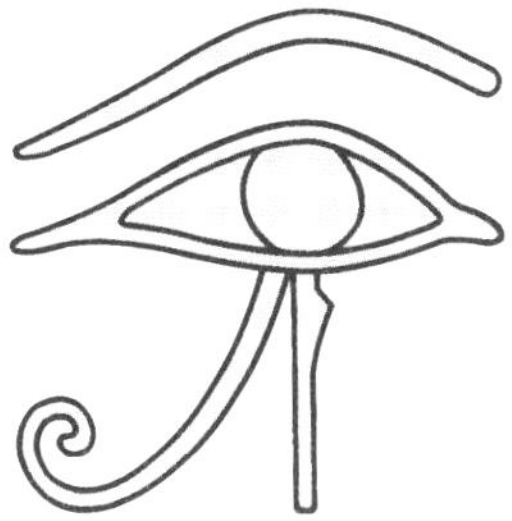

Horus's Eye

Ideogram or determinative in* wḏ3t, *literally "the healthy (or healed) eye," the name of Horus's eye.

The eye of the falcon-god Horus is shown just as the human eye, except that in the lower part it has a stylization of the vivid black spot and the feathers that appear below the eye of the predatory bird. According to ancient myth, Horus's eye was torn out by his rival Seth, the uncle who became pretender to the Egyptian throne after having killed and cut into pieces Horus's father, Osiris. Thot, the wise lunar god, patron of the sciences and writing, patiently restored and healed him. This multisemantic symbol implies a state of recovered integrity: in the astronomy it is the perfect lunar symbol and alludes to the progressive filling of the lunar sphere; in the ideology of the royalty of the Pharaohs it represents the eternal renewal of royal divinity from king to king. Wherever a weakness or faltering might menace the natural order of things, the image restores, and through its protective magic, confers a message of hope—a reflection of the Egyptian faith in the continual reintegration of universal harmony. For these reasons this was a much-loved symbol for the Egyptians. It was used in all sizes, shapes, and stones to decorate amulets to wear around the neck or in the settings of magnificent jewels; the lunettes of the stele and sarcophagi; and propitious rebuses in vase decorations and other personal objects. In an elegant graphic form it was also used in the measuring grains: the parts of the eye, which myth says were dissected by Seth, were each given the value of a fraction: the sum of the whole—equivalent to the recomposition of the eye by Thot—corresponded to the whole unit. In reality, the sum of the six fractions is 63/64; the Egyptians presumed that Thot's magic made up the remaining 1/64.

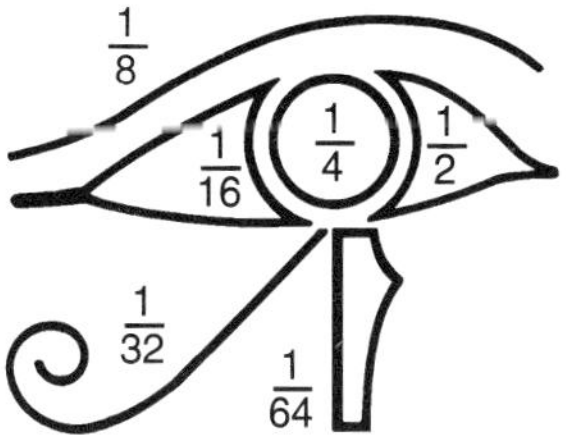

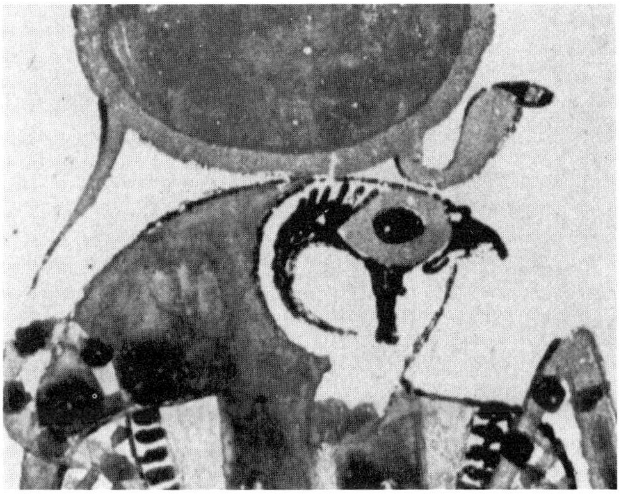

The eye of the falcon-god Horus. Detail from the stele of the harpist Djedkhonsuiufankh. Paris, Louvre.

Hair

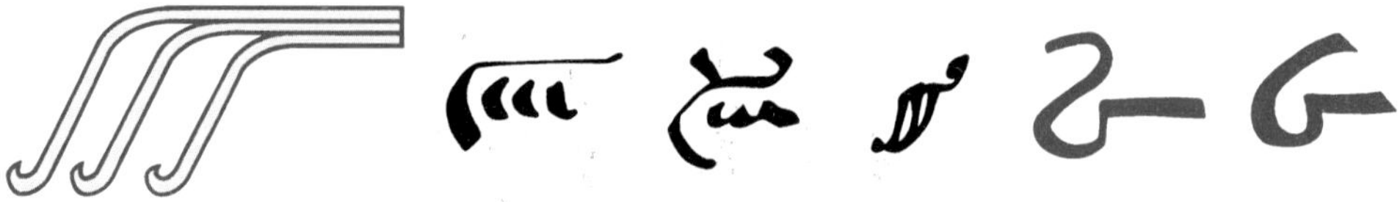

Determinative in* ỉny*, "hair," and associated words, in* ỉnm*, "skin," and in verbs and nouns concerning the notion of grief.

The lock of hair served in Egyptian writing to determine various words: the most surprising, but at the same time most revealing of the Egyptian attitude toward this physical attribute, is the word *ỉwn*, which indicates the complexion and coloring as well as the character of a person. The type and dressing of the hair are indeed significant keys to the personality and rank of an individual: a shaven head with a braid on the side indicates childhood; hair pulled high up on the head in two tight groups was part of the specific and magically functional hair style of the woman in labor; since the times of the New Kingdom, the completely shaven head and body denoted a priest. The hair of foreign populaces was very diversified and carefully observed. Just as long, loose hair suggested unseemliness; vague immodesty in the case of musicians and dancers; or an expression of pain in the case of grief; heavy, laboriously arranged wigs indicated high position, and was emblematic of those admitted to court or high functionaries. Egyptians had a real love for wigs: they made them from all kinds of human hair, in all styles according to the era and custom. Their use was not restricted to ceremonial occasions but in general to wordly events: they were always worn at banquets, where men and women balanced perfumed cones on their heads; these dissolved in the heat, dripping perfumed ointments onto their shoulders. No lady could go without; the erotic potential of the wig was irresistible for the Egyptian, as is shown in the passage from the *Tale of Two Brothers* in which the wife of Anubi revenges herself for her brother-in-law's rejection of her by giving a falsified version of the story to her husband: "he found me alone and said 'Come, let's spend an hour together in bed. Put on your wig'."

Above: *Prince with the side-lock of youth. Abydos, temple of Seti I, Eighteenth Dynasty.*
Below: *Lamenters with their hair down. Thebes, Sheikh Abd el-Qurna, tomb of Ramose, Eighteenth Dynasty.*

Nose

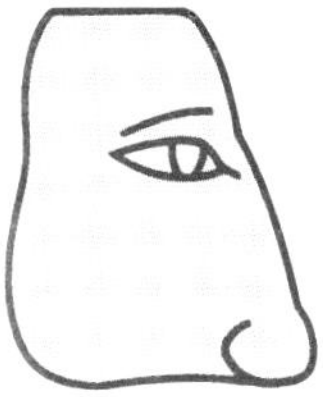

***Ideogram or determinative in* fnḏ/fnd *and* šrt, *both meaning "nose"; determinative in words connected to nose, to smell, and to joy. From* ẖnt, *"face," of which it is determinative: phonetic value* ẖnt.**

The sign for the nose, which by itself would have been unclear, includes the cheek and the eye. As the organ of respiration, through which the "breath of life" passes, it occupies an important place in Egyptian thought. Myths narrate that the demiurge Atum created the god Shu by blowing through his nose. Mutilation of statue noses was, together with the cancellation of the name, one of the means of negating life in the afterworld for that person. Egyptian sensitivity to the olfactory world conferred on the nose even further importance: the scenes in which men and gods are shown sniffing the perfume of a flower—almost always the lotus—are quite frequent. The delicacy of a perfume was considered the source of authentic pleasure, and this explains the connection between the hieroglyph and the numerous words related to joy or pleasure that are determinated by the sign of the nose.

Mouth

***Ideogram in* r3, *"mouth," and phonetically* r.**

The mouth is represented only by its outline, lengthened and with no indication of the partition of the upper lip; it is generally painted red. It would seem that the original meaning of *r3* was "fissure, cleft" and also "division," "separating element between two parts," whence came the successive meaning of "part" and also "riverbank." In ancient Egyptian anatomic theory it represented one of the seven openings in the head, as well as the principle opening of the body, associated as it was with eating and speaking. In the mythological sphere, the signs for mouth and vagina are frequently interchangeable: Nut, goddess of the heaven, conceives of the sun by swallowing it, and then giving birth to it again at dawn, just as in another legend, in the form of sow she devours the stars; the god Atum, primordial demiurge, swallows his own seed and thus initiates the procreation of the divine race; there are other examples as well.

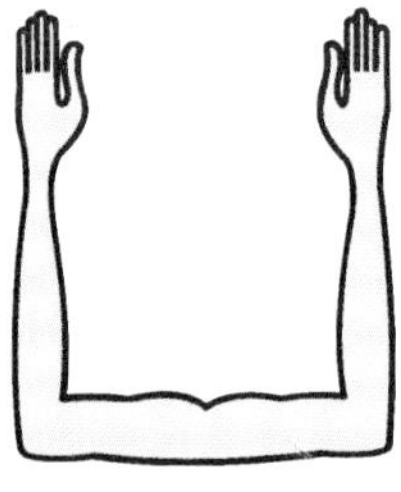

Arms

***Ideogram in* k3, *"spirit": phonetic value* k3.**

This so apparently clear sign appears very early in the hieroglyphic system, and is in reality far from being clear: to which gesture do the raised (or stretched forward: under the rules of Egyptian perspective one cannot differentiate the two) arms allude?
The fact that the sign never became a determinative makes one assume that it is a rather special gesture, probably religious and connected from the beginning to the abstract and fleeting notion, for modern thinking, of the Egyptian *ka*.
Ka is a vital power, which both men and gods possess. It is transmitted from father to son and, as such, more than an element of the individual personality, it belongs, in modern terms, to the inherited genetic patrimony of men.
The potter king Khnum forms the *ka* of a man on his wheel as he is forming the body and in the funeral rites, the *ka* reunites with the man after his death.
Of all the parts of a man's personality, in the Egyptian conception, this is the most vital, with a deep association with sexual power *(k3)* and with food, as the source of energy and life *(k3w)*.
According to one of the most common interpretations of the sign, the gesture of the extended arms could allude to the offering of food, a sacred moment in divine and funeral ceremonies. There are examples of this in some stone ritual trays from the Predynastic and Early Dynastic periods, where the hieroglyph of the arms forms the rim of the offering plate.
Another interpretation, equally plausible, places the accent instead on the passage of the vital essence from father to son: the *ka* gesture would be the metaphoric translation, through the image of the hug, the act by which the mysterious essence is transmitted.
The gods, too, may infuse their *ka* and transmit it to another god, to the king, or to common men: in the course of creation, the demiurge god gives his own *ka* to the gods.

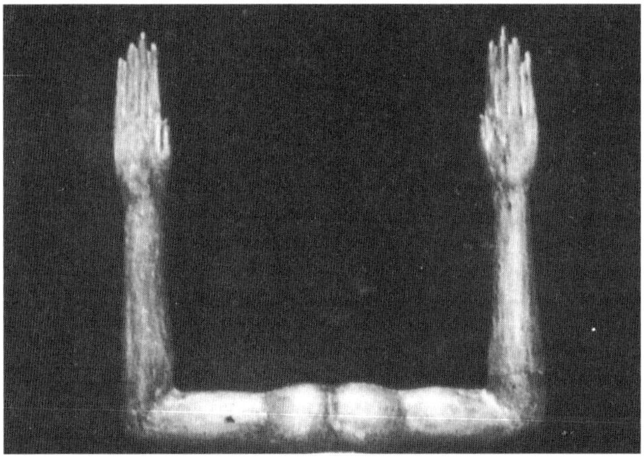

The ka-*sign on the head of Pharaoh Awibra-Hor. Dahshur, Thirteenth Dynasty. Cairo, Egyptian Museum.*

VARIANTS/COMBINATIONS

Combination of the *ka* sign with a divine standard: expresses the divine nature of *ka*.

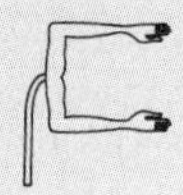

Symbol of Neheb-kau, mythic serpent and very essence of the creator god.

Arms in the Sign of Negation

***Ideogram in the adverbs of negation* n *and* nn *and in the relative negative pronouns* ỉwty, *"which does not"; determinative in various negative verbs and in the verb* ḫm, *"to ignore, to be ignorant," whence comes the use as determinative phonetic* ḫm.**

The abstract concept of negation is very clearly shown by this hieroglyph, which evidently was drawn from the ancient Egyptian battery of gestures: the slightly bent arms spread out to the sides of the body (whether slightly upward or downward is indifferent). The curve that joins them suggests shrugged shoulders; the cupped upturned or outturned palms of the hands expresses perfectly the mix of renunciation and helplessness. This last detail, essential to understanding the gesture, eventually lost its authentic meaning for the Egyptians, and it is not unusual to find the hands reversed, palms down.

It is interesting to note that while writing found in this image a universal image of negation, the language was not so concise: in ancient Egyptian each type of negation was expressed by a specific root.

Arm Offering Bread

Ideogram for* dỉ, *"to give," in antiquity for* ỉmỉ, *imperative of "give."

It seems that the triangular mark offered on the palm of the extended hand is to be interpreted as bread, a hypothesis tied more to the significance of the hieroglyph in which it appears than to any other evidence. On the other hand, the scenes of bread-making and preparation of sweets, like the piles of loaves and buns sometimes represented, show oblong loaves, conical in shape, if not so pointed, and archaeology has found innumerable conical forms for bread.

One should not exclude the possibility that the sign represents a wedge of bread or cake. To give bread is, in any case, the act of charity par excellence and it is plausible that the Egyptians used its image to show the act of giving.

VARIANTS/COMBINATIONS

Arm with a round loaf, drawing of the imperative "give," *ỉmỉ*, more often seen as *m*.

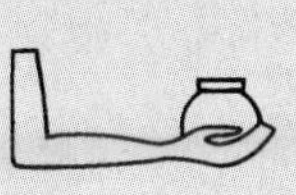

Arm with a bowl: determinative in the verb *ḥnk*, "to offer."

Arm with the Djeser-stick

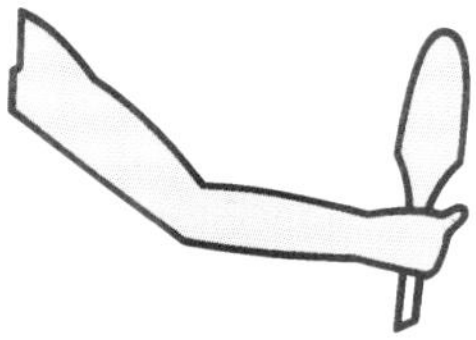

Ideogram or determinative in* ḏsr, *"to be holy," "to segregate."

An arm holding an object generally is an expression of aggression in the hieroglyphic code. The object in this hand has been variously interpreted: for some it is a special sign of power, the so-called *mks*-stick; others prefer to see the *nḥbt*-wand, which probably possessed magical powers. It is certain that the sign underwent a series of reinterpretations and re-elaborations over time: the oldest examples, which go back to the earliest dynastic era, show a long staff held in both fists and with a nodule above the handle. At one point in its long evolution the instrument was even interpreted as being a leaf of lettuce, a plant that was holy to the Egyptians and in general associated with the god Min, the fertility cult, and sexual potency.

The meaning of the hieroglyph became precise in the earliest times and it is therefore important to try to establish its original significance. Judging from the oldest images in which the staff or stick appears, it would seem to have been a weapon, like the mace with which the king squashed the heads of his enemies, but used for defense, for deflecting blows. It may be, then, that the hieroglyph represented the act of pushing off, in both the literal and magical senses, repelling evil spirits and influences.

From this action is derived the root *ḏsr* and its various meanings and, above all, that of cleansing and clearing an area of evil influences in preparation for sacred ceremonies. From there the term assumed the significance of "defining a sacred area," and then "segregate," as in separating the sacred from the profane, until it covered more generally the whole range of sacred shades of meaning. That the sacred condition is above all one of separation, this is a convention on the anthropological and linguistic level in many civilizations. *t3 ḏsr*, "the holy ground," was by definition the necropolis, ground consecrated to the dead and to funeral cults, and carefully separated from the territory of the living.

King Menthuhetep with the mace in one hand and a long staff with the ḏsr *instrument in the other. Eleventh Dynasty. Cairo, Egyptian Museum.*

Phallus

D ***eterminative of virility, used for both men and animals. Phonetic value:*** **mt.**

In the hieroglyphic system the phallus is represented erect, in its function as organ of procreation, and always circumcised, according to the practice noted by Herodotus (II, 104), adopted from the Egyptians by the Syrians and Phoenicians. The Egyptians have left us an eloquent documentation of this custom: tomb and temple scenes show young boys undergoing the procedure, immobilized by a man at each side, while the operating priest, armed with an obsidian knife, is crouched in front of him. If the texts and pictures were not enough evidence, the mummies have given incontrovertible proof. Apart from the hygienic reasons which, according to Herodotus, called for this practice, it was associated with the initiation rites for young men: a relief from the Old Kingdom shows an adolescent whose body is completely painted white (the color of death preceding rebirth) and wears an animal mask on his face, in a scene which seems to be that of the ceremonial which accompanied circumcision. The Egyptians used various terms for it, from the scientific *(b3ḥ)* to the popular (*ḥnn*, "hoe"), to the lyric (*wsr*, "the potent," *nfr*, "the beautiful," etc.). The phonetic value *mt* is the only survivor of an ancient root *mt*, found in other Hamitic-Semitic languages. In the oldest phases of the writing, the Egyptians differentiated the use of the hieroglyph *mt* from *b3ḥ*, the phallus about to eject seed: while the first was the generic determinative for virility, the second indicated more specifically the functions of the organ. The distinction was already lost, however, in the Middle Kingdom, and since then the two have been used rather interchangeably.
Sexual potency was surrounded by a magic-religious aura; venerated under the form of various cults, such as that of the holy bulls, or in notions such as the *ka*, it was protected by magic, with amulets and various formulas.

VARIANTS/COMBINATIONS

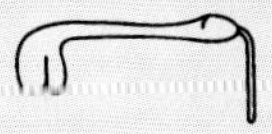

A phallus in the act of ejecting liquid. For the sign's usage, often the same as *mt*, see above.

Circumcision scene. Saqqara, tomb of Ankhmahor, beginning of Sixth Dynasty.

Man seated on his heel

Determinative in *ḥmsỉ*, "to sit."

Man hiding behind a wall

Determinative in *ỉmn*, "to hide, to be hidden."

Fatigued man

Determinative in verbs and nouns of tiredness (i.e., *wrd*, "tired") or weakness (i.e., *bdš*, "weak"; *gnn*, "soft").

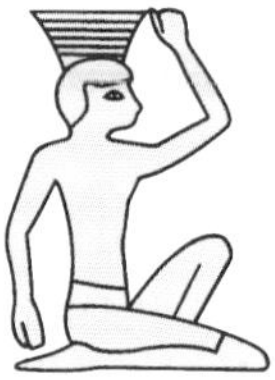

Man with basket on his head

Determinative or ideogram in verbs expressing the action of "carrying, transporting" *(3tp, f3ỉ)* and in *k3t*, "to work."

Man holding an oar

Determinative in *sḳdw*, "to navigate."

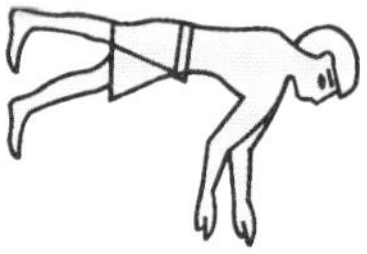

Falling man

Ideogram or determinative in *ẖr*, "to fall" and derivatives.

Adoring man

Variant of the seated man in adoration.

Man bending over

Determinative in *ksỉ*, "to bend over."

Man striking with a staff

Determinative in terms connected to physical activities and to the concept of muscular force. Ideogram or determinative in *ḥwỉ*, "strike, beat."

Variant of the preceding

Man with stick raised above his head

Determinative in *sḥr*, "to squash."

Running man

Phonogram in *ỉnw*, "messengers."

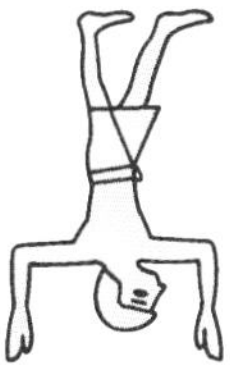

Upside down man

Determinative in *sḫd*, "to be upside down."

Man with arms extended backwards

Determinative for the act of turning (i.e., *ʿnw*, "to turn the face."

Dancing man

Ideogram or determinative in *ḫbỉ*, "to dance."

Man with a bundle on his shoulder

Ideogram or determinative for "not sedentary": *mnỉw*, "shepherd," *rwỉ*, "to wander."

Man grinding in a mortar

Ideogram or determinative in *ḫwsỉ*, "to grind in a mortar," "to construct."

Man mixing in a vat

Ideogram or determinative in *ʿftỉ*, "brewer of beer."

Man holding two imaginary animals by the neck

Ideogram or determinative in *ḳỉs* (the city Cusae), in Upper Egypt.

Syrian with a stick

Determinative for foreigner: *ʿ3mw*, "Asiatic"; *ỉwntỉw-stỉw*, "Nubian archer people."

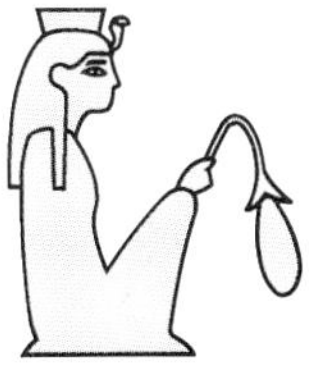

Queen with diadem and bouquet of flowers in her hand

Determinative for queen.

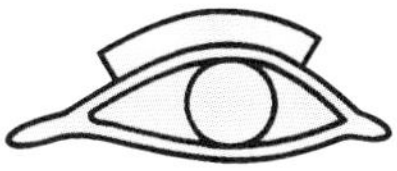

Eye made-up on the upper lid

Determinative of actions or particular states of the eye.

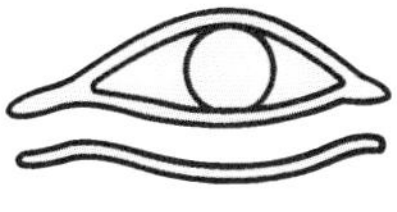

Eye made-up on the lower lid

Determinative in *msḏmt*, "galena," used as an eye cosmetic, and in *ʿn*, "beautiful," from which phonetically *ʿn*.

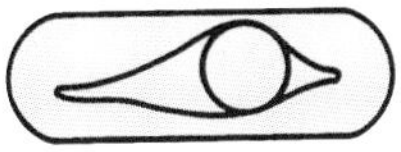

Eye in an oval

Determinative in *ʿn*, "beautiful."

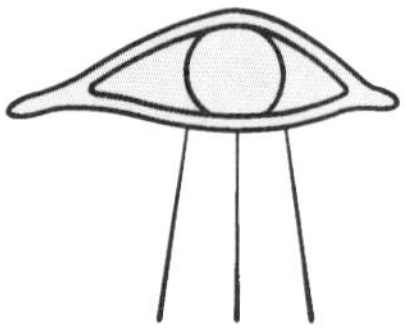

Crying eye
Determinative in *rmỉ*, "to cry."

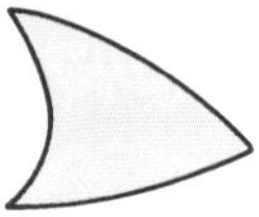

Left side of the cornea of Horus's eye
It is used only as the symbol of the fraction 1/2 in grain measures.

Pupil
Determinative in *ḏfḏ*, "pupil."

Eyebrow
Repeated twice it is the writing for *ỉnḥ*, "eyebrow."

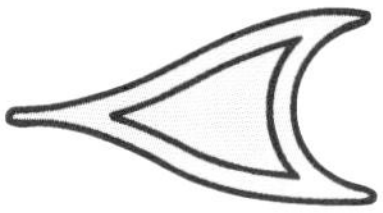

Right part of the cornea
Symbol for 1/16

Stylization of the feathers around the falcon's eye
Symbol for 1/32.

Black mark typical of the border of the falcon's eye
Symbol for 1/64.

Combination of the two previous signs
Ideogram or determinative in *tỉt*, "image," "figure."

Ear
Ideogram or determinative in *msḏr*, "ear."

Upper lip with teeth
Ideogram or determinative in *spt*, "lip," "border."

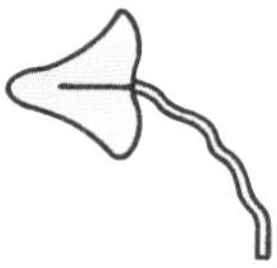

Lip in profile with liquid seeping out
Determinative in *psg*, *bšỉ*, *ḳ3*ʿ, "to spit," "to vomit," and in *sn ḳ*, "blood."

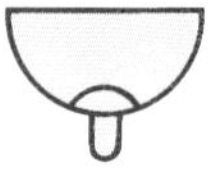

Breast
Ideogram or determinative in *mnḏ*, "breast," and in connected actions (i.e.: *snḳ*, "to suck").

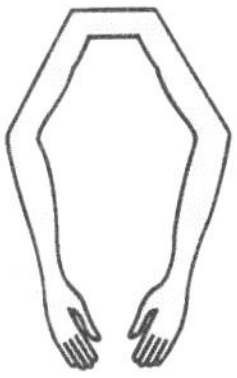

Arms extended to hug
Determinative for hugging: *ỉnḳ*, "to surround"; *ḥpt*, "to hug"; etc. Ideogram or determinative in *sḫn*, "to hug," "to search for."

Rowing arms
Ideogram or determinative in *ḫnỉ*, "to row," from which the phonogram *ḫn*.

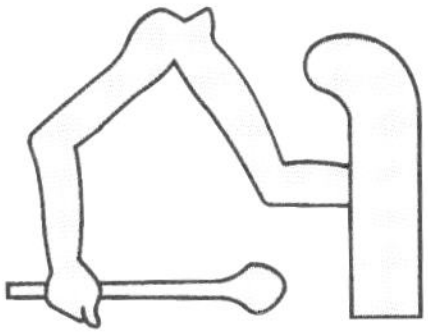

Arms with shield and ax
Ideogram in *ʿḥ3*, "combat."

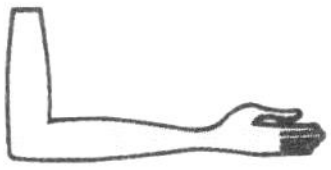

Arm
Ideogram in *ʿw*, "arm," from which the phonogram *ʿ*.

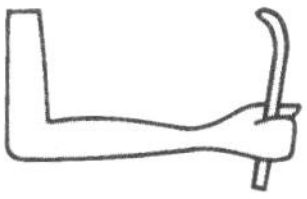

Arm with stick
Ideogram or determinative in *ḫ3ỉ*, "measure." In verbs and nouns indicating force or power, often substitutes as determinative for the man who strikes.

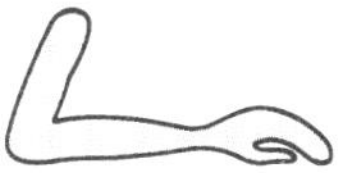

Arm with palm turned down
Ideogram or determinative in *rmnw*, "arm," and synonyms. Determinative for the movements of the arm. From *nỉ*, "to push away," the phonetic value *nỉ*.

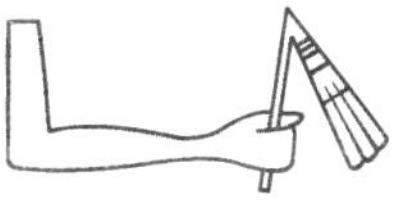

Arm with whip
Ideogram in *ḫwỉ*, "to protect."

Hand
Ideogram in *ḏrt*, "hand." Phonetic value *d* (see the Semitic yad, "hand").

Hand with cupped palm
Determinative of hand (*ḏrt*, *ḏ3t*) when written phonetically.

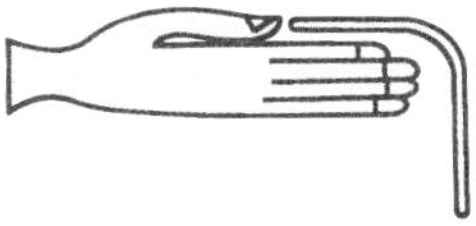

Hand with dripping liquid
Ideogram or determinative in *ỉdt*, "fragrance"; "dew," "sweat."

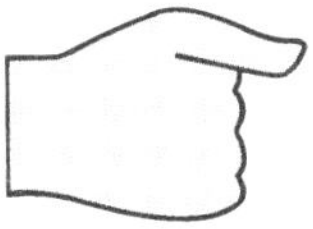

Fist
Determinative for "to grab": *3mm*, *ḫfʿ*.

Finger
Ideogram or determinative in *ḏbʿ*, "finger."

Legs in movement

Ideogram in *ỉw*, "to come." Determinative in verbs of motion.

Legs walking backwards

Determinative in *ꜥnn*, "to return"; *sbḥ3*, "to make retreat," etc.

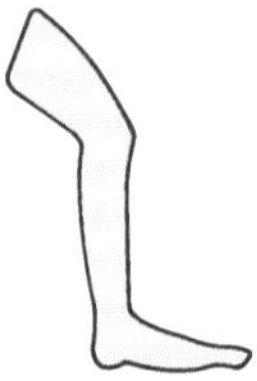

Leg

Ideogram or determinative in *rd*, "leg." Determinative for the names of the parts of the leg. From other names for leg and its parts derive the phonetic values *pds*, *wꜥrt*, and *sbḳ*.

Foot

Phonogram *b*.

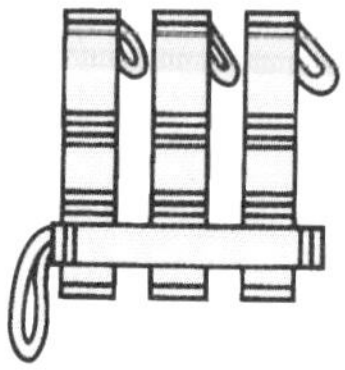

Toe

Ideogram or determinative in *s3ḥ*, "toe," from which derives the phonetic value *s3ḥ*.

Combination of legs and flowering cane

In *ỉỉ*, "to come" and derivations.

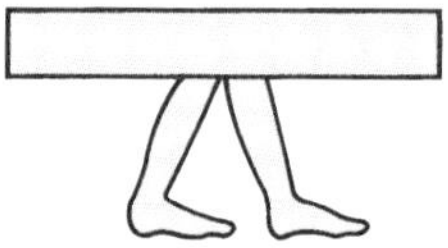

Combination of the basin š with legs

In *šm*, "to go."

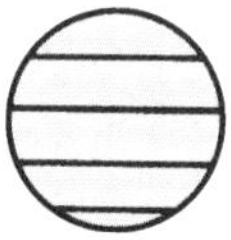

Once interpreted as an animal placenta, but probably a type of basket

Phonetic value *ḫ*.

Gods

In hieroglyphic writing, not many of the names of the gods were written in a single symbolic sign, an ideogram that would synthetically render the essence. The gods were strongly associated, from the earliest times, with a sacred animal, an emblem, or a fetish. In numerous other cases the Egyptians preferred to write their names in phonograms, alphabetic or multiconsonant, adding the generic determinative for god. In cursive writing—hieratic or demotic—this was the most common usage. The complex, multifaceted, and abstract nature of many of the gods of ancient Egypt made it impossible to render the names by a single sign. The same hieroglyphs that expressed the abstract notion of god seem to derive from the funeral cult of the archaic kings. In a phase after that of the formation of the graphic code, the Egyptians developed a series of individualized hieroglyphs for many of the gods; starting with the construction of the general anthropomorphic god, and adding the mask, animal head, astral symbol, or emblem typical of the deity.

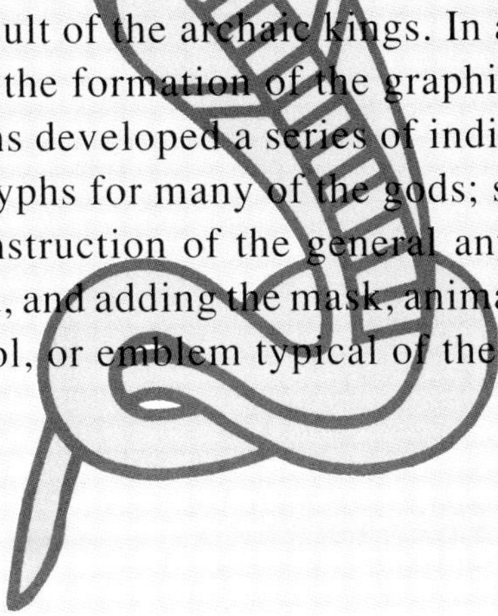

Seated God

D ***eterminative in names of gods. As ideogram, it is the first person singular pronoun, when the subject is a god or a king.***

T his is not the oldest of the images used to express the concept of godhead among the Egyptians. Much earlier than its appearance—which goes back to the Fifth Dynasty, around 2400 B.C.—it was preceded by the symbol of the divine vexillum (the ideogram for *nṯr*, "god") and by the falcon raised on a support for the statues and the sacred emblems, both found already at the end of the fourth millennium B.C. In respect to the older signs, the grapheme of the seated god gives an anthropomorphized vision of the concept of the deity. There are those who would like to read in the triad a synthesis of the evolution of thc idea of god as such in ancient Egypt—a passage from the original fetishism (the fetish *nṯr*), through animal worship (the falcon on the stand), to the cult of a god in man's likeness. In truth, this interpretation is doubtful: the use of the three graphemes does not agree with the linear development of evolution. The problem of fetishism in archaic religion is a difficult one, nor can one pass off Egyptian animal worship as being an antique phase, limited in time and culturally surpassed by later developments. It is more interesting to try to analyse the hieroglyph itself: it represents a man seated on the ground with his knees drawn up toward his chest, completely wrapped in a sudarium that hides his arms as well, and marked by the long ceremonial beard, which is the prerogative of kings and gods. Connecting these observations to the fact that the appearance of the sign in the *Pyramid Texts* happens only and always in relation to Osiris (the oldest occurrence is just as determinative of the name of the god) and to the identification of Osiris and the dead king, elements such as the squatting position and the body wrapped in a sudarium assume a new importance. One can then hypothesize that the hieroglyph originates in connection with the divine nature of the dead king and that only later was it extended to gods in general.

Gods seated at the base of the celestial vault. Deir el-Medinah, tomb of Senedjem, Twentieth Dynasty.

VARIANTS/COMBINATIONS

The falcon on a divine standard.

The divine vexillum, ideogram for *nṯr*.

Pharaoh

Determinative of king. Ideogram for writing the first person singular in discourses by the king.

The sign begins as a later adaptation of the earlier determinative of the godhead, leaving the general characteristics unchanged and refining the royal nature by the addition of a few elements: essentially the uraeus on the forehead and, above all in the variants from the New Kingdom, the short helmet-shaped wig and the substitution of the straight beard for the slightly curved beard that marked the seated god. Beginning with the Eighteenth Dynasty, it takes the place of the determinative of seated god as the writing of the first person pronoun, when the subject is the king.

Perhaps inclusion of it in the hieroglyphs for gods is inappropriate: very early—certainly already in the era in which this grapheme was formed—the Egyptians distinguished the nature of the divinity of the pharaohs from that of the numerous gods that populated their vast pantheon. The very fact that, at a certain point, they felt it necessary to create a specific hieroglyph derived from that of the god, to designate the king, is an eloquent demonstration. However, this choice is justified by the common genesis of the two signs, the divine origins of Pharaonic royalty, and by the fact that in the ancient world the image of the pharaoh as the object of divine cult was well established; Alexander the Great and the Caesars who came to this land to satisfy their mythomania also have been adored as gods, and had illustrious predecessors in the pharaohs themselves, such as Amenophis III or Ramses II, who did not have the patience to await divine destiny *post mortem*.

Head of King Seti I with the ureo on his forehead. Abydos, temple of Seti I, Nineteenth Dynasty.

VARIANTS/COMBINATIONS

King wearing the crown of Upper Egypt: ideogram or determinative for *nsw*, "king," and determinative of the name of the god Osiris.

King wearing the crown of Lower Egypt: ideogram or determinative in *bìtì*, "King of Lower Egypt."

Standing king with staff and sceptre: determinative in *ìty*, "sovereign."

Ra

Ideogram or determinative in* R‘*, name of the sun god.

The seated god with the sun's disk on his head, around which the divine cobra is coiled, is the image for Ra, the sun god, destined over time to incorporate the principal gods of ancient Egypt. However, like the majority of cosmic gods, his history is lost in a fog that obscures the time and place of the origin of his cult. The first solid evidence of his name dates to the reign of Djoser in the Third Dynasty (around 2630 B.C.). His overwhelming confirmation takes place between the Fourth and Fifth Dynasties and starts in the city of Heliopolis, which remains the canonic center of the development of his theology. At the beginning, the cult was clearly astral: the name designates the star of which the god is the personification. The etymology is obscure: the Egyptians liked to connect it to the verb *ỉ‘r*, "to climb," in reference to the rising of the sphere into the sky. Almost always they preferred to write the name with the two monoconsonant signs, *r* and ‘, and the grapheme of the disk of the sun, rather than with the anthropomorphic hieroglyph. Only in the Middle Kingdom did the use of this hieroglyph as a determinative become the usage. The cursive script—hieratic and demotic—almost entirely ignores the ideographic usage and generally preferred the falcon on the standard as the determinative.
From the syncretism with the heavenly falcon-god Horus came the falcon-headed variant.

Ra-Harachte seated on his throne. Thebes, Valley of the Queens, tomb of Nefertari, Nineteenth Dynasty.

VARIANTS/COMBINATIONS

Falcon-headed variant of Ra's name.

Atum

Ideogram or determinative in* ỉtmw, tmw, *name of the god Atum.

The hieroglyph represents the god in his classic anthropomorphic iconography, with the double crown of Upper and Lower Egypt, which also relates him to the circle of the dynastic gods. It is an iconography that must have taken form in the period between the Fourth and Fifth Dynasties, when the fate of the Egyptian state was in the hands of kings who gave strong support to the solar heliopolitan religion and associated the origins of the dynasty and the monarchy in general to the sun god. Atum was then incorporated into the solar cycle and became the evening manifestation of the sun, the tired and aged god who sets, only to be reborn at dawn. But prior to this time Atum was the principal god of Heliopolis, the embodiment of the creator, who by masturbation or spitting, depending on the version of the myth, gave life to the divine couple Shu-Tefnut, the principals of humid air and of dry air, from whom descended the nine principal gods of Egypt, the great Enneade.

Shu

Ideogram or determinative in* šw, *his own name.

The ostrich plume that characterizes the god, carried in its anthropomorphic form on his head, is itself a hieroglyph, the ideogram that expresses the notion of lightness and vacuity, connected to the nature of the god. His name in fact signifies "empty" and the god represents the personification of air. The mythic imagination visualizes him as the god who with extended arms raises the body of the sky goddess Nut, distancing her from the earth god Geb: a powerful image that invokes the air that intervenes, at the moment of creation, between earth and the vault of the skies.
The placement between sky and earth not only makes him the god of wind, but also the god of light, often assimilated to the sun god. His body is made of fog and clouds, called the "bones" and "walls" of Shu in the texts. Shu also belongs to the Heliopolitan circle: Atum created him as the first of a pair of cosmic principles, together with his sister Tefnut, moisture.
Nut and Geb are descended from them, and in turn are the parents of Osiris, Isis, Seth, and Nephtis.

Horus

***Ideogram in the name of the god* ḥrw.**

The simple image of the falcon distinguishes the god Horus, one of the greatest Egyptian gods, for the importance of his cult and theology and for the political implications of his religion.

At first one of the numerous falcon-gods venerated almost everywhere in Egypt as heavenly gods (his name *ḥrw* seems to mean "the distant"), he was given powerful influence by the affirmation of the monarchy in Upper Egypt, becoming the dynastic and national god. The city of Hierakonpolis was at the center of the movement to conquer and unify predynastic Egypt, and in fact the Greeks gave the city the name "city of the falcon."

From these earliest times, the essence of the god seems to be thus characterized doubly as heavenly god and dynastic god. The pharaoh is the living Horus, the incarnation, repeated at every coronation, of the god that founded Egyptian royalty.

The oldest of the names in the royal protocol is inscribed in a rectangle that represents the royal palace, over which the image of the falcon dominates: an effective rebus to express the idea of Horus living in his palace. The falcon Horus was from very early on associated with the cult of the sun, a union which is already certainly active in the *Pyramid Texts* (Fifth Dynasty), but perhaps already in the First Dynasty. It is more difficult to understand the mysterious meanderings that carried the falcon-god into the circle of Osiris: here Horus is the son of Osiris and Isis, heir and revenger of his father against his uncle, Seth, with whom he battles fiercely for the crown and in the end is the undisputed and only winner.

Horus pours the water of life on Queen Hatshepsut. Detail of reliefs from the temple of Karnak, Eighteenth Dynasty.

VARIANTS/COMBINATIONS

Falcon with whip: determinative in *bik*, "falcon."

Falcon on the hieroglyph for gold: the image of "the golden Horus name," part of the royal protocol.

Osiris

***Ideogram or determinative in the name of the god* wsỉr.**

The hieroglyph is borrowed from one of the most common iconographies of Osiris in man's image with the elaborate *atef* crown often associated with this god. The iconography and the hieroglyph are both relatively late. In general the Egyptians preferred to write the god's name by a rather enigmatic writing: the grapheme of the throne followed by that of the eye, whose phonetic value is, in fact, *wsỉr*. The etymology of the name and the original nature of this god, who exercised a deep and lasting effect, long beyond the era of the civilization of the pharaohs, continue to be the topic of discussion and various but not conclusive hypotheses. In recorded history, the theology, cult, and iconography of the god had undergone profound changes; this makes it very difficult to trace the early phases: he was already a funerary god, in which at first every deceased king found his identification, and subsequently, every dead man. His holy city, Abydos in Upper Egypt, does not have any traces of the god's earliest history in the Predynastic and Early Dynastic periods: at that time, he was a jackal god, Khentamenti, who was in time incorporated by Osiris. Whether Busiris on the delta, often cited in connection with the god, was the real place of origin and diffusion of the cult is not certain.

In myth Osiris is killed and cut into pieces by his brother Seth. With pious love, his sister and wife Isis recomposed the body after a long search for the dispersed members. Osiris's son, Horus, has the obligation to revenge him and restore the broken order, reigning on his father's throne. This is the founding myth of the pharaonic royalty: the death of King Osiris, which interrupts the harmonious cosmic flow, is healed by the elevation to the throne of the new Horus. King of the kingdom of the dead, Osiris is also soon incorporated into the solar cycle: he is the sun of the night, dead, who embodies the regenerating principle of life.

Osiris with the atef*-crown, on his throne. Thebes, Valley of the Queens, tomb of Nefertari, Nineteenth Dynasty.*

Hathor

***Ideogram or determinative in the name of the goddess* ḥwt-ḥrw.**

The hieroglyph shows Hathor as a woman whose head is crowned by a pair of bovine horns through which the solar disk shines. The crown synthesizes her original nature as heavenly heifer, but in very early times the fusion of anthropomorphic and bovine elements had already taken place: the goddess is shown with a woman's face, but with the bovine ears and tall horns. She is thus a very ancient goddess, certainly associated with the sky: her name—as is better explained in the variant with which it is rather frequently written—means "house of Horus" and probably indicates the deep skies in which the falcon-god resides. The antiquity and diffusion of her cult, soon assimilated with that of other heifer divinities venerated in the Nile Valley, veil her origin. In a later era, she is often called *Nwbt*, "the Golden," which for some indicates an origin in the "city of gold," Ombos, in Upper Egypt, the region where the cult of the god Horus was also developed, and with whose name she is connected. Here, on the site of Dendera, rose the most famous of her sanctuaries. But others prefer the papyrus thickets of the delta as her place of origin. Of the Egyptian pantheon she represented one of the most complete incarnations of the female principle: mother and heavenly nourisher as well as goddess of love, joy, and rapture.

Hathor enthroned. Thebes, Valley of the Queens, tomb of Nefertari, Nineteenth Dynasty.

VARIANTS/COMBINATIONS

The bounds of the palace *ḥwt* with the falcon inside: *ḥwt-ḥrw*, "Hathor."

Seth

Ideogram or determinative in* sth̲, stš, swtỉ, *variant forms of the god's name.

The name of the god whom the Egyptians associated with confusion and cosmic and social disorder is often expressed by the hieroglyph of a god with a human body and an animal's head. This is the famous animal of Seth, itself a writing of the name, about whose zoological identity many theories have been put forward: ass, antelope, giraffe, okapi, and so on. It seems more probable that the animal is chimerical, a member of the fabled desert fauna.
The zoomorphic variant is encountered frequently as determinative to a broad series of words, all connected to the idea of suffering, violence, and perturbation, including the atmospheric: even the words for tempest, rare occurrences in the stable Egyptian climate, carry this determinative.

VARIANTS/COMBINATIONS

The mythic animal Seth.

Nephtis

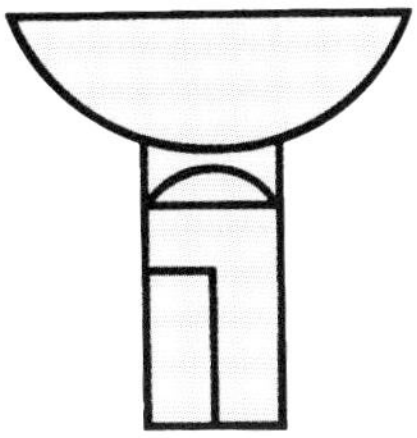

***Ideogram in the name of the goddess* nbt-ḥwt.**

As opposed to the other hieroglyphs, this one commonly used to indicate the goddess Nephtis is a pure transcription of the name *nbt-ḥwt*, "lady of the house," and does not give us much information as to her nature, which remains rather evasive. Nephtis belongs to the heliopolitan Enneade: together with Isis, Osiris, and Seth, she is the child, according to the myth, of Geb and Nut. As are Isis and Osiris, Nephtis and Seth are a couple, but, consistent with Seth's negative nature, a sterile one. One has the impression, however, that the goddess was a later creation of dualistic Egyptian thought, a result of the need to give Seth a companion and as a counterpart to the "positive" couple Isis-Osiris. Nevertheless, her image is not negative, and together with Isis she performs the lamentations at the side of the dead Osiris.

VARIANTS/COMBINATIONS

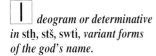

Anthropomorphic variant of the goddess's name.

Thot

Determinative in hb, "ibis": ideogram or determinative in the god's name ḏḥwtỉ.

The image of the ibis erect on the standard-bearer is at least from the Fourth Dynasty the most used writing of the name of Thot, one of the most important in the Egyptian pantheon, and whom the Greeks assimilated to their god Hermes. As ensign to be carried in processions, it makes its debut as early as the end of the fourth millennium B.C., on a cosmetic palette known as the "Battlefield Palette"; but it is not possible to say whether this was already associated with the god Thot in that distant era. It is, however, certain that, beginning in the Fourth Dynasty, the tie between Thot and the *Ibis religiosa*, now extinct, was already indissoluble and that it would last until Roman times. The late Egyptian necropolises have given us hundreds and hundreds of these holy birds, more or less carefully embalmed and buried in the intricate web of underground galleries alongside the baboons that were also sacred to the god: those of the ancient Hermopoulis Magna, canonical center of the god's cult, and those of Saqqara, the necropolis of ancient Memphis, are among the most impressive.

Papyri and *ostraka* of the Greco-Roman period furnish precise accounts of the administration and personnel of real economic-religious institutions, the temples dedicated to the cult of the holy animals. We know of the lesser and greater dishonesty of those who subtracted food destined to the animals or profited from their burial. But we are still ignorant of the deeper significance of the tie between the ibis and the multiform god of science and writing, magic arts and lunar phases.

Wood, bronze, and gold leaf group of Thot in the form of an ibis and the goddess Maat. Twenty-sixth Dynasty. Hanover, Kestner Museum.

VARIANTS/COMBINATIONS

Variant in the god's name; in human form with an ibis head.

Anubis

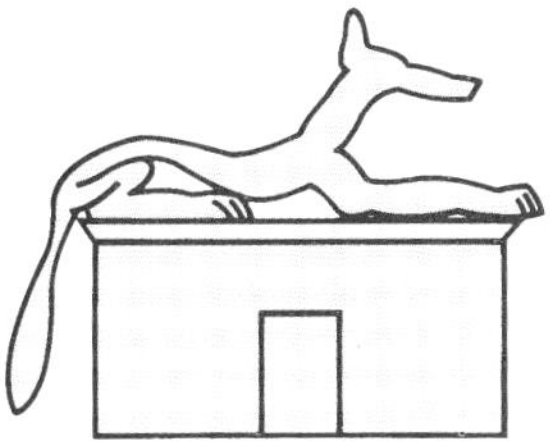

Ideogram or determinative in the god's name* ỉnpw, *ideogram in the title* ḥry sštȝ, *"in charge of the secrets."

Anubis belongs, with Wepwawet, god of Assiut, and Khentamenti of Abydos, to the canine gods. The animal or animals from which it derived its zoomorphic form was generically classified by the Egyptians under the collective term *sȝb*, which we translate as "jackal"; but it is not so easy to identify the exact species, which from time to time are hidden within the various gods. Anubis was represented lying on his stomach or, as in the hieroglyph illustrated here, stretched out on a chest, the mysterious container from which was derived the epithet "keeper of the secrets," also given to some priests. The tie between Anubis and embalming suggests a relationship between the chest and the sarcophagus or the cases for canopic vases, which were the containers of the organs extracted in the course of mummification. Jackals and dogs were frequent visitors to the urban periphery, and as such their association with the world of the necropolis and the dead is only natural. Their wanderings and meanderings among the tombs identified them, certainly already deep in the past, as benevolent powers charged with the care of the dead. It was only a short step from this thought to the association of them, by embalming, with the care and rites for the defunct.

As with the many animals connected with gods, the dog and jackal, which are identified in the black Anubis, were part of the wide circle of sacred animals, raised by the temples which were dedicated to them and then mummified and buried at the expense of the pious faithful, who in doing so earned merit points for the afterworld.

Anubis on the chest, as painted on the wall of Pashed tomb. Deir el-Medinah, Nineteenth Dynasty.

VARIANTS/COMBINATIONS

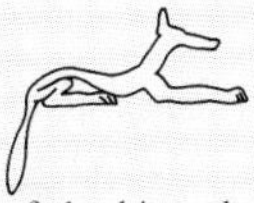

Variant of the hieroglyph, with identical value.

God with a dog's head: ideogram or determinative in the names of canine gods.

Wepwawet

***Ideogram or determinative in* wp-w3wt.**

The hieroglyph does not represent the animal, but rather the image that was carried in procession, on its typical standard. It appears as a wolf or black jackal (the interpretations swing between these two), usually standing, but sometimes lying down.

The name means "the opener of the way," the outrider, perhaps originally a general epithet for hunting dogs and jackals, which in any case seems to have gained a place at the head of royal processions for Wepwawet. The predynastic images frequently show its insignia preceding the king in processions, reviewings of the troops or prisoners, and religious rituals.

Its divine nature is synthesized in two different ways: as the warrior, and as the funerary god, both frequently connected to the canine divinities.

The Greeks called him Ophois, based on the later Egyptian pronunciation of the name of the god, and interpreting it as wolf, called the city of Asyut, seat of his cult, "Lycopolis."

Jackal

Ideogram or determinative in* s3b, *"jackal," and associated words.

Besides Anubis and Wepwawet, the black jackal loaned his likeness to many gods, of both the warrior and funerary types. Among the divine beings a special category of jackals, which were known only by the generic name of the species, *s3b*, was made up of the beings that in the hereafter would draw the solar boat through the night. These are also nicknamed *sṯ3w*, from the verb meaning "to drag" a boat. It was a tiring duty, but one well known to the ancient Egyptians, required in those places where the navigation by oars or sail was impossible as, for example, at the level of the cataracts in the Nile. A part of the crew had then to drag and guide the boat by means of hawsers from the banks. The imaginary underground landscape that was traversed by the sun in the course of its nighttime voyage was, in contrast to the easy daytime navigation, sometimes represented as a sandy world with a scarcity of water and full of insidious dry spots where the boat could fetch up. In the mythology and geography of the solar circumnavigation, the jackals were associated with the Occident.

Amon

I ***deogram or determinative in the god's name* ỉmn.**

The hieroglyph belongs to an advanced phase in the theological elaboration concerning Amon, when the original nature and cult were remodeled to create a powerful national god for the Theban dynasties. The completely anthropomorphic appearance of the hieroglyph makes the abstract essence of the high god evident and hides the more ancient characteristics. The crown with its double plume could relate him on the one hand to Min of Coptos, with whom Amon, according to some interpretations, shares more than one element, or on the other hand to Montu, ancient warrior god of the Theban region. It is not even certain whether the area from which he came was Thebes, which gave much power to his fortunes beginning in the Eleventh Dynasty. His name means "the hidden one," and it was already borne by one of the members of the Ogoade of Hermopolis Magna, the eight paired principles, of the yet unformed creation, from whom, according to the cosmogony elaborated in this religious center, the cosmos would be developed. A famous theory, no longer unanimously accepted today, would have it that the god, born at Hermopoulis, moved to the Theban area because of political events. Others see a god of the wind, whose cult would have been diffuse in the ancient region between Hermopoulis and Thebes.

In the Twelfth Dynasty, in the process of reorganizing Egypt and solidifying its control of the entire country, Amon was made from an obscure god into a national and dynastic divinity, calling on the powerful solar theology of the Memphite dynasty of ancient Egypt as an obligatory step. Amon became Amon-Re, beginning a syncretistic process through which then every god with nationalistic pretenses would have to pass. Venerated in all of Egypt, his historical sanctuary is the imposing Karnak, where he was worshiped together with the goddess Mut and the lunar boy Khonsu.

Amon places his hands on Queen Hatshepsut. Cusp of an obelisk at Karnak, Eighteenth Dynasty.

Mut

P ***honogram in the name of the goddess*** **mwt.**

Mut was in reality not a vulture-goddess, as the hieroglyph would have one believe, and as was thought in the past. Recent studies have modified earlier theories and hypothesized that the name of the goddess should rather be connected to the noun *mwt*, "mother": the hieroglyph would then be only the phonogram *mwt/mt*. In fact, the iconography of the goddess does not represent her as a vulture, nor even in animal form: the cast-off vulture's skin that sometimes adorns her head is typical of many female godheads and would seem to be connected to the relationship between Mut and the queen, perhaps specifically the queen-mother, a tie that would lead back to the attractive hypothesis that saw in Mut an ancient mother goddess. Unfortunately, the evidence that would sustain this interesting theory is still missing. At Thebes she was worshiped together with the powerful Amon and the lunar god Khonsu, making a triad with them—a structure that recalls the family model, even though frequently the mythological setting of real relationship was lacking.

Goddess with a Leonine Head

I deogram or determinative in names of goddesses, Sekhmet in particular.

The silent apparition of lionesses, thirsty or hunting, at the mouths of desert wadis frequently disturbed the life of the inhabitants of the valley in antiquity. Their majestic stride and the terror they aroused proclaimed them as goddesses and men hoped to placate their terrible ferocity and ingratiate themselves by dedicating cults and sanctuaries to the lionesses, often close to the wadi where they so suddenly appeared.

The numerous goddess-lionesses incarnated the disquieting and untamed aspects of the female principle and sometimes the features of the more reassuring—but no less enigmatic—cat were substituted. Sekhmet, "the powerful," was the only one consistently of leonine aspect, and sometimes pernicious: plagues and epidemics were attributed to her deadly arrows, and often her priests had the duty of curing them.

The principal place of the cult was Memphis, where beginning in the New Kingdom, it appears in the company of Ptah and as mother of Nefertem.

Ptah

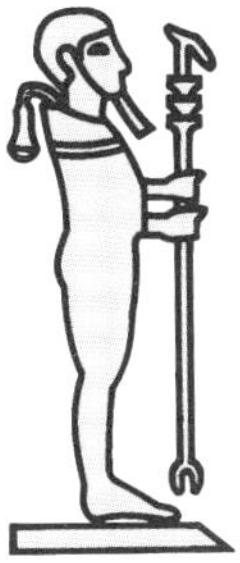

Ideogram or determinative in the name of the god **ptḥ**.

Ptah belongs to the gods having mummiform iconography: he is shown standing on a pedestal, tightly wrapped in a type of sudarium, from which only his hands, holding the long user-staff, emerge. In the hieroglyphic image, just as in the drawings, the body, which is more modeled by than covered by the sudarium, is emphasized. The texts also underline the corporal quality of the god: if Re is the face—they say—Ptah is the body. Unlike the other great gods, he does not wear a crown, rather a clinging blue-cowled beret, the same that one sometimes sees worn by blacksmiths and artisans in the scenes of the tombs of the Old Kingdom. His beard is also different from the godly pattern, as it curves upward and recalls instead the royal beard.

The relation between the mummiform iconography and the intimate nature of the god is not clear; even though Ptah was soon fused syncretistically with the necropolis god Sokar, he is not a funeral god. One can not exclude, in fact, that the unusual dress may have nothing to do with the sudarium, nor with the bandages of mummification, but may instead be a close-fitting ceremonial costume.

Until the New Kingdom, the hieroglyph includes the drawing of a chapel, inside which is depicted the god: the grapheme thus represented him as a statue. It is possible that this iconography relates to the other—and much more important—aspect of the god: his being the artisan god. In this form he has his origin at Memphis, where he is patron of artists and trades. In the capital, residence of the court and center of pharaonic art, the artisans, tied to the royal palace and to the temples, had a privileged role: the delicate mission of sculpting the statues, the true replicas of the personalities of gods and men, which were then animated through the appropriate rituals.

Corporality, representation as statue, patron of artists and sculptors: these are, perhaps, the three key elements of this god's personality.

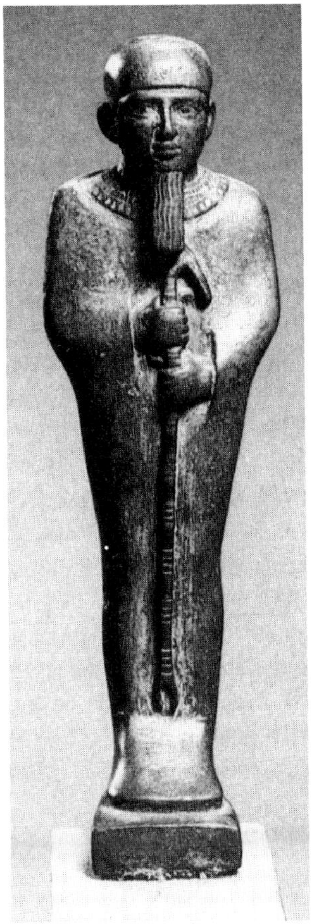

Ptah, bronze and electrum, Twenty-sixth Dynasty. Cairo, Egyptian Museum

VARIANTS/COMBINATIONS

Ancient variant of Ptah.

Sokar in the Holy Boat

***Determinative in the name of the god* skr *and his boat* ḥnw.**

Sokar and his processional boat were, from the very beginning, so closely tied that frequently the hieroglyph of the boat served as ideogram for the god's name. Its singular appearance rendered it certain of identification, but the fundamental element in it remained the god himself, shown in the form of a falcon on his boat.
The strange boat, with the back-turned head of an antelope at the prow, had an important role in a very ancient procession that took place around the walls of Memphis and was probably originally connected to the royal boat. Many diverse aspects flowed together into the personality of Sokar: god of the Memphis necropolis, he was also patron of metallurgy and blacksmiths, a dominant factor in the Old Kingdom and quite early associated with Ptah and Osiris.
The close relationship with these gods finally obscured his original character.

Heh

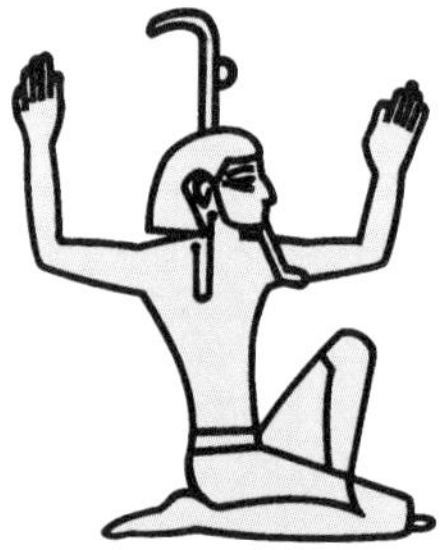

***Ideogram or determinative in the divine name* ḥḥ*; phonogram* ḥḥ.**

Heh is the personification of innumerable quantity. In fact, the hieroglyph also serves to write the word *ḥḥ*, "millions." It is shown as a divine personage seated on the earth with his arms raised. Often it has on its head the sign of the carved palm frond, which represents the summing of the years, an accessory auguring good fortune, because the years of a reign must be above all innumerable. He is not usually a single god, but occurs in association with other Heh, forming couples, quartets, and even octets. They represent together the pervasiveness of the air, a sort of infinite duplication of Shu, who sustains the heavenly vaults. For this reason, in the temples of the Greco-Roman era, the symbol is often offered by kings to the gods of air and sky. The king receives it in exchange for a promise of a reign of many years.

Min

I***deogram or determinative in*** **mnw.**

In the religion of the Egyptians the god Min held a preeminent post as the god of fertility: the erect phallus, characteristic attribute of the god, was an immediate and evident sign of his sexual potency.

The ithyphallic god Min, with his emblem and characteristic sanctuary behind him. Temple of Luxor, Eighteenth Dynasty.

Much less transparent are the other features in his iconography: the two tall plumes on his head, the body once again restrained by a tight-fitting tunic, the arm brandishing a whip behind his shoulder. In the hieroglyph the other arm is not usually visible, but other images of the god show him grasping his penis at its base.
The god's pose is part of his oldest iconography: it occurs on the strange stone giants, datable in the Second Dynasty, that at the end of the last century were found at Coptos, the historic center of his cult. On these disquieting and rough statues Min was associated with a series of symbols, among which is lightning, the enigmatic emblem of the god that often served to write his name. Besides this are other signs, coupled or repeated twice—shells of the *Pteroceras* type, the bone-appendix of a sawfish, an elephant with a bird, a bull with a hyena—which soon disappeared from the classic iconography, but remain as the isolated and fragmentary witness to the original nature of the god. In particular, the shells and appendix of the sawfish would seem to sustain the hypothesis of the god's origin in the remote Eritrean lands: the Egyptians themselves frequently associated this god with the fabulous Punt or the Medjai nomads of the eastern desert. He is sometimes called in the texts "the black of skin" and explicitly labeled as a foreigner. The typical hut, with its conical roof often associated with his image, is certainly exotic and would seem to depict a primitive sanctuary.
Sometimes at the god's shoulders are shown two or more heads of lettuce, a sacred plant, whose juice was considered to be an aphrodisiac. The offering of the plant was part of the ritual of the Min cult. The fact that the lettuce was sometimes drawn above the orderly reticulation of the rows of a field reminds us that Min was also a god of vegetation.

VARIANTS/COMBINATIONS

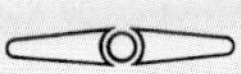

Emblem of Min.

Khnum

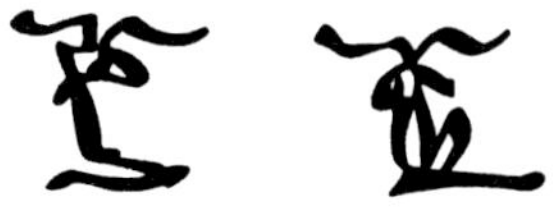

***Ideogram or determinative in* ḫnmw.**

It originally may have been a purely animal divinity: that *Ovis longipes paleoaegyptiaca,* soon extinct and illustrated by the variant. But already in the Old Kingdom the god was anthropomorphized, and only the head of the ram remained. Thus the animal that represented its divine manifestation on earth did not lose its holy character: the necropolis of the sacred rams at Elephantine has given us their mummified bodies buried in sarcophagi of gilded wood. On this island, at the height of the first Nile cataract, Khnum had his most illustrious cult, where the god held the bridle of floods and could, as the Ptolemaic "Famine stele" narrates, intervene as he pleased to end seven hard years of famine. Khnum was also the potter god, who modeled humanity on his wheel, as developed in the myth of creation in the temple of the god at Esna.

VARIANTS/COMBINATIONS

The ram, writing of the god's name.

Montu

***Ideogram or determinative in the name of the god* mnṯw.**

The hieroglyph repeats the classical iconography of the god, with the head of a falcon surmounted by the solar disk and the two plumes fixed to the disk.
Originating in the Theban region, of which he was always considered the unchallenged lord and was worshiped in numerous temples of the zone, from Armant to Medamud and Tod, Montu came out of the relative obscurity of his former life to shine with a new—but short-lived—light in the Eleventh Theban Dynasty. It seemed as though he might become the new dynastic god of Egypt, but he was soon supplanted by Amon.
The brief parenthesis of national glory did, however, have its mark on his personality and iconography: the bellicose Theban dynasty that brought unity to Egypt at the cost of long years of hard-won victories left him with the character of a warrior god, patron of war and its arts.
In the tradition of the New Kingdom he followed the king into battle as his protective genius; the sovereign who stood out in the arts of war and sport was "one versed in the art of Montu."
The predatory falcon and the aggressive bull were his animals.

Maat

Ideogram or determinative in the name of the goddess **m3ʿt.**

As is frequently the case for the gods which the ancient Egyptians represented entirely in human form, Maat is an abstraction rather than a real goddess, a disembodied personification of an ideal image of principle to which men, kings, and gods were meant to adhere. As such, she was not the object of a real cult and was not worshiped in her sanctuaries until the New Kingdom. Her symbol, worn on her head, was the plume, an expression of the levity connected with ethical behavior. A man's heart placed on the scales of the divine judgment should not outweigh the feather placed on the opposite plate. Magistrates and high priests wore the figure of the seated goddess, in lapis-lazuli or gold, around their necks.

The concept of order that the goddess personified was above all socially based: respect for Maat—in which the real "cult" of the goddess consisted—was effective in the complex ethical and juridical norms that regulated Egyptian society. By it the rapport between subjects and pharaohs was formed as an equal exchange: the king rewarded obedience with social benefits and a well-functioning state, which the subjects depended on to a large extent. At the same time, the king was bound to the gods to maintain social and religious order by fulfilling cult and ritual duties. Thus, he put the gods in the position of being able to keep the unchanging cosmic equilibrium, on which man and gods depended for life.

This was then a rule of mutual dependence, a machine in which every element was a precious gear and interacted with the others.

Figurine of the goddess Maat. Detail from a group of gods, Twenty-sixth Dynasty. Hanover, Kestner Museum.

Sobek

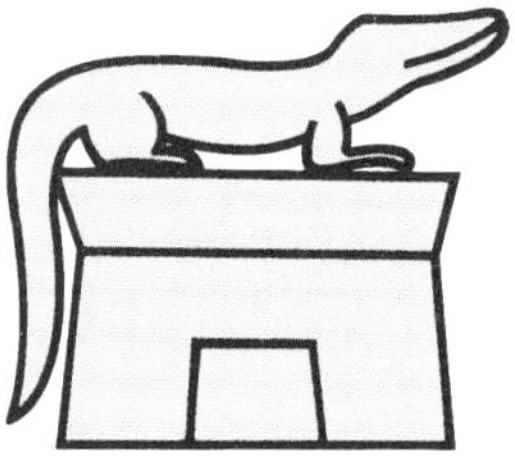

Ideogram or determinative in **sbk.**

The image of the crocodile on the holy chest identifies the divine nature. An older variant reproduces the crocodile god as a cult image, perhaps a fetish, or a mummified crocodile, with only its head emerging from a type of sudarium or bandages in which it is wrapped. It is an archaic form that this animal shares with other divine cults, primary among them the falcon fetish of Hierakonpolis. Originally Sobek was a crocodile-god, connected to water and fertility, perhaps because of the popular belief that saw in the massive presence of crocodiles an indication of the depth of the flood, and thus of the abundance of the crops. He was worshiped in Fayum, which was the reptiles' favored habitat, rich in lakes, canals, and swamps. Later he became a primordial divinity and a creator god and realized his universal aspirations in the classical syncretistic process with the sun god, giving origin to the form of the god Sobek-Re.

VARIANTS/COMBINATIONS

The archaic crocodile fetish.

Selket

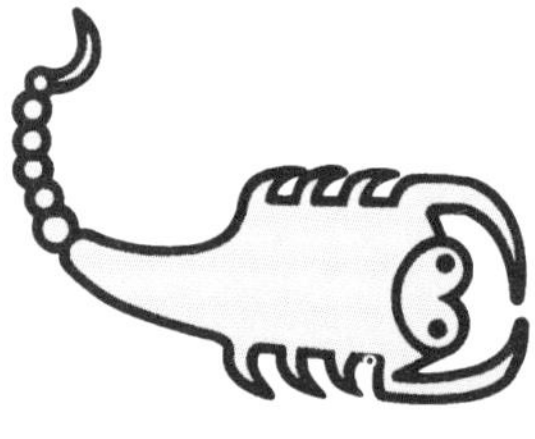

Ideogram or determinative in the name of the goddess **srḳt.**

The classical version of the hieroglyph shows the insidious outline of the frightening Egyptian scorpion. Abbreviated forms, apparently lacking the head and without the deadly tail, were often preferred in the inscriptions in funeral chapels, magically reducing the sign, which was potentially animate and dangerous, to impotency. On the basis of these altered signs it had been deduced that the goddess originally represented by the grapheme did not have the nature of a scorpion, and that this was the image of a headless larva. The later confusion with the image of the scorpion would have caused a radical turnaround in the original significance of the goddess, a hypothesis that is unacceptable today. Selket belongs to the group of witch goddesses associated with Isis, and she had a corps of specialists in curing the devastating effects of the creature's sting.

VARIANTS/COMBINATIONS

Magically stylized version of the hieroglyph.

Uraeus

Determinative in* i͗ʿrt*, "Uraeus," and in the names of many goddesses.

The enraged cobra, menacingly upright (the name *i͗ʿrt* is connected to the verb *i͗ʿr*, "to rise, to climb") and with his throat distended, pictured the serpent as he was symbolically carried on the Pharaoh's forehead and by the god Re, as protection against enemies. Sculpture and two-dimensional representations of the king and god never omit this ornament, which some would have derived from a nomadic-Libyan context. It was seen, in this function, as the flaming eye of god, which with the ardor of its flames annihilates his enemies, and it symbolized, clearly, the fiery nature of the crowns. The name "uraeus," which is commonly used for it, is the latinized form of the Greek *ouraios*, which Horapollon was first to mention, forming it after the Egyptian word. Since *i͗ʿrt* is feminine in the ancient Egyptian, the hieroglyph was used as ideogram or determinative for feminine gods, and first of all the goddess Wadjet of Buto in the Delta, herself a divine personification of the uraeus and of the crown of Lower Egypt. Her name, which means "the green," is generally interpreted as a euphemistic substitute for *dšrt,* "the red," the word for the crown.

The Two Ladies

Ideogram in* nbty*, name of the two protectresses of Egypt.

The counterpart of Wadjet of Lower Egypt is Nekhbet, the vulture-goddess of ancient Nekhen or Hierakonpolis, as the Greeks called it, worshiped in the nearby sanctuary of Nekheb (today el-Kab). Together, vulture and cobra, represented by the two signs *nb*, became symbolic of the unification of Lower and Upper Egypt and were incorporated into the royal protocol. They introduced there the so-called name *nbty*, "of the two ladies," the epithet that indicated the two protectresses. In theory, in the choice of that particular name the sovereign was making reference to the policy he intended to adopt vis-a-vis the two territorial and cultural realities of unified Egypt. But it was really dealing with, once again, an artificial construction of the dualistic Egyptian thinking. As Wadjet became an integral and essential part of the king's crown, the vulture's remains worn on the queen's head were perhaps associated with Nekhbet's role in Egyptian royalty.
In historic times, the goddess did not seem to have been more than the personification of the white crown of Upper Egypt, functional within the ideology of the new state.

Bes

***I**deogram or determinative in the name of the god* **bs.**

The grotesque shape in the hieroglyph—a dwarf frontally shown, with the outsize face of a hybrid monkey-lion mask and crooked legs with a long animal's tail hanging—belongs to one of the minor gods who was very dear to popular fantasy.

Alien from the demonic characteristics that the first glimpse of his repugnant appearance might suggest, he belongs, along with Thoeris, to the domestic and family world: he was a protector of the home and children, especially tied to the delicate phase of delivery and defender against harmful animals.
This last was probably the oldest quality. The natural ambience of his activity logically causes his image to appear on a broad range of objects of daily use, from headrests, where he watched over the sleepers, to toilet articles.
His rapport with dance and music was also close, as he used these to placate the enraged goddesses.
Connections with the solar cycle indicate him as a sort of popular form of the sun god.

Thoeris

***I**deogram or determinative in the goddess's name* **t3-wrt.**

Thoeris too belongs to the lesser-known group of popular gods, as she lived more in the home than in the temples. The hybrid and monstrous form—half hippopotamus, half crocodile—which also provokes laughter, is indicative of her domestic sphere of action, like Bes: a world essentially made up of women and children.
The goddess, with her great belly and hanging breasts, is the good-humoredly disrespectful image of a pregnant woman and she is in fact the protector of pregnancy, delivery, and breastfeeding. The hieroglyph puts into her hand the symbol of magic protection *s3*, which was probably originally the image of the fisherman's lifesaver, worn about the neck, and from which the amulet type of protection is derived. There are small votive statues of the goddess, still wearing fragments of pregnant women's costumes, or others with holes in the breasts—holes that would allow milk to be placed inside and pour out, thus perhaps taking on magic properties.

Neith

Ideogram or determinative in the goddess's name **nt.**

The goddess, who as an emblem carries in the hieroglyph the red crown of Lower Egypt (this, too, is called *nt*), has an interrupted history in ancient Egypt: after a swift rise at the beginning, she spent two millennia in the background, and came back into the foreground with the Twenty-sixth Dynasty, which originated at Sais, her place of cult and origin. She was apparently associated with the hunt and war at first, as her other emblems show: two bows tied together or two crossed arrows. This second emblem had a name and independent being: it was Hemesut, which seems to have been the feminine counterpart of *ka*, the vital and procreative force. The red crown characterizes instead the goddess as a dynastic divinity, tied to Lower Egypt. A Libyan origin, proposed by some scholars, has not yet been confirmed.

VARIANTS/COMBINATIONS

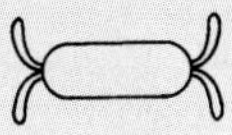

Variant of the goddess's name.

Seshat

Ideogram or determinative in the name of the goddess **sš3t.**

When her name is not written, as it frequently is, with the enigmatic emblem of the rosette with the upside-down crescent bow, Seshat is shown as a woman with her head surmounted by the same strange instrument. In classic times she was the goddess of writing and sums: her name seems to have been read *sẖ3t*, "scribe." Horapollon (II, 29), in describing this symbol, relates it to the muse, the innumerable, and Moira, or the Greek notion of fate. The three definitions delimit Seshat's functions well enough: muse, as she was compiler of the royal annals; goddess present in royal jubilees, where she wishes innumerable celebrations to the king; and, at last, goddess of destiny, as the one who counts the years of life and reign of the pharaoh in the magnificent coronation ceremonies.

VARIANTS/COMBINATIONS

Variant for the name of the goddess.

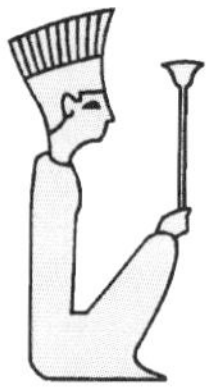

Anukis
Ideogram or determinative in the goddess's name *ʿnḳt*, worshiped in the area of the first cataract.

Apis bull
Ideogram or determinative in the name of the sacred bull, *ḥp*.

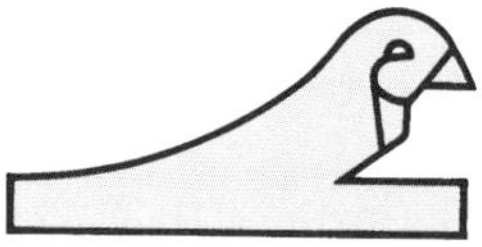

Crouching or mummified falcon
Determinative in *ʿšmw/ʿḫmw*, "divine image, idol."

Tatenen
Ideogram or determinative in the name of the Memphite god of the earth, *t3-ṯnnt*.

Soped
Ideogram or determinative in the name for the falcon–god of the Orient, *spdw*.

Hapi/Nile
Ideogram or determinative in the name of the hermaphrodite genius of abundance and of the flood, *ḥʿpy*.

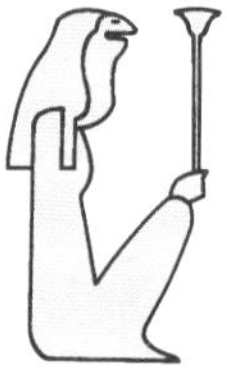

Renenutet
Ideogram or determinative in the name of the serpent goddess of the flood deposits and of fertility, *rnnt*.

Nefertum
Ideogram or determinative in the name of the young god of the Memphite triad, *nfr-tm*.

Animals

The ancient Egyptians regarded the animal world with attention and love, an attitude that became the source for innumerable lively scenes painted in the tombs and temples, rich in colorful detail, as well as for the many hieroglyphs that refer to the various known animals. In these hieroglyphs, even in the necessary generalization of a graphic code, the accurate observation of the animals by the Egyptians is always present. Especially in the hieroglyphs of the Old Kingdom, which are the most detailed, scholars have been able to identify the exact species represented. Almost no animal was considered too insignificant or unworthy of appearing in their graphic code: the larger mammals are amply represented, but so are reptiles, small insects, fish, and even the humble centipede.

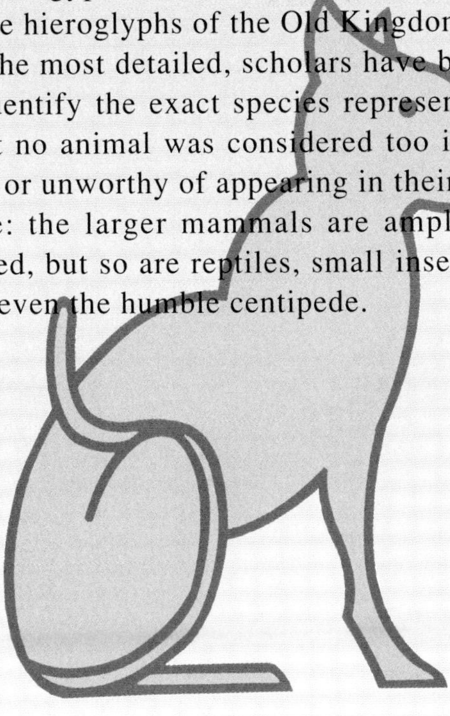

Bull

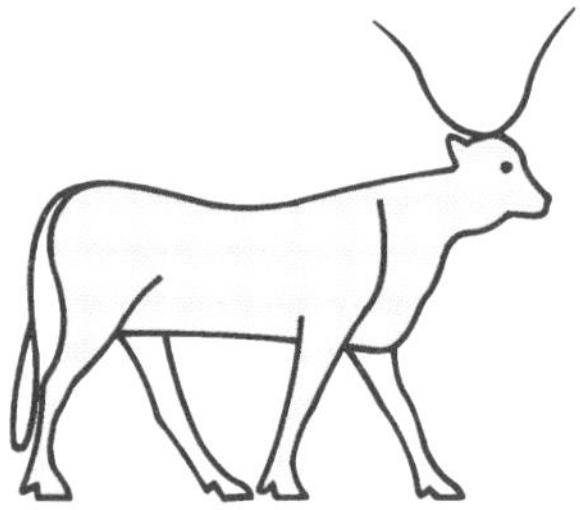

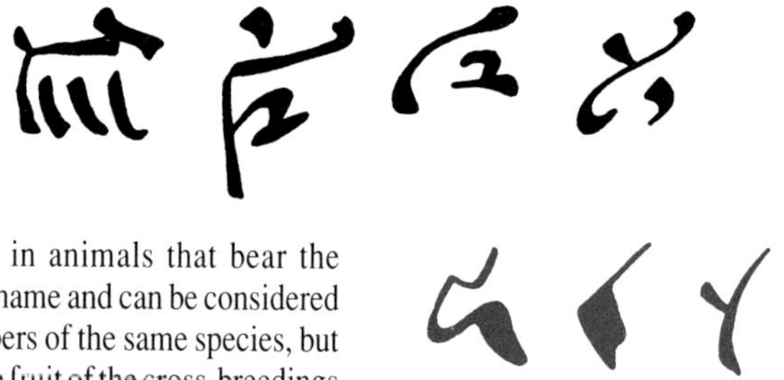

Ideogram or determinative for various bovine species* (k3, ỉḥ, ỉw3, ng)*; determinative for cattle.

Even though the drawing appears accurate enough to our eyes, to the ancient Egyptians this hieroglyph represented an abstraction, formed over time as the synthesis of bovine characteristics. It does in fact sum up (and represent ideographically) the distinctive traits of the various bovine species that were to be found from the remotest times in the Nile Valley and adjacent areas. The oldest hieroglyphs often show significant variations on the formula, according to the species or the gender. The same careful adherence to realistic detail is even more evident in the representation of bovines in typical scenes—very common in tombs—of cattle-raising, butchering, and, in general, of animal life.

The bovines, indicated by the names *k3*, *ỉḥ*, *ng*, *ỉw3*, etc., are shown with different builds, sometimes robust and large, with short, massive legs, sometimes thinner. Even the horns vary; although frequently tall and in the shape of a lyre, they are sometimes short and rounded, and may even be lacking in either gender. In many cases, the variants can be noted in animals that bear the same name and can be considered members of the same species, but are the fruit of the cross-breedings effected by the Egyptians in order to better the species. In the later period, and perhaps earlier, the Egyptians kept oxen as well as bulls in their herds: texts mention castration, even the most detailed images and hieroglyphs provide no means of distinguishing the castrate from the bull.

The greatest distinction seems to be between *ng* and *ỉw3*: the former are usually bellicose and left to roam wild, and are often the protagonists of the battles of the bulls in the typical scenes of animal life; the latter are slower and thicker, lords of the stalls and triumphant participants in the proud parades of cattle that the cattlemen liked to organize for their noble patrons.

The sacred Apis bull was chosen from the ranks of the frightening *ng*.

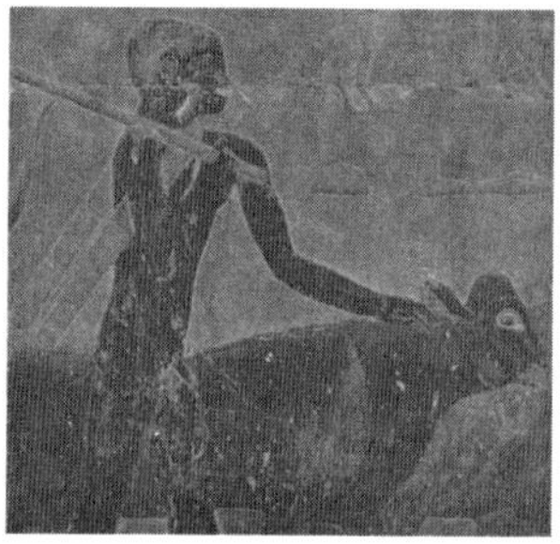

Left: *Bulls led to be butchered for funeral offerings. Saqqara, tomb of Niankhkhnun and Khnumhotep, Fifth Dynasty.*

Right: *Bull at a ford. Saqqara, tomb of Ti, Fifth Dynasty.*

VARIANTS/COMBINATIONS

This shows the fighting bull, its head aggressively lowered, ready to gore. It is a variant of *k3* and determinative in *sm3*, "fighting bull."

Horse

I ***deogram in the word* ssmt, *"horse." Determinative for similar words.***

T he hieroglyph and the word "horse" enter into Egyptian language and writing fairly late, and were probably the gift of the Hyksos (the Egyptian word indicating the "princes of foreign lands"), who were the first foreigners to dominate Egypt toward the end of the first half of the second millennium B.C. The word *ssmt* is of Semitic origin *(susim)* but the Egyptians soon adopted the epithet *nefer*, "the beautiful," for common use in designating this noble animal, an eloquent testimony of the prestige it enjoyed in their eyes. In late inscriptions the sign for horse, in a typical graphic pun, is substituted by "beautiful." Beginning in the New Kingdom, the horse became a real status symbol: princes and nobles contended for the most beautiful horses with the most elegant trappings, and they liked to aggrandize their own skills as charioteers in the inscriptions and have representations, on their own tombs, of themselves driving.
According to the Asiatic tradition, it was not dignified to mount the animal—they preferred to be drawn in light carts. The Egyptians took over this practice, and it is not until the Hellenistic era that one finds a king illustrated in the saddle of a fiery charger. The hieroglyphic variants of the stylized sign capture the nervous and pawing grace of the animal, figured always at full gallop or in the act of rearing. The quicker hieratic and demotic preferred to substitute the phonetic writing for the ideogram, and signs that were more generic and more quickly drawn for the determinative.

Pharaoh Ramses III in battle, on a chariot drawn by two horses. West Thebes, funerary temple of Medinet Habu, Tenth Dynasty.

Ass

Determinative in* ʿ3, *"ass."

The sign was used more as a determinative than as an ideogram, to distinguish the *ʿ3* from numerous words with the same sound but different meaning. Almost always the hieroglyph for ass is preceded by that for phallus, emphasizing the negative aspect of lust (as opposed to the bull's more venerated sexual potency). This aspect is not in evidence in the hieroglyph, however, where the most visible trait is the long ears. Though a dutiful and patient beast of burden, the ass was the object of Egyptian ancestral repugnance, a sentiment that is buried in a mythic complexity that is difficult to unravel. There are many different elements: from the sexual, cited above, to the wildness of the onager, abundant in ancient Egypt, to the association of the ass with the world of Asiatic nomads.
From quite early on, the ass was connected with the animal of the despicable god Seth (in hieratic, the sign for this animal often substitutes for the determinative of ass) and shares with him the iconoclastic fury: the sign of the ass is sometimes shown with the counter-charm of a knife stuck in its back in hieroglyphic texts.

Parade of asses. Saqqara, tomb of Ti, Fifth Dynasty.

Young Goat

Phonetic value* ìb, *from the word* ìb, *"young goat." Used also as determinative for small farm animals.

The hieroglyphic represents a young goat, either still without horns, or, in some epigraphic variants, with horns just beginning to show.
The small upturned tail distinguishes him from the very similar images of calves. In the first years of the New Kingdom, the hieroglyph was substituted by the representation of the young goat upright on its hind legs, perhaps in the act of jumping, which with its greater plasticity renders the nervous nature of the young goat. This version would seem to be associated with the capricious tendency of goats to disdain the grass of the pastures, preferring instead the leaves of trees and bushes, as faithfully observed and depicted in numerous scenes by the Egyptians. Differing from the bovines, shown in placid attitudes in the pastures or in parades before the lords, the goat is typically shown in ancient Egypt in a rampant position: the greedy goat is pictured by the artist in the act of stretching up from its hind legs toward the lower branches of acacias or other trees.

Swine

***Determinative in words indicating pigs:* rrì, š3ì.**

The hieroglyph is often seen in the *Pyramid Texts*, just as the animal itself was present in Egypt from the earliest times (neolithic kitchens have given us the remains of bones). It descended from a type of wild boar: *Sus scrofa ferus*. The oldest and most detailed epigraphic variants draw with synthetic realism the long snout and the thin spine with its tough bristles: the animal was still quite close to its wild state and much more disquieting than the well-fed modern domestic animal.
Its feral nature, together with its voracity, is probably responsible for the ancient Egyptian aversion to the beast, considered impure, yet not unappreciated at table. In traditional myths the pig is always shown eating: according to a version of the myth of Horus's eye, the eye (a lunar symbol) was devoured periodically by a large black pig; in another common cosmic legend, the great celestial sow devours her piglets, the stars, at daybreak.

Ram

D*eterminative in the word* b3, *"ram," and its synonyms. Determinative also in the name of the god Khnum.*

The hieroglyph draws the image of a large ovine, with a pair of spiraling twisted horns that sit horizontally on its head. There is often a little beard, typical of the male of the species.
Scholars have identified in the hieroglyph a drawing of *Ovis longipes paleoaegyptiaca*, a breed that existed from prehistory in Egypt and was extinct in the Middle Kingdom (by the first half of the second millennium B.C.). Shortly before its extinction, a new breed appeared in the Nile Valley, destined to take the place of the former: the *Ovis platyra aegyptiaca*, characterized by its smaller size, large tail, and, above all in the males, by thick horns that curve forward around the ears. This must be the ram sacred to Amon of Thebes.
The disappearance of *Ovis longipes paleoaegyptiaca* did not cause the abandonment of the hieroglyph *b3*, however, as its long life continued to follow the parabola of Egyptian writing. It had by then given its likeness to many ram-headed gods in the Egyptian pantheon, besides being itself the drawing of the sacred ram worshiped in many places in ancient Egypt: they continued to affix long horizontal horns of gilt wood to their mummies, in memory of the extinct ram-*ba*!

Herder with rams. Above the herd, the hieroglyphic text of the so-called "Herder's song," Saqqara, tomb of Ti, Fifth Dynasty.

Cat

D ***eterminative in the onomatopoeic and almost universal* miw, *"cat."***

T he domestic cat was much loved by the Egyptians and, like many other animals in that country, was protected by powerful taboos, mummified and rendered godly after death, to the joy and haughty disdain of many right-thinking Greeks and Romans. It appeared relatively late, and so the hieroglyph is also of a fairly late period.

Its predecessor seems to have been a wild and aggressive feline, probably more similar to the representations of the Heliopolis cat, which in the *Book of the Dead* kills the evil serpent Apophis. The lively scenes of the Old Kingdom, even though crowded with varied fauna, do not have images of the domestic cat, which will have to wait for the beginning of the second millennium B.C. to make its entrance into Egyptian life, and occupy—naturally—a place of importance. The proud and indifferently absorbed aspect is what is fixed by the hieroglyph and then adopted in the innumerable little statues representing the cat goddess Bastet (sovereign of an interesting domestic female ambient, of which joy and love are part). But the tomb scenes, with their little pictures of private life, show also the cat's more playful and vital aspects: we find it frequently curled up under the chair of the noble patron or greedily devouring a fish. It is often portrayed in hunting scenes, or fishing in marshes, or in precarious equilibrium on a branch that bends under its weight as it stretches to catch a bird. According to some, Egyptian hunters used the animal to flush birds from the swamps. The beautiful hieroglyph, which entered the graphic system long after its formation, was only rarely used for this purpose and was almost always a determinative. Hieratic and demotic, which almost always drew from a more historic reservoir of signs, preferred to use instead the phonetic writing with more generic determinatives.

Left: *The cat of Heliopolis. Tomb of Inerkawi, Twentieth Dynasty, West Thebes, Deir el-Medinah.*
Below: *Cats painted on a chest of a mummified cat. Late period of Ptolemaic era. Turin, Egyptian Museum.*

Reclining Lion

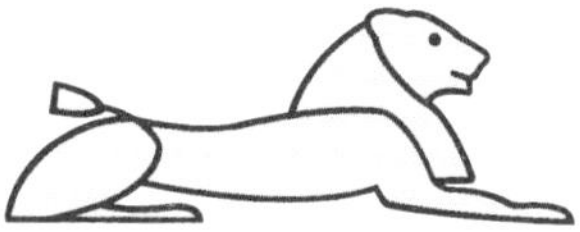

Ideogram in* rw, *"lion," whence the phonogram* rw *and, later,* r*; sometimes abbreviation for* m3ỉ, *another name for lion.

Quite common in prehistory and still present in the valley in the late pharaonic period, the lion, for the most part feminine, was an important element in royal symbolism and divine iconography.
The Egyptians knew the members of *Panthera leo* that were common in Africa and the Near East —the Berber lion *(Leo barbarus)*, the Senegalese and the Persian lions *(Leo persicus)*—and drew them first with the common name *rw*, then with *m3ỉ*. This second name was frequently qualified more specifically as *m3ỉ ḥs3*, "ferocious lion." In the graphic hieroglyphic code, the Egyptians showed the feline in two ways: reclining in majestic indolence *(rw)* or erect, in the act of striding forward (*m3ỉ*). The reclining pose is the one represented from Predynastic times, by an ample sculptural repertory; later the iconography of the Sphinx will develop from it. If this reclining pose is more apt to express the hieratic aspects of royalty, as conceived by the Egyptians, the erect lion, especially in the earlier phases, seems to relate to the ferocity and aggressive power. The lion was a much loved iconography in the New Kingdom, when the sovereign is pleased to have himself represented in the act of leaping

with his chariot onto the enemy lines and pitilessly trouncing them. The metaphor of the warrior king, strong and courageous as a lion, is curiously rendered in these reliefs by placing the majestic feline beside the king, as his companion in battle. But for some, these were real lions trained by the Pharaoh. As to the kingly quality of the animal, the Egyptians had no doubts: from prehistoric beginnings, on numerous Predynastic tablets, hunting the lion is a king's prerogative, an ac-

tivity that draws more on the sacred world of ritual and the deep African roots of pharaonic kingship than on hunting skill. In the infinite silence of the desert the two adversaries faced each other as equals: identification of king and feline is part of the mysterious interpenetration of hunter and hunted that unites and ritually heals what the bloody violence of hunting lacerates.

Above: *Ivory pawns in the shape of crouching lions, used in the "serpent's game." End of fourth millennium B.C. – beginning of third millennium B.C.*
Cairo, Egyptian Museum.
Below: *Pink granite statue of a guardian lion of King Nectanebo I, Thirteenth Dynasty, c. 370 B.C.*
Rome, Vatican Museum.

Hippopotamus

Determinative in words designating the animal: **db, ḫ3b.**

The hieroglyph shows the massiveness of the pachyderm, with its great body sustained by short thick legs.
It is not by chance that in the Late Period the sign was often used to write the word "heavy" (eg., *dns, wdn.*)

The agricultural society of ancient Egypt feared the hippopotamus's devastating voracity, which it associated with the evil forces in the world. A text exalting the scribe's profession reads, "Do you not remember the sad fate of the farmer? When it is time to register the crop, the reptile has taken one half, and the hippopotamus, the other."
Hunting the hippopotamus, one of the king's ancient privileges, thus took on a ritual significance as the act of annihilating a manifestation of evil. In the female hippopotamus, instead, the prominent belly recalled the image of pregnancy and the animal symbolized female fecundity. In this benign mode it was differentiated from the hieroglyph and shown in an upright position, in the likeness of the hippopotamus goddesses Thoeris ("the Great") and Opet ("the Harem"), who protected maternity and delivery.

Elephant

Determinative in **3bw,** ***"elephant," from which the phonetic value*** **3b;** ***in the Hellenistic age, determinative of the new term for elephant:*** **dnhr.**

Common in prehistoric times in the area of the Nile Valley, by the historic era it was practically unknown, and was sometimes shown with fabulous features, even though the ivory from its tusks was widely imported from the south. Up to the New Kingdom, when the wars of Tuthmosis III brought the encounter with the elephants of the Upper Euphrates Valley and the hunts by the king and his valiant men, his name and the hieroglyph that represents it is mostly remembered in connection with the city of Elephantine (today an island in front of Aswan), the *3bw* of the ancient Egyptians, or "city of the elephants." This was, in fact, the marketplace for African ivory *(3bu)*, derived from the elephant tusks as well as, probably, from rhinoceros horns.
The elephants returned to Egypt, and to the Egyptian texts of the Hellenistic era, when, having become a powerful instrument of battle, they were captured and imported into Egypt by the Ptolemies.

Gazelle

D*eterminative in* gḥs, *"gazelle."*

The gazelle in the hieroglyph is the *Gazella dorcas*, characterized by the rather short tail and the double curve of the horns. Even though it was bred quite early, it was never considered a real domestic animal by the Egyptians: as in the case of most desert animals, the image retained its sense of wildness. Since it was part of the hostile desert landscape, and not of the civilized world, they associated it with the evil forces of the god Seth. Only in places where the desert acquired another economic and cultural value did the gazelle take on the positive character that the Egyptians attributed to the animal world and become sacred to the god of the place, and worshiped as well. Together with the other antelopes common to the Nile Valley, such as the white long-horned oryx (e.g., *m3-ḥḏ*), we see a double personality: on the one hand, in the numerous scenes in private tombs, it is a domesticated animal, sometimes on a lead held by the herder, or in the act of eating, sleeping, or suckling its young; on the other hand, in religious scenes, as a sacrificial victim it is the annihilator of hostile powers. Between these two aspects are the representations of hunts in the desert, in which the gazelle is both the prey valued for its meat and the symbol of the enemy to be vanquished.

Gazelle in flight or pierced by arrows in the course of a hunt. West Thebes, Sheikh Abd el-Qurna, tomb of Userhat, Eighteenth Dynasty.

Giraffe

Ideogram for "giraffe" **(mmy)*****; determinative and sometimes abbreviation of the verb*** **sr,** ***" to announce, to foretell."***

The hieroglyph delineates in absolutely clear lines the long neck and small head of the gracious animal, which was not an unusual presence in the savannas that once bordered the prehistoric Nile Valley, an area that is now only desert. In the historic era the giraffe and its tails were imported from the African hinterland and from the fabulous Punt. In paintings of the tombs of the noble Thebans the lithe beast is often depicted in the parades of the African tributes, hobbled and led by black servants or, an amusing detail, with a small monkey grabbing its long neck. Rather mysteriously, the hieroglyph of the giraffe appears as determinative or abbreviation of the verb *sr*, "to announce, to foretell," and related nouns that have the meaning of oracle or prophecy. We cannot now say with certainty whether this is due to the animal's miraculous prophetic qualities or to a hypothetical term *sr*, "giraffe," still unknown.

Desert Hare

Phonetic value **wn.**

The hieroglyph emphasizes the long and broad ears of the desert hare *(Lepus aegyptiaca)*, giving the animal, even though it is shown crouching, a watchful air —tense and ready to run.
The animal, very common in Egypt, is frequently shown in desert landscapes and hunting scenes. In the tombs at Beni Hasan the hieroglyphic captions to the scenes on the walls designate the hare as *sẖ‘t*. The existence of the verb *wn*, "to run," written with the biliteral sign *wn* (the hare) and determined by the running legs, leads one to suppose that the phonetic value *wn*, with which the hieroglyph appears quite frequently in Egyptian texts (think of the very common verb *wn*, "to exist, to be," or the homonym *wn*, "to open," or the noun *swnt*, "sale," and so on), may be derived from an ancient epithet for "runner," worthy of an animal that is well noted for its running speed.

Baboon

Determinative in* i͗ʿn, *"baboon," and its synonyms; determinative in the verb* knd, *"to be furious."

From the very beginning of their history the Egyptians knew and drew two types of African monkey: the cercopith *(gf)* and the dog-faced baboon with its elongated canine head, and long fur on the shoulders of the males. To the latter category belongs the *Papio hamadryas* or sacred baboon, the one shown in this hieroglyph.
A native of the Sudan and Abyssinia, but imported early on into Egypt, it was consecrated to Thot, the god of writing and sciences who also played a complex role in solar theology. Although more deliberate than the agile and playful cercopiths, the baboon also had an important part in the daily life of ancient Egypt, and it is in this role that the hieroglyph shows it. Far from the fixed hieratic quality of the seated pose of the sacred animal, this recalls the companion of everyday life, which in many tomb scenes appears as it is led on a leash in front of the lord by a servant, or plays funny games with the children of the house or other animals, or is up in a fig tree, intent on eating the fruit. The Egyptians appreciated its quick intelligence, using the animal as an example for unwilling students, and its sexual lustiness, using its excrement in recipes for aphrodisiac ointments. But they did not forget the less attractive aspect of the beast's personality, as is clear in the use of the sign as determinative of the verb *ḳnd,* "to be furious."

Gathering figs: the men work, the baboons devour. Beni Hasan, tomb of Khnumhotep, Twelfth Dynasty.

Egyptian Vulture

***Ideogram in 3, "vulture," from which the phonetic value* 3.**

The bird shown in this sign, one of the so-called Egyptian alphabetic signs, is the Egyptian vulture *(Neophron percnopterus).* In the oldest examples the wings are gray or blue; they are green in the later images.
The more detailed portrayals are careful to show the characteristically unfeathered area at the base of the beak and the thinly feathered neck, details that give the vulture's neck its typical look of wrinkled leanness.
In general, though, it is difficult to distinguish it from the sign *tiw (Buteo ferox,* a variety of buzzard), which in respect to the hieroglyph of the vulture is characterized only by the greater rotundity of the back of the head. The word *3*, "vulture," from which the hieroglyph derives its phonetic value, is found only in the oldest phase of the Egyptian language, in the *Pyramid Texts*. In those texts the *Neophron percnopterus*, as do other species of vultures, also loans his body to a divine being: the Great Vulture, which flies over a dead king, as a sign of his divine power.

Vulture

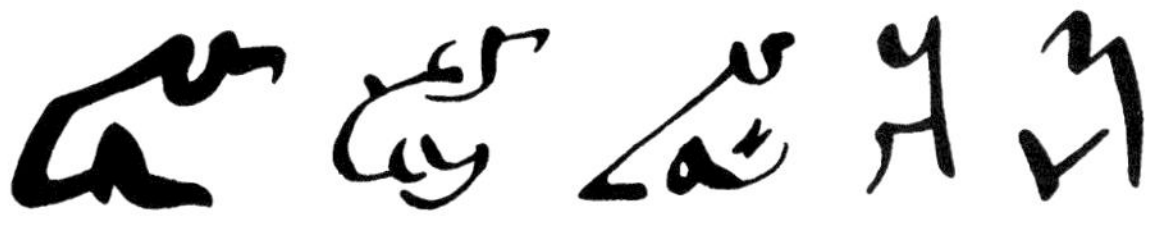

***Phonetic values:* nr *(from* nrt, *"vulture"),* mwt /mt.**

The hooked beak, the deep curve of the neck, and the hump on the back are the distinctive features of this sign, which represents without doubt the vulture of the *Gyps fulvus* species. *Nrt* is the Egyptian name for this vulture from the times of the *Pyramid Texts*, and the hieroglyph functions as both determinative and, at times, as ideogram. From this develops the autonomous phonetic value *nr*. The roots of the other phonetic value *mwt, mt* are more obscure, but are probably connected to the name of the famous vulture-goddess Mut *(Mwt).*
The goddess was from the very beginning a mother goddess, whence the name: *mwt* is also the word for "mother" in Egyptian. Classic authors record that according to the Egyptians there were no male vultures, an affirmation which can be associated with the unique representations of the androgynous Mut. In the later period the vulture frequently represented the female principle, associated with the scarab, which represented the male. In the enigmatic writing, the two signs paired are given the names of the goddess Neith and the god Ptah, according to Horapollon (I, 13): as he recounts, this signified that in being demiurge divinities, they unite in themselves the two principles.

Owl

P*honetic value* m.

Of all the birds used in the hieroglyphic system, the owl is the only one shown full face. More precisely, the hieroglyph shows the head full face, leaving the body in profile. The reason for this uniqueness is probably to be found in the intense individuality of the owl's gaze, which the Egyptians undoubtedly perceived as a distinctive personality trait of the bird, such that it unequivocably distinguished it from other species. However, it must be noted that the owl, like all nocturnal birds of prey, has limited peripheral vision and compensates for this by the ability to rotate its head a full ninety degrees, a quality that perhaps did not escape the perceptive Egyptians (thus is pictured, also, Anthea's owl on Greek coins).
Whether the owl was considered bad luck in ancient Egypt, we do not know. Some evidence leads one to suppose that it might have been: the writing of the verb *ḥsḳ*, "to cut a bird's neck," written by a composed hieroglyph of the owl with its body crossed by the alphabetic mark *k* (perhaps originally from the sign for knife, which is very similar), though more compelling is the curious fact that ali the mummies of owls that have been examined have had their heads cut off. Even the Egyptians were not immune to the effect of the disquieting gaze of the bird of prey! It is not certain where the phonetic value is derived from: presumably from the ancient name of the animal, which is lost. The demotic *3mwlḏ* and its Coptic derivative, which both designate the owl, are probably composed substantives in which the first part, *3mw/mw*, echoed the original name and perhaps was connected in an onomatopoeic way to his lugubrious call.

Owl painted with great detail on a sarcophagus panel, Eleventh Dynasty. Cairo, Egyptian Museum.

VARIANTS/COMBINATIONS

Monogram composed of two owls, phonetic value *mm*.

Combination of the owl and the arm with bread to express the phoneme *m(ỉ)*: this is in fact the archaic phonetic value of the arm with bread as ideogram, in the imperative of the verb "to give."

Guinea Hen

I***deogram in the Egyptian name of the guinea hen*** **(nḥ)*****; whence the phonogram*** **nḥ.**

The model from which this hieroglyph derived has been identified as the *Numida meleagris*, commonly known as the guinea hen. This bird, now common far south of Egypt in Africa, was portrayed by the Egyptians from the very earliest times of their civilization, indicating that at that time its habitat was more northerly. On the other hand, hieroglyph images of the bird vary and are often imprecise, making one think that the animal was already rare in ancient Egypt and perhaps observed only further south or west. In its quality as an exotic bird, it appears among the examples shown in the botanic garden of the Karnak temple, which is dedicated to the depiction of foreign fauna and flora. A distinctive trait of the hieroglyph is the two frontal protuberances, which correspond to the crest and tuft of filaments that sprout above the beak of the *Numida meleagris*. The examples that have retained their color show that the bird was painted black with lines of white marks.

Rechit Bird

P***honetic value*** **rḫyt** ***(from the name of the bird itself).***

The upturned crest, the long legs, and, in general, the form of the body and head with its short hooked beak identify easily in this hieroglyph the crested lapwing—a bird of European origin that habitually migrates in the winter toward northern Africa and is quite common in Egypt, above all in the Nile Delta. As a phoneme, *rḫyt* soon came to designate a category of men, that, together with the *pʿt* and the *ḥnmmt*, were the entire nucleus of humanity subject to the pharaoh. The *rḫyt* have an ambiguous role: on the one hand they are identified as foreigners, often with heavily hostile connotations: on the other they are sometimes Egyptian subjects. It is typical of the Egyptian genius for symbols to have identified a migratory bird that comes from the north, but that every year established itself in the swamps and nests there as the image of the integrated foreigner.

VARIANTS/COMBINATIONS

Lapwing with its wings superimposed, to prevent its flying.

Hoopoe

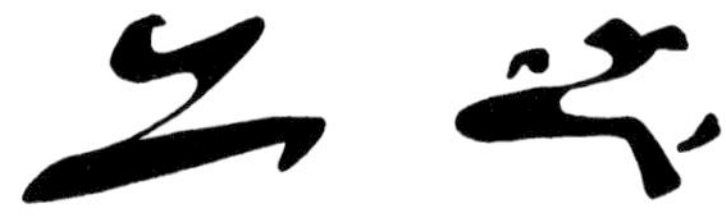

P ***honetic value* ḏb.**

It is not difficult to recognize in the hieroglyph the hoopoe *(Upupa epops)*, with its magnificent plumage and characteristic crest, quite common in Egypt. The classic writers frequently mention this bird, and Pliny (*Hist. Nat.* X, XLIV, 1–13) observes its capacity to contract or expand its crest at will, a fact that the Egyptian artists had also noticed: in the numerous portrayals of the bird, the crest is sometimes shown closed, like a pointed brush, sometimes half spread, and sometimes fully open.

Even though the common bird appears often in temple and tomb scenes, strangely enough we do not know its ancient name, which is perhaps *ḏb*, judging from the phonetic value taken by the hieroglyph. Only in the late period do the demotic texts give us the name *ḳwḳwpdt*, which in Coptic has the sound of *cacupat, cucufat*, evidently the same as the Greek *kukupha* (and of our hoopoe); but it is not clear who loaned and who borrowed the name, which is probably onomatopoeic.

Horapollon (I, 55), in his bizarre explanations of hieroglyphs, associates the sign of the hoopoe with gratitude: it is the only dumb beast, he says, that cares for its parents in their old age.

This legend is found in many ancient sources and may have had its roots in ancient Egypt: there are quite a few images of children carrying the bird by its wings, the cheerful companion of their play; and so are there statuettes of the infant god Harpocrate, with a finger in his mouth and a hoopoe in his left hand.

If in the first scenes it is difficult to perceive any symbolic intent, one should not exclude that this is instead present in the late iconography of Harpocrate and that the hoopoe, for associated reasons, seemed more in the popular credence than in a zoological reality to have assumed in the late period the symbolic value recorded by Harapollon.

The hoopoe in a swampy landscape. From the temple of Userkaf at Abusir, Fifth Dynasty. Cairo, Egyptian Museum.

Bird-ba

I ***deogram in the word* b3, *"soul"; phonetic value,* b3 /b.**

W hatever the relationship may have been that united the great African stork, known as jabiru *(Mycteria ephippiorhynchus seu senegalensis)*, to the Egyptian concept of the *ba*, which we incorrectly translate as "soul," is not known. The similarity in sound between the name of the bird and that of the *ba*, the understandable Egyptian tendency to represent the more spiritual aspects of mankind as birds, which were thought to ascend toward the sky after death, may be sufficient explanation. Or were there other associations, more intimate and by now intangible, which gave the *ba* the form of that white long-legged bird? Today the jabiru inhabits the area of the White Nile but the Egyptians were certainly able to observe it in closer regions: prehistoric documents abound with images that note precisely the swelling on the upper part of the beak and the caruncle that mark the male. The representations of the historical age, with their uncertainties and variants, demonstrate that only in the hieroglyph was there a memory of the jabiru. The term *ba* and the related concepts *Ka, Akh* do not have an exact equivalent in any modern language. The translation "soul," conventionally used, introduces a dualistic separation between body and spirit, which is appropriate to other philosophical systems and totally alien to the Egyptian conception.

The *ba* belongs to men as well as to kings and gods, for whom it may be visualized as a manifestation of their supernatural power. For the common man it is rather a personification of the vital forces—both the mental and the physical—which after death are brought into existence by appropriate rituals. The Egyptian *ba* may also be conceived as a different way of being in the life of the afterworld.

Above: *The bird-*ba *as the soul with human arms and head. Anhai Papyrus, Nineteenth Dynasty. London, British Museum.*

Below: *The jabiru storks, pictured with a giraffe and other animals on the handle of an ivory comb, Predynastic era (Carnavon ivory). End of Fourth Dynasty. New York, Metropolitan Museum of Art.*

VARIANTS/COMBINATIONS

Triplication expresses plurality and abstraction for the Egyptian. The monogram composed of three jabirus side by side, *b3w*, signifies in fact "power, whole of the divine manifestations."

Phoenix

D ***eterminative in* bnw, *"phoenix."***

T he grey heron *(Ardea cinerea)*, which in the flood season came back to inhabit the waters of the valley and rose in majestic flight at dawn, is the basis for the Greek legend of the phoenix. From the Egyptian name *bnw* (pronounced *boinu*), the Greeks drew their own name, *phoenix*. The bird, especially venerated in the region and theology of Heliopolis, was immortalized in an elegant hieroglyph that reproduced its long straight bill, the double tufts of its head, and its long legs for wading. Its cyclical return with the birds connected it with the regenerative power of those waters (the same bird, perched on a stand, is the ideogram for *bʿḥ*, "flood") and with the concept of regeneration: it became the living image for cyclically renewed life and for every hoped-for rebirth.

In funerary texts, among the various transfigurations that the spirit of the dead must pass in order "to go out into the light," some of the most important involved the phoenix. From the beginning the phoenix was a solar bird: its glorious morning apparition in the Egyptian skies, the illusion of its rising like the sun from the waters as it lifted in flight; its cyclical return—even though the cycle was much longer than that of the star—lent itself excellently to this association. Water and sun, Osiris and Ra, the dead father who is reborn in his son, the death from which life is regenerated: these are the basic elements of the Egyptian symbolism of the grey heron, later converging with the classic myth of the phoenix, which is consumed by flame and reborn from its own ashes. According to some versions of this myth, the phoenix's cycle was 500 years long; for others it was 1,461: this was the so-called sothiac period, which intervened between one coinciding of the heliacal rising of the star Sirius with the Egyptian New Year and the next. The beginning of a new sothiac period signified the birth of a new era to the Egyptians, the general renewal of the cosmos. Thus, even though it is detached from the Egyptian myth in more than one detail, the classic versions of the legend took the sense of the return of the phoenix.

The phoenix as the divine transfiguration of death. Kha's Book of the Dead, *Eighteenth Dynasty. Turin, Egyptian Museum.*

Duck

***Determinative in* st *(perhaps* s3t*), "duck": whence its phonetic value* s3.**

The two long feathers at the end of the tail and its lively colors allow us to identify the duck, and more precisely, the *Dafila acuta*, in this hieroglyph. The brilliant coloring is purposefully exaggerated to distinguish it from the quite similar sign for the goose *(gb)*. In order to avoid an easy confusion, the Egyptians usually accompanied the two hieroglyphs with their phonetic complements. As a phonogram, the sign was used to write the word *s3*, "son," and this explains the frequency of its appearance in the Egyptian inscriptions that were always careful to identify a person by patronymics and matronymics: "The N son of N son of N" and so on, going back sometimes far enough to cite the long genealogies recounted to Herodotus by his Egyptian interlocutress. Horapollon himself (and the late tradition of mixed Greco-Egyptian culture, from which he drew) saw a causal connection rather than

the purely phonetic one that relates duck to "son": "When they want to write son, then depict a goose. Because this is the animal that shows the most affection for its offspring, and if someone chases one in order to capture it with its young, the father and the mother offer themselves spontaneously to the hunters so that the young be saved.
And it is for this reason that the Egyptians have thought it just to worship this animal." The duck was in fact sacred to Amon – Ra and Geb and, in the late period, placed in a relationship to Harpocrate.

Above: *Detail of a limestone relief painted with cranes, geese, and oxen. Saqqara, tomb of Ptahhotep, c. 2450 B.C.*
Below: *The very famous Ducks of Meidum wall painting. Meidum, tomb of Nefermaat and Atet, Fourth Dynasty. Cairo, Egyptian Museum.*

Duck Prepared for Cooking

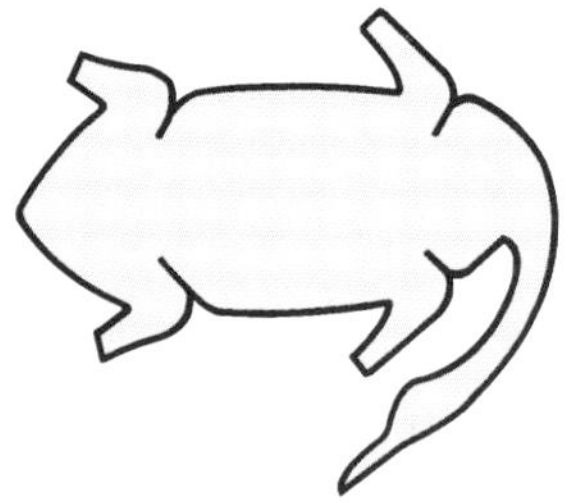

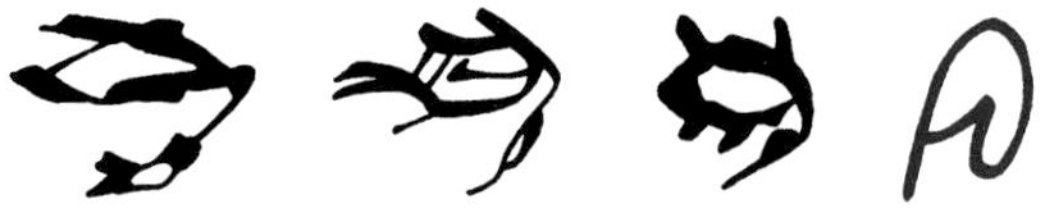

***Determinative in the verb* wšn, *"twist the neck (of a bird)." Phonetic value:* snḏ.**

Plucked and gutted, wings tied and the neck dangling crookedly, the poor bird is ready to be cooked and put on the table, as this drawing so clearly shows. Even more than as hieroglyph, the sign is always present in the overflowing heaps of food that the Egyptians showed in front of the deceased in the classical scenes of funeral banquets. Besides being among the desired objects of the Egyptian afterlife, the prepared duck or goose was also among the most appreciated foods: holiday food for the poor, frequently served at the more sumptuous tables, it could be prepared in a great variety of ways—roasted on the spit, grilled, or even stewed. There were also refined procedures, carefully represented in all their detail in the tombs, for conserving the meat in large vases, with salt or immersed in fat. Other scenes show the poor animal being fattened and stuffed with balls of sweetened and dampened bread. The image of the appreciated food must have disturbed the conscience of the greedy Egyptians: the hieroglyph serves as determinative for the verb *wšn,* "to twist the neck," and to write the verb *snḏ*, "to have terror."

Cormorant

***Phonetic value* ʿḳ.**

The thin and sinuous neck, the hooked beak, and the long tail are the essential characteristics of the bird as represented in this hieroglyph. These characteristics have led one to think of the cormorant, (*Phalacrocorax carbo*), an aquatic bird and able fisher, which was still common in the Fayum cane brakes at the end of the last century. The form of the long neck and the aquatic characteristics could also belong to the *Anhinga*, and the hieroglyph may have undergone contamination from diverse signs over the ages. The derivation of the phonetic value *ʿḳ* is not known.

There is no text which allows us to affirm that this was the true name of the cormorant. In the *Triumph of Horus*, a sacred representation that comes to us on the walls of the Ptolemaic temples, the god Horus who fights with the hippopotamus Seth is compared to the bird-*ḥbs*, which dives into fishy waters; many scholars believe that this gives the name of the cormorant. If so, one may not exclude that *ʿḳ* was its popular name. The verb *ʿḳ*, in fact, means "to enter, to penetrate" and it is possible that the ability of the bird to immerse his neck under water to catch fish may have won him the nickname "immersionist."

Lizard

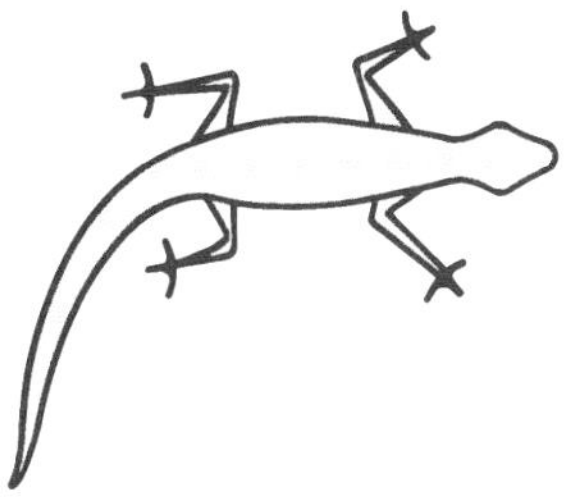

Determinative in ʿš3, "lizard" (from which phonetically ʿš3), in* ḥnt3sw *and its synonyms.

This hieroglyph is a synthetic and universalizing characterization of the numerous types of lizard *(Lacertidae)* that were common in Egypt; from the frightening monitor lizard that could be as long as three meters (the "earth crocodile" that Herodotus had seen in that country), to the common small lizard. The examples from the New Kingdom depict instead the gecko. The members of this numerous family, phenotypically suspended between the crocodiles and the serpents, were perceived as hybrids by the ancient Egyptians, who likened them to one or another group, and according to the case, consecrated them to the gods and the places connected to the crocodile or to the serpent. The creature's great diffusion perhaps suggested one of its names, *ʿš3*, "multiple" or "innumerable quantity." The synthetic abstractness of the hieroglyph does not reflect the Egyptians' capacity to observe and depict the individual characteristics of the various members of the family: for example, the monitor lizard is distinguished, in Egyptian portrayals, by having its head turn backwards, a movement of which the aquatic reptile is incapable, but at the same time is typical of the "earth crocodile."

Frog

***Determinative in the name of the frog-goddess* ḥḳt *and in the nouns that designate the animal* (ʿbḫn, ḳrr).**

In antiquity, as today, the Egyptian bogs were overrun with frogs, in such great quantity that the tadpole, in Egyptian *ḫfn(r)*, was used to write the number 100,000 *(ḫfn = ḫfl)*. Not even this minute and humble inhabitant of the swamps could escape from the omnipresent Egyptian respect for the animal world: the frog-goddess Heqet figures in the Egyptian pantheon, though her role is not very clear. In the cosmogony of Hermopolis, the primordial divinities are eight creatures, with either serpents' or frogs' heads. An association with the aquatic world and the muddy bottoms full of life is certainly at the origin of this conception. It may be that this is the idea behind the explanation that Horapollon gives (I, 25) of the hieroglyph of the frog, symbol, as he would have it, of "not yet formed" man. In Egyptian texts, beginning in the New Kingdom, the frog becomes a symbol of rebirth: the cryptographic value of the sign was *wḥm ʿnḫ*, "repetition of life," an allusion to cyclical renewing. Because of this symbolism, the little statues of the animal were a New Year's good luck gift and Christianity inherited the symbol as an allusion to the resurrection.

Crocodile

***Ideogram or determinative in names indicating the animal* (msḥ, ḫnty).**

The Nile crocodile (*Crocodilus niloticus* Laur.) is extinct today in Egypt, although it was common in ancient times and infested not only the waters of the rivers, but also the canals, the swamps, and the great Faium Lake. Frightening to both animals and men, it was the object of the Egyptians' holy terror and became a symbol of hateful abomination and of one of the most important gods. The hieroglyph shows it with its long snubbed snout and closed jaws, the stubby body rough with scales and, at the base of the head, sometimes, a sort of ear, which is probably a deformed version of the great scales on the nape that are often well defined in the larger portrayals in tombs. In their decorations the crocodile is a constant fixture of the aquatic world: in the scenes of beasts wading in the shallows there is frequently a crocodile, waiting on the bottom, with its sharp conical teeth giving the large mouth an even more terrifying aspect, ready to attack some hapless calf. The captions to these scenes carry a magic formula to counteract this possibility, spoken by the cowherder who, kneeling on the bow of a boat, leans over the water with his index finger pointed. Other times, the tricky animal attacks a hippopotamus that has already been wounded by fishermen's harpoons. His sneakiness offers material for many injurious comparisons with various enemies: the Asiatic nomad is like the crocodile waiting by the river, capable of attacking along deserted roads, but not adventuring into the well defined cities. Among the despised characteristics of the crocodile, his voraciousness and bottomless appetite were proverbial; so much so that the hieroglyph served significantly as determinative for the verbs *skn*, "to be avid," *ḫnt*, *ʿfʿ*, "to be greedy," and related adjectives. His aggressiveness was also considered typical and the verb *3d*, "to be aggressive, furious" is also determined by the sign. Only the power of love could have the best of the crocodile: "My sister's love is on yonder side, the river is between our bodies; a crocodile waits in the shallows. I enter the water and brave the waves, my heart is strong on the deep; . . . the flood as land to my feet. It is her love that gives me strength, it makes a water-spell for me." (Ostrakon, Cairo no. 25218; Miriam Lichteim, *Ancient Egyptian Literature*, vol. II: The New Kingdom, Berkeley, 1976, p. 193).

The god Horus on crocodiles. A magic stele against the bites of harmful animals, Ptolemaic era. Cairo, Egyptian Museum.

VARIANTS/COMBINATIONS

Crocodile with its tail curled. Determinative in the verb *s3q*, "to collect."

Horned Viper

***Ideogram in* fy, *"viper," whence phonetically* f.**

A hieratic papyrus of the late period, now in the Brooklyn Museum, contains the description of thirty-eight reptiles. Each column of this *Treatise on Ophiology*, as its editor, Serge Sauneron, has called it, carried an accurate description of the physical characteristics of the serpent, so that it can be recognized, even from the look of its bite and its consequences, including the prognosis. In some cases, it also includes the appropriate treatment, if such existed. It considers each serpent to be the manifestation of a god. In a second part of the treatise are more commonly given the recipes for treatment and antidotes against poison. Six sections are reserved for the different types of vipers the Egyptians knew and called collectively *fy*. We read in the section relative to the horned viper *(fy ẖr dbwy*: viper having two horns): "His color is similar to that of the quail; it has two horns on its forehead; the head is broad, the neck narrow, and the tail thick. If the bite's opening is ample, the face of the wound swells; if the bite is small, the one bitten will become inert, but [...] [He will have] fever for nine days, but will survive. It is a manifestation of Horus. One may draw the poison by making him vomit abundantly and by exorcisings [...]."

Cobra in a Position of Rest

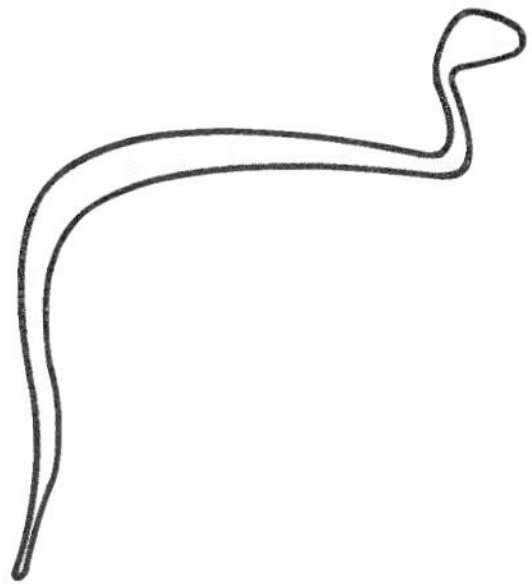

***Ideogram in* ḏ, ḏt, *"cobra," whence phonetically* ḏ.**

The name *ḏ* and its female variant *ḏt* are documented in the *Pyramid Texts*, but the serpent's more common name is *ỉʿrt* (variant, *ʿrʿrt*), the same as the erect serpent (the uraeus placed on the king's forehead).

But different from this, the resting cobra does not take a place in the iconography of the divine forms of the reptile.

The cobra is quite common in Egypt. The Egyptian *Treatise on Ophiology* gives the following description: "As to the serpent cobra, it is the color of sand. If it bites someone, he will feel pain in one half [of his body] where he has not been bitten and will not feel pain in the half that has been wounded. This is a pain that I will deal with. Execute all the operations that are necessary and give him numerous emetics, just [use] the knife, once he has vomited. It is a manifestation of Seth. The bitten do not die."

The strange observation about the pain of the bite finds no comparison in modern medical texts.

Tilapia Nilotica

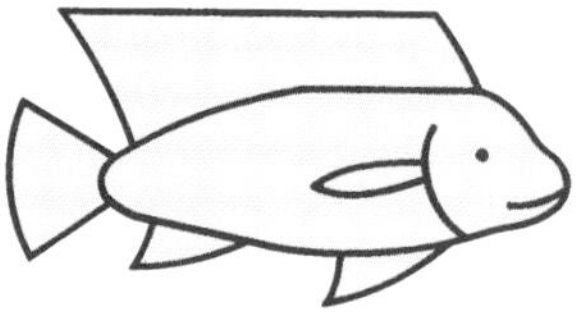

***Determinative in* ỉnt, *"Tilapia," whence phonetically* ỉn.**

This fish, belonging to the family of the Cichlids and very common in Nile waters, was among the most pictured in Egyptian art. Among zoologists it is famous for the female's unique practice for protecting its young: immediately after depositing her eggs, she takes them into her mouth, where she keeps them until the small fish are completely formed. Even after having been let go, the little ones frequently return to the mother's mouth for refuge. It seems that the Egyptians were aware of this surprising habit: a type of decoration that appears on various objects from ancient Egypt shows easily recognizable examples of the *Tilapia*, placed in a circle or facing, touching their mouths to the globular mass that may represent the agglutinated eggs they are about to engulf. A fractured echo of the observations made by the ancient Egyptians about the habits of this fish is perhaps transmitted by Herodotus (II, 93), according to whom in certain fish the females swallow the seed emitted by the males during the descent of the Nile toward the sea; in the mating season, while on the return upstream, the eggs deposited by the females are swallowed by the males.

The Egyptian religious symbolism of this fish shows the influence of the knowledge of this singularity: gestation by swallowing and successive rebirth are fundamental elements of the solar cycle (the star was swallowed by the celestial mother at sunset and delivered at dawn) and this explains the existence of a common decorative motif in which the *Tilapia*, with a lotus flower in its mouth, is a clear symbol of rebirth after death.

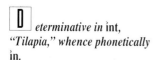

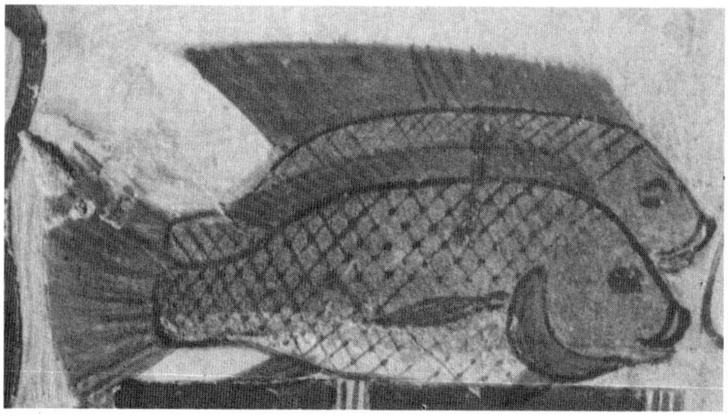

Above: *Detail of two* Tilapia *in a fishing scene. West Thebes, Sheikh Abd el-Qurna, tomb of Menna, Twentieth Dynasty.*
Below: *Two splendid examples of the fish presiding on a tray among the offerings to Menna. West Thebes, Sheikh Abd el-Qurna, tomb of Menna, Twentieth Dynasty.*

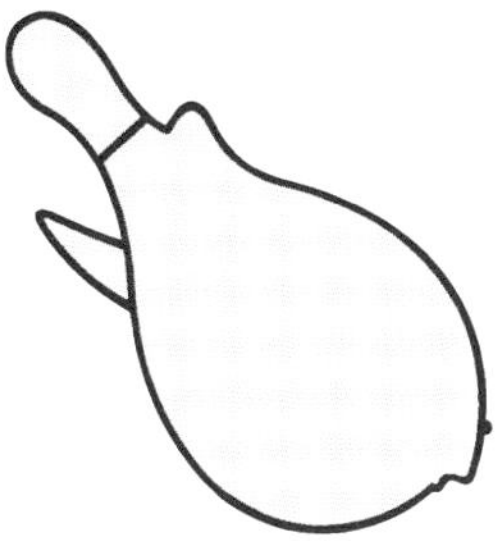

Puffer Fish

Determinative in the name of the fish* špt, *literally, "blown-up fish," and in like-sounding words* (špt, *"blow up"*; špt, *"to be discontent").

The puffer (in Egyptian modern vernacular, "fahaka") is a fish that has the singular ability of being able to fill itself with air. According to Nile fishermen, the fish rises to the surface in order to fill itself with air; this remarkable change in its size prevents it from being eaten by its predators. The ancient Egyptians, careful observers of nature, certainly knew of this peculiarity of the fish, which they realistically represented in relief and painted versions in numerous tombs: its name, in fact, *špt*, is certainly connected to the verb *špt*, "to blow up, to blow oneself up." The members of the family of *Tetraodontidae* derive their name from the four sharp teeth in their rather strong mouths which are used to break the mollusks and shells on which they feed. Their strong bite is frightening, and even a dying fish can puncture an incautious fisherman's finger. The *Tetraodontidae* are all poisonous and the fahaka is no exception. It seems that at Kom Ombos there was a taboo against killing and eating this fish. At Elephantine the fish enjoyed a special veneration that was connected to the flooding, and the ancient Egyptians imagined the springtime return of the mullets toward the south as a type of holy pilgrimage "to the chapels of the fahaka." It is hard to say whether the use of the puffy hieroglyph of the fish as a determinative and sometimes abbreviated writing for the verb *špt*, "to be angry, to be discontent," is to be associated with the angry puffing of the fish when it is bothered, or to the anger of the fisherman when he finds the inedible creature in his nets. More likely, it is just a phonetic use of the determinative, influenced by the sound of the fish's name.

A Tetrodon painted with other fish and swamp plants. West Thebes, tomb of Nebamon, Eighteenth Dynasty. London, British Museum.

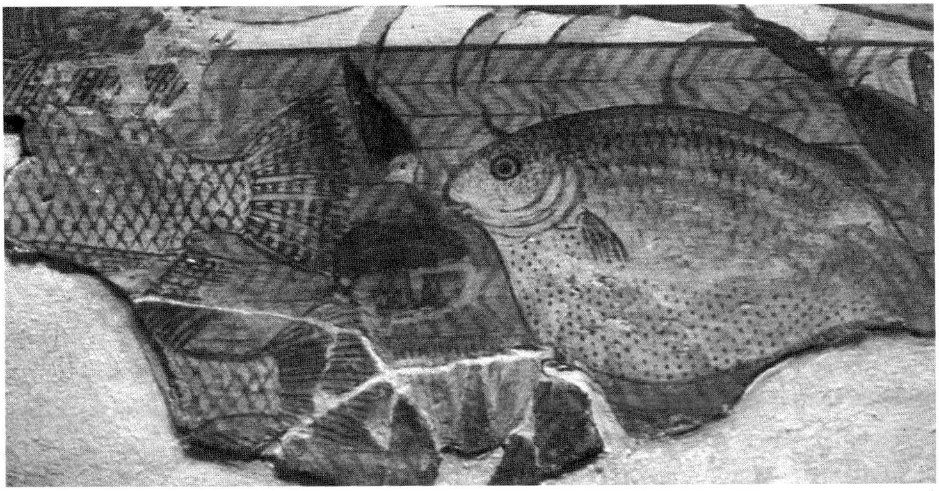

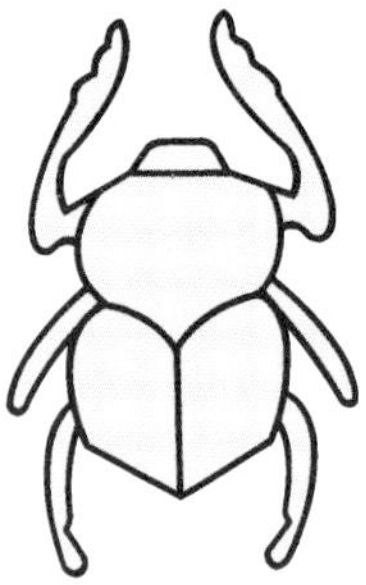

Scarab

I*deogram in* ḫprr, *"scarab," whence phonetically* ḫpr.

That a humble coleopterus, moreover dung-beetle, which shapes dung into little balls and deposits its eggs in them, could become for the Egyptians the image and symbol of the highest sun god, is a little difficult for us to understand. But the Egyptian culture, so deeply rooted in nature, did not have these problems: the black insect that tirelessly pushes the ball and miraculously draws out from it its progeny is a magnificent subject for suggesting the idea of the demiurge "that comes into existence on its own": *ḫpr* is the Egyptian verb that expresses the idea of assuming a form in the cyclical flow of existence, and *ḫprr* was the name of the insect that so fortunately consented the characterization of an otherwise abstract notion. If this association between scarab and self-generation was formed in that workshop of the Egyptian religion—Heliopolis, the seat of the solar cult —one understands how the Egyptian theologians who loved to dwell on the powerful hieroglyph images could have seen in the little ball an image of the solar disk, and in the scarab a manifestation of the god Khepri, the morning form of the sun god.

But the play of analogies and deep connections established between things on the thread of their assonances did not stop there: *nḥp* is the name of the little ball of dung and *nḥp* is the verb "to shape on a potter's wheel," another of the demiurge's activities in the Egyptian cosmogonies. The ball can also be the image of the subterranean world, into which the sun is closed during the night, like a larva, which the sun drills into with its rays in the morning in order to emerge in the eastern sky. Plutarch explained it all very well: "As to the scarab, they pretend that the species has no female, that they are all male and place their eggs in a type of material, which they shape into a sphere and roll along with their hind legs, imitating in this way the course of the sun."

A well-loved symbol, it became very early a potent amulet and loaned its characteristic form to seals: the inscription was carved on the flat belly. Besides scarabs with the names and titles of private persons, there are also many with names of royalty or with enigmatic inscriptions of a religious nature. One peculiar category was that of the so-called "scarabs of the heart," an amulet placed on the mummy, over the heart, and carried protective formulas for the precious organ and for the deceased.

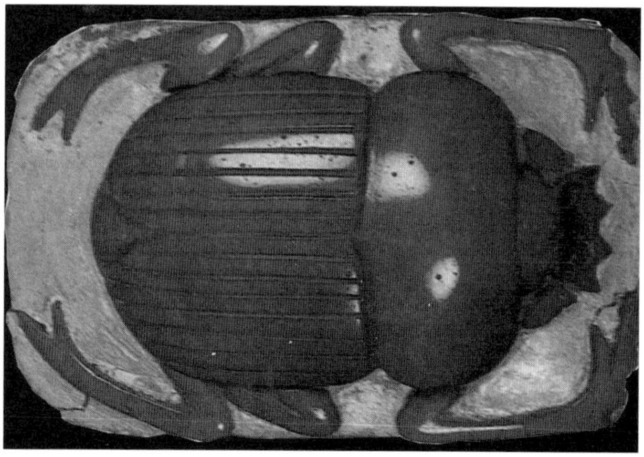

Plaquette of gold-leafed wood with a scarab in blue glaze. Greco-Roman era. Cairo, Egyptian Museum.

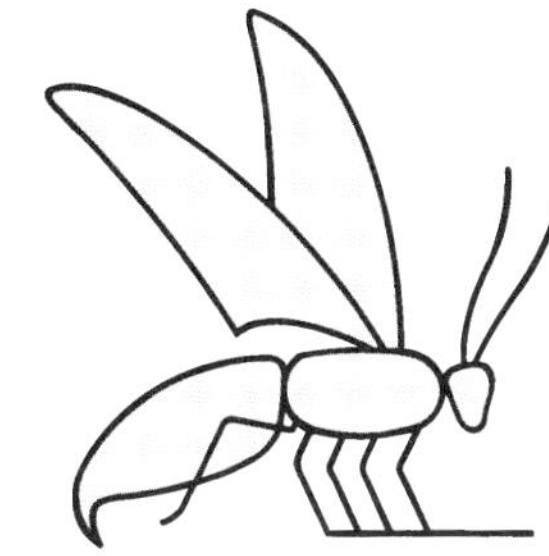

Bee

***Ideogram for "bee": phonetic value* bi͗t.**

As ideogram *bi͗t* designates both the bee and its honey. Bee keeping has been documented in Egypt from the third millennium, but was probably already practiced in Neolithic times. In the *Papyrus of the Signs* found at Tanis in the Egyptian delta, a collection of hieroglyphs with comments and explanations in hieratic for each sign, the bee is the first grapheme illustrated. *bi͗t* is in fact also the symbol of Egyptian royalty of Lower Egypt and, as such, opens that which was for the Egyptians a sort of encyclopedia, hierarchically ordered, of existence. In royal protocol, the title that preceded the name Pharaoh was *n(y)-swt-bi͗t*, "He who belongs to the rushes and the bee," where the rushes were the emblem of Upper Egypt and the bee of Lower Egypt. Here on the broad delta plains apiculture must have had a tradition and importance dating back thousands of years, and it was in the religious circles of precisely the central delta area where the symbolism of the bee developed. At first it was especially tied to the sacred royalty of the divine ancestor kings: the focal center of these concepts seems to have been Sais, where the principal temple, dedicated to the warrior goddess Neith, was called "Castle of the Bee" and the bee itself was the animal associated with the goddess's cult. The culture of late Egypt, known for combining different hieroglyphs to weave complicated and multicolored fabrics of symbolic references, has left one extravagant cryptograph based on the hieroglyph *bi͗t*. It is in the *Myth of the Eye of the Sun* (6, 31–33), a narrative-philosophic text that comes down to us on a demotic papyrus of the Roman era: "the beekeepers, when they want to solicit her (the bee) to swarm, call her with a whistle made of cane. . . . When they want to write the word 'honey' they use the figure of Neith with a cane *(kš)* in hand, since it is she who purifies *(kš)* the temples of Upper and Lower Egypt."

Details of bees on a honeycomb offered to the deceased. West Thebes, tomb of Tjenro, Eighteenth Dynasty.

Millipede

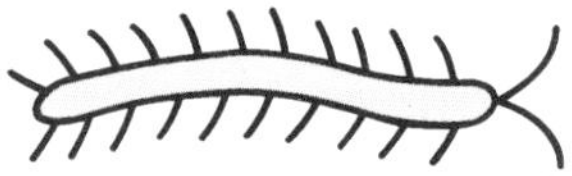

Determinative in the word* sp3, *"millipede"; phonetic determinative in* sp3, *"litter."

The millipede *(Scolopendra)* in fact has neither one thousand nor one hundred feet, but rather forty-two, as the Egyptians knew very well. The Egyptian example *(Scolopendra adhaerens)* is about twenty-five centimeters in length, so the legs could easily be counted. Its bite was to be avoided and the Egyptians warded off its danger and ingratiated the creature by making it divine: it is the god Sepa, worshiped in the Heliopolitan area and invoked in the *Pyramid Texts* in protection from the harmful subterranean creatures. The innate comic and slightly disrespectful sense of the Egyptians attributed the same term to the portable throne, which is frequently pictured in scenes from the Old Kingdom. The throne, used only by the pharaoh in solemn ceremonies, was carried on the shoulders of twenty men, led by a chief of porters: forty-two legs that moved in unison, irresistibly suggesting the image of the litter-millipede. But the image also lent itself to other allegories: the forty-two legs recalled the idea of the provinces (nomoi) comprising Egypt, of the forty-two reliquaries of Osiris, and so forth.

Forequarters of a Lion

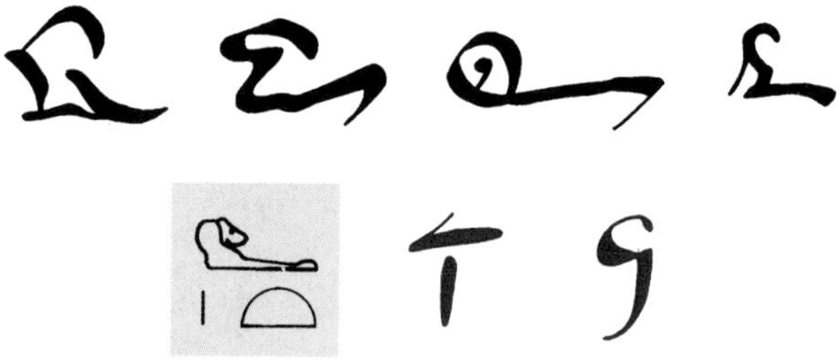

Ideogram in* ḥ3t, *"front part," and derived nouns.

In describing the concept of frontality, a drawing of the front of a man would not have had the necessary clarity, but an animal figure, lying down and in profile, as the lion is presented in the hieroglyphic system, was much more apt; and perhaps there were other not strictly graphic considerations involved: *ḥ3t* is that which is in front, but also that which presides, and the figure of the lion had more of the necessary charisma than any other mammal. The hieroglyph was ideally divided in two on a vertical axis: the forequarters of the lion, with the head and forepaws, was *ḥ3t*; the hindquarters, with thighs and erect tail, was *pḥwy*, "posterior, behind." *ḥ3ty*, "that which stands in front," is also the name for the heart, perhaps because the Egyptian concept perceived the heart as the seat of emotions, thought, and will, and thus the supreme organ of the body.

Bovine Horns

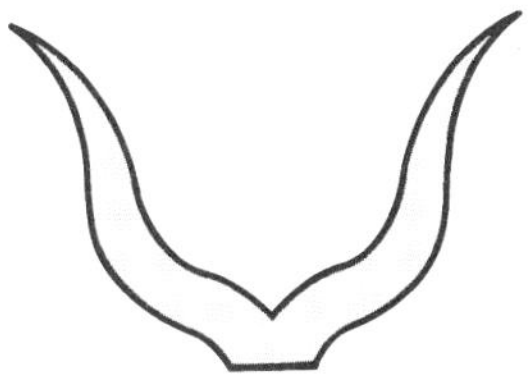

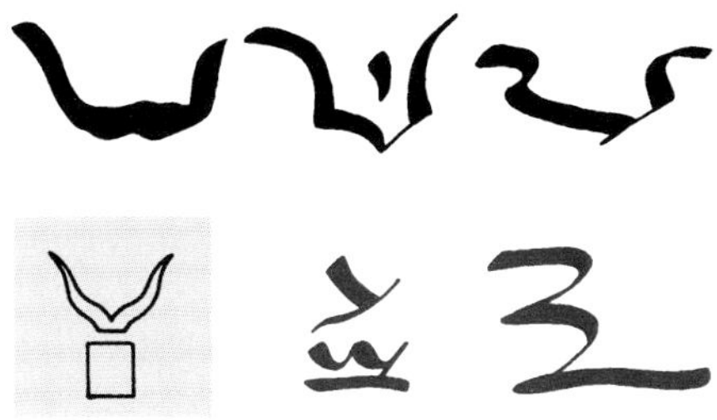

***Ideogram in* wpt, *"top of the head, forehead"; whence phonetically* wp.**

The hieroglyph with the long lyre-shaped horns did not originate in order to illustrate these typical bovine appendages, but rather to render the sagittal line of the cranium, whether animal or human. The median line is impossible to render neatly in man, but is well marked in quadrupeds at the point where the horns grow: the more detailed versions of the sign have a vertical line that crosses the joining of the horns in perpendicular, showing the anatomical characteristic of which the hieroglyph is ideogram. From the original technical significance of "sagittal line" and "summit" it passed over to indicating the broader notion of "forehead." As summit, *wpt* is also "the beginning" and the noun *wpt* may also have this meaning; so too, the sagittal line is the line that ideally divides the cranium into two symmetrical halves, and from this comes the meaning of "division" and the verb *wpỉ*, "to divide, to separate."

Elephant Tusks

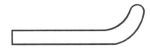

***Determinative in* nḏḥt, *"elephant's tusks," in names designating teeth:* nḥḏt, nḥdt, ỉbḥ; *and in related actions (e.g.,* psḥ, *"to bite"). From* ỉbḥ, *"tooth," phonetically* bḥ.**

The tusk of an elephant is much more visible and understandable in the drawing than the tooth of a man or other animal would have been. For this reason the Egyptians used it to determine all types of teeth. One of the terms used in Egyptian texts to designate human teeth is *nḥḏwt* (plural of *nḥḏt*), clearly a metathesis of the noun *nḏḥt*, the real elephant's tusk. It is probable that the word indicated more specifically the molars.

The phonetic value *ḥw*, generally attributed to this hieroglyph, does not seem to have any relation to it: *ḥw* was in fact also the name of an instrument used in the so-called ceremonies of the "Opening of the mouth," a ritual of statue animation that was also practiced in funeral rites: it is probably the drawing of this instrument, rather similar in form to the elephant's tusk, which determines the name of the god Hu and the family of words *bỉꜣ*, connected to the idea of metal and mineral.

Animal Tongue

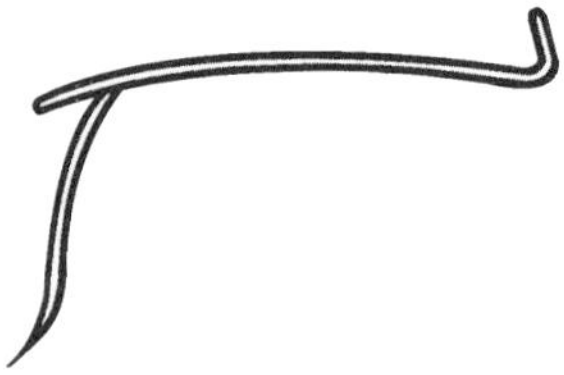

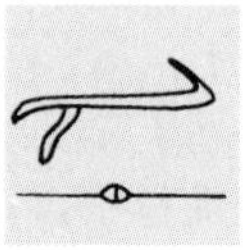

***Ideogram in* ns, *"tongue"; whence phonetically* ns.**

The sign represents a tongue, probably bovine, in a conventional image. The examples from the Old Kingdom, which are more realistic, show the base of the tongue more clearly, and at a certain distance from it, a protuberance. After the Old Kingdom it became increasingly customary to use it for the title "superintendent, responsible (for a given duty or function)." It is one of the graphic puns the Egyptians loved: the Egyptian title was in fact *ỉmy-r*, literally, "one in whom is the decision (or: the capacity to decide, judge)." But the word *r* also means, not in a metaphoric sense, "mouth" and *ỉmy-r* is thus also "that which is in the mouth," or: the tongue.
The term itself also has a frequent metaphoric use: "The tongue is… the sword of mankind: it is stronger in discourse than any weapon," as King Kheti says at the end of the third millennium B.C. to his son, Merikare.

Bovine Leg and Hoof

***Ideogram in* wḥmt, *bovine "hoof," whence phonetically* wḥm.**

There was a controversy over the interpretation of this sign for many years: the hoof of a quadruped was perceived clearly, but the precise animal from which it came was the object of discussion. Fundamentally, there was a wavering between the ass's hoof or the oxen's. The second is now universally accepted and confirmed by the existence, in a tomb of the Third Dynasty at Meidum, of a colored, quite detailed hieroglyph representing a hoof that is clearly cloven and with a spotted black-and-white hide. The two details definitely exclude the ass and make the domestic oxen the best choice (the wild bulls are to be excluded, as their hides were red – brown in color). The hieroglyph also clearly depicts one of the two small nails on the back of the hoof, which in horses is substituted by a tuft of hair. The reading of the sign, which once also wavered between *wḥm* and *whm*, has been defined in favor of the former transcription.
The sign was conceived by the Egyptians as the ideographic representation of the hoof and not of the whole leg, which is included only for the sake of clarity.

Hoof and Lower Thigh of Ox

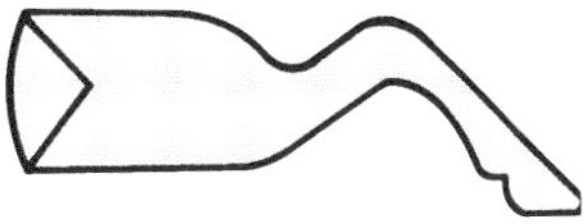

Ideogram or determinative in **ḫpš*****, "foreleg," "arm."***

The hieroglyph shows an ox's hoof and, more exactly, the right foreleg. This was the first piece of the animal that butchers would cut and use for offerings. It is possible that the custom, which has come down to us for the most part in ritual contexts, was connected to religious beliefs, but there were probably good practical reasons as well: it was the only leg unfettered by the immobilizing ropes of the sacrificants. Butchering scenes, which are very numerous in temple and tomb, show the procedure in meticulous detail. First the beast was thrown to the ground, a difficult task that was achieved by immobilizing the hind legs and the left foreleg, then putting leverage on both the free leg and the horns

A thigh in the group of offerings placed in front of the deceased. Funerary stele of Amenemhat, Eleventh Dynasty. Cairo, Egyptian Museum.

to tip it over. It is interesting to note that until at least the Eighteenth Dynasty the hieroglyph was not subject to the conventional rules for the orientation of the signs, but followed a different code: the hieroglyph with the thigh on the right and the hoof on the left was generally used to write *ḫpš*, to indicate "strength," while in order to signify the cut of meat prepared for offering, the hoof was on the right. The lists of offerings, which contained the quantity and quality of the various victuals offered to the deceased, never lack a rather plentiful choice of cuts of beef, which, together with fowl, breads, wine, and beer, were intended to be enjoyed at the fictitious funeral table. The hoof with its thigh was always first, just as it almost always appeared, carried by one or more servants, in the long offering processions portrayed on Egyptian tomb walls.

Heart

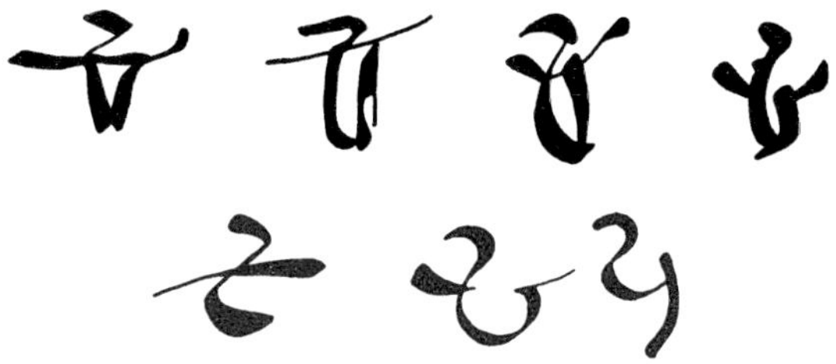

I ***deogram in ỉb, "heart," determinative in its synonym,* ḥ3ty.**

Very different from the conventional rendering of the heart in Western or modern cultures, the hieroglyph which represents the cardiac muscle is for us, at first glance, not very evocative. It looks more like a vase with a neck and handles than our image of the heart. Nonetheless it is a relatively faithful representation of the section of the heart of a sheep, as can be seen clearly in the more archaic versions, in which the "neck" and "handles" correspond to the junctures of the arteries and veins. Sometimes the upper part is painted a lighter color than the red-brown of the rest, and this may indicate the layer of fat that covers the organ. The Ebers papyrus (dating from the beginning of the Eighteenth Dynasty, sixteenth century B.C.) gives us a treatise on the anatomy of the circulatory system, which even though imprecise and containing some extravagant theories, is an attempt to understand it in a rational manner, so can be defined as scientific. In medical texts such as this, the term often used for the heart is *ḥ3ty*, while *ỉb* is the preferred term in literary and liturgical texts and refers to the heart as an anthropological rather than anatomical reality. However, in the late period, *ỉb* is definitely substituted by *ḥ3ty*. Egyptian doctors well knew the value of the pulse as a diagnostic tool: "The heart speaks in the vessels of all the members," says the first chapter of the treatise on the heart. In the Egyptian conception, the heart was supreme: "The actions of the arms, the movement of the legs, the motion of every other member is done according to the orders of the heart that has conceived them" *(The Memphite Teology)* and the same text subordinates the five senses and the word to the heart: "It is the heart that draws from the senses every judgment and the tongue pronounces that which the heart has thought." It is not only the physical, but also the sentimental and intellectual center of life. The heart has its place in all the vocal expressions of mood, spiritual attitudes, and character traits: "broadness of heart" expresses happiness; "to wash the heart" means "to calm a desire"; "to immerse" it alludes to hiding one's thoughts; "to enter into the heart [of someone]" is to be his friend.

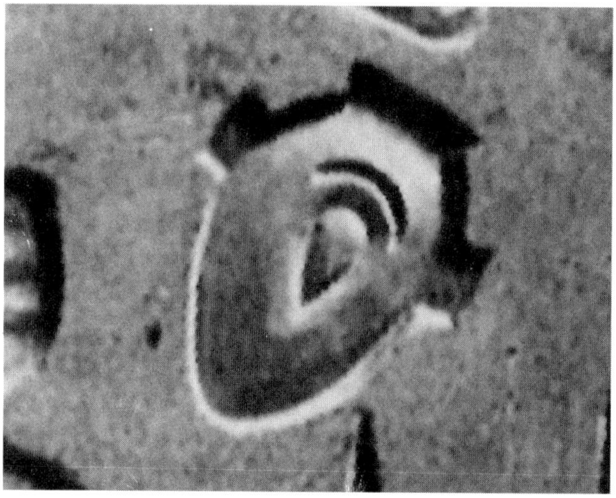

Heart of a sacrificed animal, placed among the funerary victuals. Sarcophagus of Ashait, Eleventh Dynasty. Cairo, Egyptian Museum.

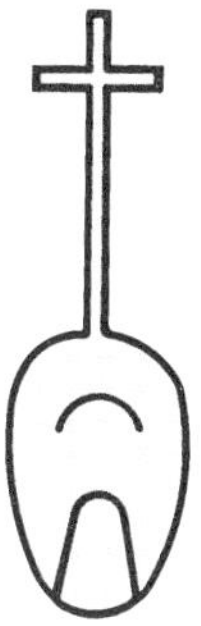

Heart with Trachea and Esophagus

Phonetic value:* nfr*, in the adjective* nfr*, "good, perfect," and in related words.

At first confused with the lute, the sign seems instead to portray the heart with a long canal, which until now has generally been identified with the trachea. The more detailed examples, above all those in the texts of the Old Kingdom, show clearly that the lower part of the sign is identical with that for the heart. In earliest times, one frequently finds, instead of the single horizontal upper cross mark, a couple of lateral projections at the top. But note that not even the more precise epigraphic variants of that era show the horizontal striations characteristic of the tracheal cartilage, a detail that becomes quite common in later examples.

It is thus probable that this detail is a later reinterpretation, influenced by the assimilation of the sign *sm3*, which shows the lungs and the trachea. The identification of heart/trachea is supported by one of the explanations in Horapollon (II, 4), according to which "the heart suspended on the trachea indicates the mouth of a good man." This affirmation has been correctly placed in relation to the meaning of the sign *nfr*, "good." However, it must be said that there is no known term *nfr* meaning "trachea." One theory that is gaining credit sees the upper canal as a representation of the esophagus: in fact there are examples from the Ptolemaic era of the word *nfrt* with the meaning of "throat," "esophagus," and it is worth remembering that the Egyptian word for stomach was *r–ib*, literally "mouth of the heart." This theory would supply the phonetic value *nfr* which is assumed by the hieroglyph.

It has been noted that from an anatomical point of view, the combination of the heart and the esophagus (or the trachea) is improbable; so it has been proposed instead that the lower part of the sign be interpreted as the stomach. The question of what was represented is still open. In historic times, the sign was bound to the meaning "good, perfect" and used as such, not only in texts, but in many symbolic images or cryptographs auguring good fortune.

The hieroglyph nefer *on a container of bronze worked with gold that belonged to the Divine Votaress of the God Amon. Twenty-fifth Dynasty. Paris, Louvre.*

Feather

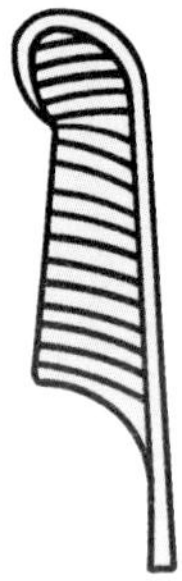

Ideogram in* šwt, *"feather"; whence phonetically* šw. *It may substitute the hieroglyph of the goddess Maat and thus carry the ideographic value* m3ʿt, *"truth, justice."

The white ostrich feather, which the hieroglyph reproduces as a universal and easily recognizable symbol for every kind of feather, large or small, monochrome or colored, suggested the idea of lightness to the Egyptians. The feather was associated by them with everything to do with levity and imponderability. *šw* is the Egyptian adjective that expresses emptiness or absence, and Shu *(šw)* is the name of the god who represents the principle of air; in the myth Shu, as impalpable air, interposed himself between Mother Sky (Nut) and Father Earth (Geb) and separated them, at the beginning of time. A feather is also the only possible term of comparison for the levity that a pure and guiltless heart should have in facing the judgment of the otherworld, the judgment of all men after death. In the depictions so often found on funeral papyri, the scales held by the god Anubis bear on the one side the heart of the deceased and on the other the feather of truth—always in miraculous equilibrium. The feather is thus the perfect symbol for the goddess in which the abstract idea of Maat is incarnated, that complex concept that regulated cosmic equilibrium and the relations between gods and mankind: it is an evanescent deity, object of an abstract cult, but omnipresent in rituals, represented iconographically by a small seated female figure, her head bound by a tape to which an emblem is affixed: the feather. In rituals, it is the perfect offering: kings owe nothing else to the gods other than respect and maintenance of this supreme rule of harmony, natural and ethical, cosmic and social; in practical terms it may be translated into a series of ethical, juridical, and ritual norms, but the whole of the concept is not exhausted in them.

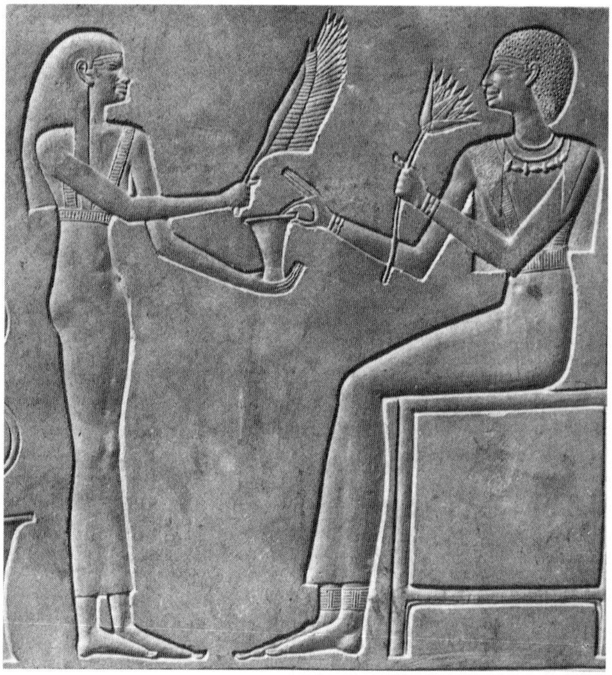

A handmaiden waving a feather fan passes ointments to her lady. Sarcophagus of Kawit, Eleventh Dynasty. Cairo, Egyptian Museum.

Egg

Determinative in* swḥt, *"egg," and in the names of goddesses.

The question as to whether the egg or the chicken came first did not torment the ancient Egyptians; they did not know of roosters and hens before the New Kingdom, when the texts mention the astonishing bird "that gives eggs every day." Naturally, the Egyptians knew of and ate the eggs of various birds, from the goose and duck to the pelican. Strangely enough, though, the scenes of daily life do not show them eating this nutrient food: it is certain that the priests were not allowed to eat them, and it seems they were not considered worthy of the funerary table, as they never appear there.
Tomb scenes show the abundant quantities of ostrich eggs that were imported from the desert and from Nubia—not to be eaten, one hopes, given the distance to be traveled and the heat in that area.
Beginning in the Nineteenth Dynasty, the texts often use the hieroglyph of the egg to express the child-parent relationship: it is in fact a deformation of the hieratic sign of the duck *s3*, but evidently the sign for the egg lent itself wonderfully to the exchange. In the theologists' cosmogonic speculations, the creation of the world often begins with a miraculous egg deposited on a hill that emerges from the primordial waters. In general, as with all circular or closed symbols, the egg expresses very well the idea of the birth of life from death: it may thus be used in the sense of "sarcophagus" or of "sudarium."
The implications of this type of association explain the taboos that could surround the egg and make one understand why in dream texts it was considered bad luck to be seen eating an egg.
Like the birds, eggs were carefully placed in the necropolises of sacred animals, in large pots, and like the mummies eggs were often wrapped in linen bandages.

Two large baskets of pelican eggs. West Thebes, tomb of Horemheb, Eighteenth Dynasty.

Heifer
Determinative in the word *bḥs*, “heifer.”

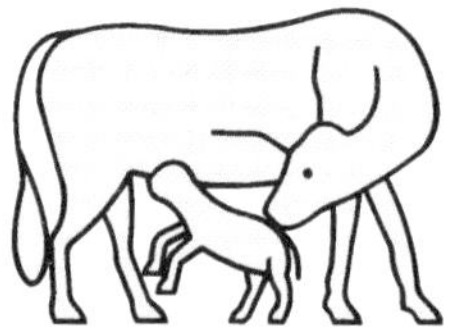

Milking cow
Determinative in the verb *3ms*, “to show care.”

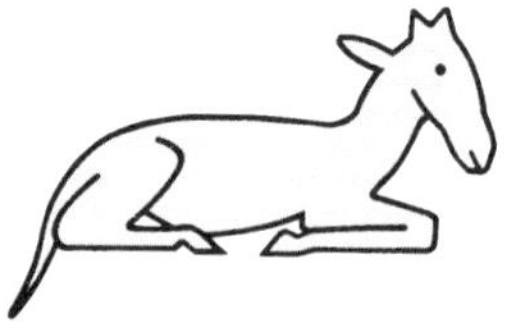

Young deer or the like, new-born
Phonetic value *ỉw*.

Hound
Determinative in *ỉw*, “dog.”

Lion
Ideogram or determinative in *m3ỉ*, “lion.”

Panther
Ideogram or determinative in *3by*, “panther.”

Ibex
Determinative in *n3w*, “ibex.”

Goat with a cylindrical seal around its neck
Ideogram or determinative in *sʿḥ*, “rank, position.”

Monkey
Determinative in the word *gf*, “monkey.”

Head of angry bull
Determinative in *ḏnd*, “anger.”

Head of hippopotamus
Phonetic value *3t*.

Ox head
In offering formulas it means *k3*, “bull.”

Antelope head

From *šs3w*, the animal's name, phonetic value *šs3*.

Ram's head

Determinative in *šft*, "head of ram"; from that, determinative and abbreviation in *šfyt*, "prestige, dignity," and *šfšft*, "respectful fear" inspired by god.

Leopard's head

Determinative or abbreviation in *pḥty*, "strength."

Animal head and neck

Determinative in words indicating the throat and related activities: *ḫḫ*, "throat," *ʿm*, "to swallow," etc.

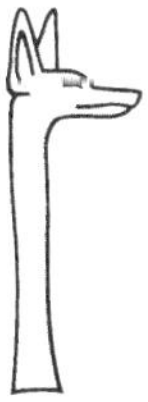

Canine head and neck

Ideogram in *wsrt*, "neck"; whence phonetically *wsr*.

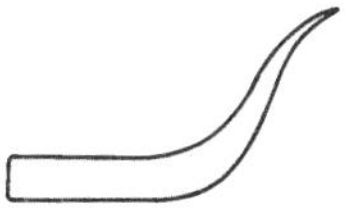

Horn

Ideogram or determinative in words indicating a horn: *db*, *ḥnt*, *ʿb*. From the latter, the phonetic value *ʿb*.

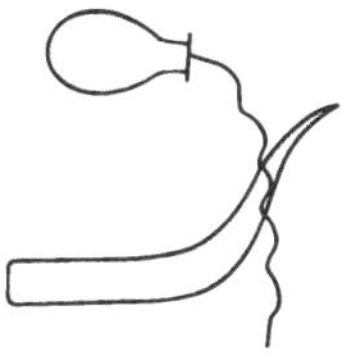

Combination of the horn ʿb with the libation container

Determinative in *ʿbw*, "purifications."

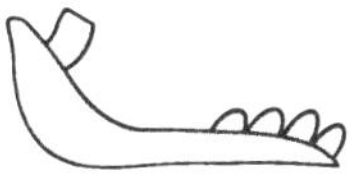

Ox jaw

Determinative in *ʿrt*, "jaw."

Bovine ear

Ideogram in *msḏr*, "ear," and in the verbs related to it: *sḏm*, "listen." From *ỉdỉ*, "to be deaf," the phonetic value *ỉd*.

Goat's hide

Ideogram in *ḥnt*, "skin"; whence phonetically *ḥn*.

Bovine hide

Determinative in words indicating skins and in general names of mammals.

Bovine hide

Variant of the former.

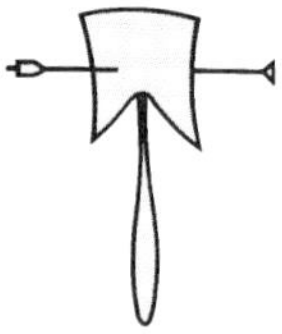

Bovine hide pierced by an arrow

Ideogram or determinative in *stỉ*, "pierce, perforate"; phonetically, *st*.

Belly

Determinative in *šdw*, "belly," whence phonetically *šd*.

Fly-whisk made from three fenek skins tied together

From the name of the instrument *mst*, in its phonetic value *ms*.

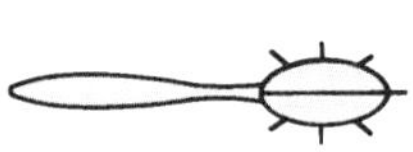

Animal belly with teats and tail

Ideogram in *ẖt*, "belly, body"; phonetically, *ẖ*.

Tail

Determinative in *sd*, "tail"; whence phonetically *sd*.

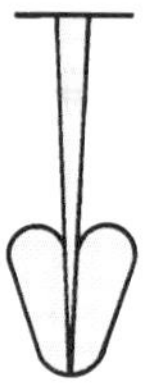

Lung and trachea

From *smꜣ*, "lung"; phonetic value, *smꜣ*.

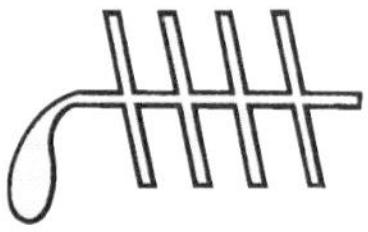

Spine with ribs

Ideogram or determinative in *ỉꜣt*, "back, spine." Determinative in related words.

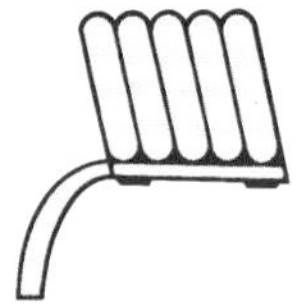

Spine with marrow

Ideogram in *ỉmꜣḫ*, "spine," from which *ỉmꜣḫ*, "dignity, to be revered." *ỉmꜣḫw* is originally the functionary to whom the king gives the funerary offerings.

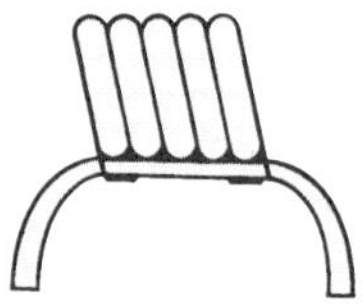

Spine with marrow issuing from both ends

Phonetic value *ꜣw*.

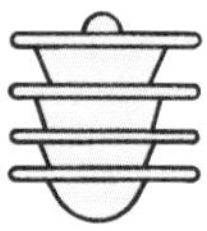

Vertebrae

Determinative in *psd*, "back, spine."

Rib

Ideogram or determinative in *spr*, "rib," whence phonetic value *spr*.

Rib of the ox

Determinative in *spḥt*, "ox rib," a cut of meat often mentioned in the lists of funeral offerings.

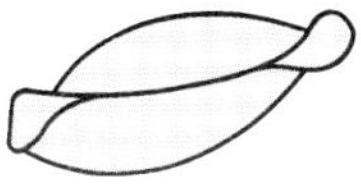

Bone with meat on its sides

Determinative in names for the thigh bone, *ỉwʿ* (phonetically *ỉw*), and for the tibia, *swt* (phonetically *ỉsw*).

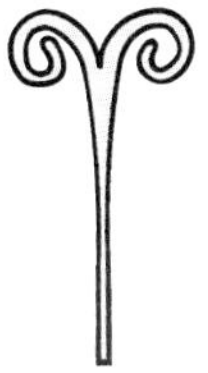

Heifer's uterus

Ideogram or determinative in *ỉdt*, "vulva."

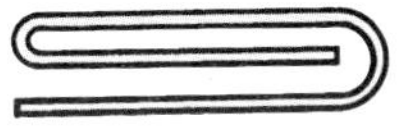

Intestine

Ideogram in *ḳ3b*, "intestine," from which the expression *m-ḳ3b*, "in the middle of" and the verb *ḳ3b*, "double." Ideogram in *pḫr*, "to turn, to go around," and derivatives, whence phonetically *pḫr*.

Cut of meat

Determinative in names for parts of the body. From *ỉwf*, "flesh," often used as a cryptograph for *f*.

Excrement

Determinative in *ḥs*, "excrement."

Monogram formed by two vultures

Phonetic value *33*.

Combination of the vulture 3 and the sickle m3

Phonetic value *m3*.

Long-legged vulture [Buteo ferox]

Phonetic value *tỉw*.

Crested ibis [Ibis comata]

Ideogram in *3ḫ*, "spirit, luminous energy"; whence its phonetic value *3ḫ*.

Pink flamingo

Determinative in the bird's name *dšr*, from which the semi-phoneme in *dšr*, "red," and derivatives

Black ibis [Plegadis falcinellus]

Ideogram in the bird's name *gmt*; whence its phonetic value *gm*.

Egret [Ardea ibis]

Determinative in the bird's name *sd3*, phonetic value *sd3*.

Ostrich [Struthio camelus]

Determinative in *nỉ*w, "ostrich."

Swallow or other member of the Hirundidae family

Phonetic value *wr*.

Sparrow [Passer domesticus aegyptiacus]

Determinative in names meaning "small," and from this, in a defective sense, "bad, lacking," etc.

Goose [Anser albifrons]

Determinative in the goose *gb*; phonetic value *gb*. Determinative in names for types of geese and for birds in general.

Flying duck

Ideogram in *p3*, "to fly," phonetic value *p3*.

Landing duck

Determinative in *ḫnỉ*, "to land, to stop," from which the determinative phonetic value *ḫ*n. For unknown reasons, phonetic value *ḳm(ỉ)*.

Duck being fattened or widgeon [Anas penelope L.]

Ideogram in wš3, "to gain weight," and in the name of the bird.

Quail chick

Phonetic value *w*.

Monogram made up of two quail chicks

Phonetic value *ww*.

Combination of the chick w and arm ꜥ

Phonetic value *w*ꜥ.

Combination of w with m3

Phonetic value *m3w*.

Duckling

Ideogram in *ṯ3*, "nestling"; whence its phonetic value *ṯ3*.

Three ducklings in the nest
Determinative in *sš*, "nest."

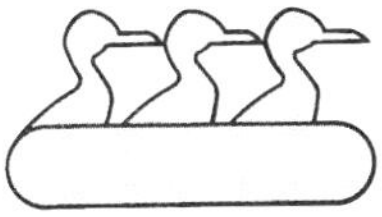

Ducks swimming in a swamp
Ideogram or determinative in the word *ỉwn*, which indicated a small swamp where birds were attracted and caught in a net. Ideogram and phonogram, *ỉwn*.

Monogram consisting of two plovers
Phonetic value *rḫt* in the word *rḫty*, "washer."

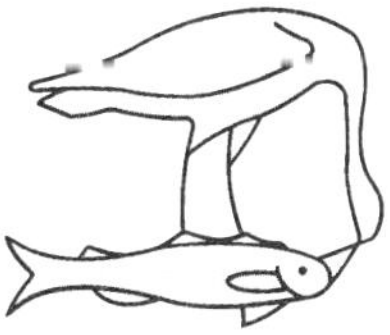

Heron catching a fish
Determinative in *ḥʿm*, "to catch a fish."

Goose pecking at grain
Determinative in *snm*, "to nourish."

Heron's head
Phonetic value: *m3ʿ*, *wšm*.

Spoonbill head [Platalea leucorodia]
Phonetic value: *p3ḳ*.

Vulture's head [Gyps fulvus]
From the Eighteenth Dynasty, used as cryptograph for *rmṯ*, "people."

Wing
Determinative in *ḏnḥ*, *dnḥ*, "wing," and in verbs denoting the act of flying.

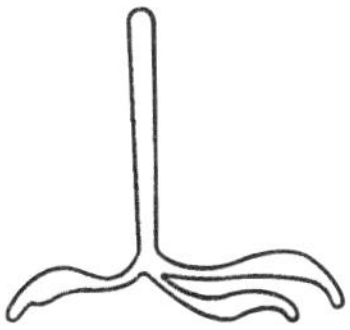

Bird's foot
Phonogram *š3* in *š3t*, name of a foreign land.

Tortoise
Ideogram or determinative in *štỉw*, "tortoise."

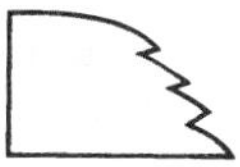

Crocodile hide
Phonetic value: *km*.

Tadpole
From *ḥfn(r)*, name of the animal; its phonetic value, *ḥfn*. It is the sign for the number one hundred thousand.

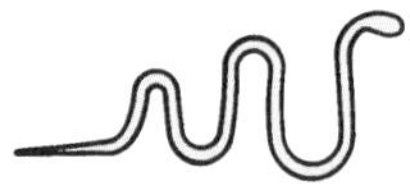

Serpent
Determinative in the word *ḥf3w*, "serpent," and synonyms.

Locust
Determinative in *snḥm*, "locust."

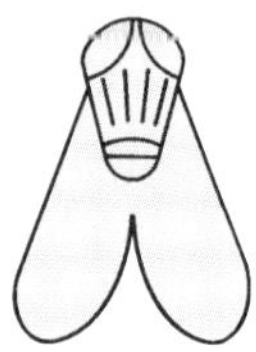

Fly
Determinative in *ʿf(f)*, "fly."

Mullet [Mugil cephalus]
From the name *ʿdw*, phonetic value *ʿd (ʿḏ)*.

Oxyrhynchus [Mormyrus kannume]
From the name *ḫʿt*, phonetic value *ḫ3*.

Barbus bynni
From the name *bwt*, phonetic value *bw*.

Petrocephalus bane
From the name *bs*, phonetic value *bs*.

Shell of bivalve
Phonetic value: *ḫ3*.

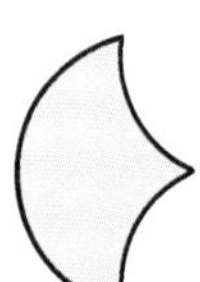

Fish scale
Ideogram or determinative in *nšmt*, "scale."

Trees and Plants

In a land surrounded by deserts, where sand and dryness are always ready to erode the cultivated earth and turn it into an extension of the dunes, that which is green is precious; it is treated with care and infinite love. The Egyptians' intimate knowledge of the plant world is documented in medical and magic texts, which reveal a rich vegetal pharmacopeia and abundant terminology. In scenes sculpted and painted in civic and funerary monuments, gardens were often proudly displayed, with all the plants and trees that lived in them.Notwithstanding, plants did not have a large place in the hieroglyphic system. Perhaps the Egyptian view of the plant world was more synthetic: the signs tend to group various examples by their similar characteristics (trees with diffuse branches, grasses and shrubs, wooden parts, roots, etc.). Among the plants, papyrus and the lotus flower appear most frequently.

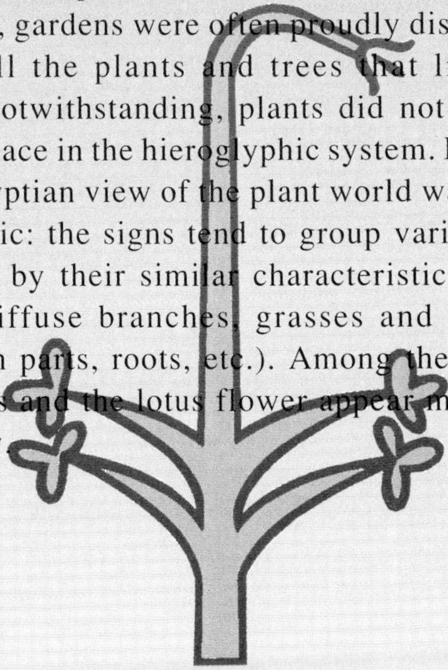

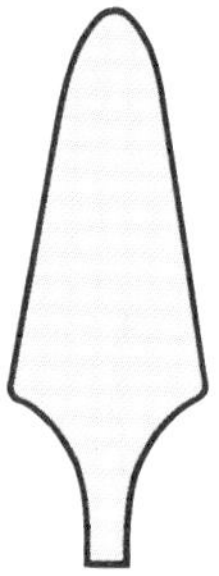

Tree

***Determinative in the names of many trees and shrubs, among which is the tree* ỉ3m *or* ỉm3*; whence its phonetic value* ỉ3m, ỉm.**

The category of botanic names determined by the sign of the tree is the largest of all. The hieroglyph serves as determinative and iconographic model to a great number of species. Its phonetic value seems to connect it particularly to the tree-*ỉm3* , so that there has been a recent proposal from Nathalie Baum to identify the tree as *Maerua crassifolia* Forsk., which is scattered through large parts of Africa, tropical Arabia, and Palestine, but is now disappearing in Egypt. Whatever the origin of its phonetic value and of the original model, the sign very early became the synthetic abstraction for the concept of tree—or better, of everything vegetal that was composed of a trunk and branches, whether tree or shrub, regardless of its form or stature. This is the only common denominator to be found among the innumerable plants determined by the sign for tree, making the hieroglyph an enormous container-sign. In the Graeco-Roman era there were many possibilities for reading the sign, connected to the names of trees which the hieroglyph usually determined: *b3ḳ*, *nht*, *ẖt*, *šn*, etc. The abstract nature of this hieroglyph tends to diminish any search for detail in its graphic rendering, despite the jumbled variety apparent in paintings of trees. In the hieroglyph, usually only the outline is indicated.

Sometimes the branches are indicated inside the closed outline.

Above: *Detail of the painting in the tomb of Pashed. Thebes, Nineteenth or Twentieth Dynasty.*
Far left: *Farmer under a tree, drinking from a goat-skin. Thebes, tomb of Nakht, Eighteenth Dynasty.*
Left: *Woman with child and fruit, in the shade of a tree. Thebes, tomb of Menna, Eighteenth Dynasty*

Grass

***P**honetic values* **ḥn** *(from* **ḥnỉ**, *"cane"); * **ỉs** *(from* ỉsw, *"canes"). Determinative in names of plants and flowers.*

Originally this sign represented aquatic plants, typical of swampy habitats, as can be deduced by the nouns from which it has drawn its phonetic values. The oldest epigraphic examples show a great variety of forms. Individual renderings tend to reproduce with greatest possible fidelity the real appearance of the plant The determinative seems in these cases to be more a persistence of the ideographic phase of the writing, featuring individual and meticulous representation, than a principle of classification for the various nouns. Eventually, the hieroglyph became fixed in the form with three stalks, and its function as determinative became specific to grassy plants.

In the late period and in documents about daily life there is a tendency toward greater synthesis and to the grouping of the words into a few classes of determinatives. This has the effect of making it easy to find the sign for grass in the place of other, more specific determinatives. In demotic texts, for example, it is generally used for all different kinds of plants.

Branch

***P**honetic value* **ḫt** *(from* **ḫt**, *"wood"). Determinative in names of objects made of wood and of wooden parts.*

The classic form of this hieroglyph, represented as a branch with twigs, developed only with the beginning of the New Kingdom. In fact, in the earlier period this represents a trunk of wood stripped of its branches and knots, with the exception of the one at the end, more than it does a branch. This aspect of the hieroglyph explains the literal meaning of the term *ḫt* as "worked wood, timber," and the fact that it primarily functions as determinative for the names of things made out of wood (tools, furniture, parts of ships and buildings, etc.). It is only secondarily that it designates the woody parts of plants (roots, bark, etc.) or is used as determinative of names of trees or plants. In any case, the generic word for

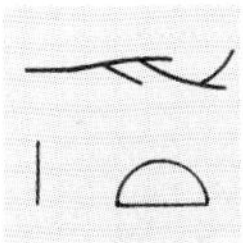

"tree" also derives from the Old Kingdom *ḫt*, and the term enters into the formation of botanic names of trees and shrubs.

Even though they were quite expert artisans and workers in ebony, the Egyptians did not have good quality wood. That which was indigenous was reserved for the productions of daily life.

Palm Branch

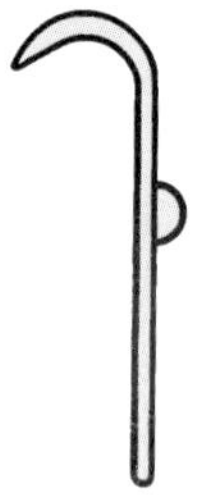

Phonetic value **rnp, tr.**

The most credible interpretation is that this sign represents a palm branch, stripped of its leaves and notched for use as a measure. According to other scholars, the character with the single eyelet is just an abbreviation for a date palm branch with all its leaves. In either case, the ancient Egyptian word for "year" was *rnp, tr*, and was very closely connected to the idea of annual growth and the cyclical renewal of vegetation. The Egyptian verb *rnp* in fact meant "to be fresh, vigorous" and also "to renew youthfulness, renew itself." It is worth remembering the different interpretations scholars have given to the hieroglyph, and understanding it rather as the representation of a branch with a bud. In the commentary—sometimes abstruse—to hieroglyphics written in the Roman era by Horapollon, the relationship between the palm branch and the year is explained in this manner: "They [the Egyptians] still write the word year in another way, by painting the palm branch, since this tree alone of all trees produces a new branch with each new moon, so that the passing of a year corresponds to the growth of twelve branches."

In the ancient Egyptian concept of the world, the idea of cyclical return (of vegetation, floods, the sun rising every morning, the moon at the end of the lunar cycle) was of fundamental importance. Around it they constructed their belief in an otherworld, and an entire system of funerary rites to guarantee their admittance.

Pashed drinks in the shade of a palm. Tomb of Pashed at Deir el-Medina. Nineteenth or Twentieth Dynasty.

VARIANTS/COMBINATIONS

A graphic pun that starts with the combination of the branch with *t*, to write the word *tr* "season."

Another version of the same word combines the branch with *r*.

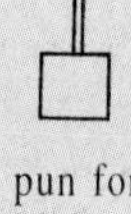

A graphic pun for *rnpỉ* "to be young," which combines the branch with *p*.

Flooded Country, Swamp

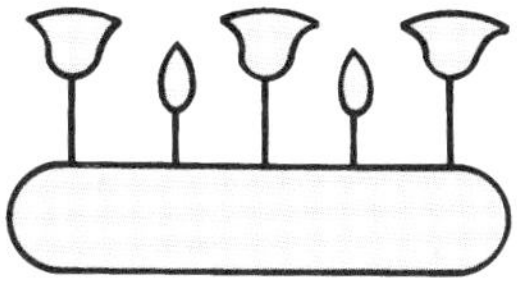

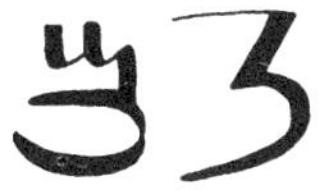

Ideogram in š3, "flooded country," whence its phonetic value š3. It is also the ideogram in the word 3ḫt, "season of the flood."

This sign expresses an element that was once one of the most characteristic of the Egyptian landscape: the country submerged by floodwaters, with tufts of plants emerging. Today, this spectacle can no longer be admired, because of the building of the Aswan dam.
The base of the hieroglyph is usually oval, like the sign for island, and suggests the scattered little islands that peeked above water during the flood season. Perhaps for the ancient Egyptian there was no sight more beautiful and reassuring than this, caused every year by the miraculous summer growth of the Nile waters, full of fertile mud and innumerable fish which filled the basins and canals prepared for them.
This ideogram also represents the vast swamps which were common in northern Egypt and in the Fayum.
There, the noble Egyptians hunted and fished amidst the cane brakes, papyri, and aquatic plants: "One happy day, when we go down towards the swamp: that we can take birds [...and many fish] from its waters...Oh, if I only were [always in the country, to do these] things that my heart desired, when the swamp was my city and the inhabitants of the swamp [were my companions!]" (from "The Pleasures of Hunting and Fishing," papyrus in the Pushkin Museum, Moscow).

Hunting and fishing in the swamps. Thebes, Tomb of Menna, Eighteenth Dynasty.

Lotus Flower

Ideogram or determinative in the word* sšn, *"lotus flower."

The delicate beauty of the lotus is such that the Egyptians almost did not dare to alter its pure lines by excessive stylization. The hieroglyph renders its graciousness in a drawing that remained practically unchanged through different scribal traditions and epochs, and even in the rapid hand of the scribes writing hieratic and demotic. While the difference can be seen in artistic representations, in the graphic code it is impossible to distinguish between the two species of *Nymphaea* known in Egypt—the blue *Coerulea* Sav. and the white *Nymphaea Lotus* L. Because of this, it is not certain to which of the two the word *sšn* refers. It may more likely be the blue lotus, the more sacred and appreciated of the two, with its delicate and sweet perfume. The Egyptians imagined the blossom that opened each morning above the water as the crib of the sun of the primordial morning. As the living symbol of the Egyptian idea of beauty—its hieroglyph can write, allusively, the adjective *nfr* "beautiful," and "beautiful" was its popular name—it was an almost obsessive element in their art. Decorative friezes are composed of alternating lines of budding calyxes; its petrified image repeats itself in the so-called lotus columns; carpets of lotus open under the keels of nobles' boats in tomb scenes, and they are never lacking in banquet scenes. Finally, the lotus was borrowed in sculptural form for the splendid goblets of blue Egyptian faïence.

Left: *Lotus flowers and buds offered to Osiris. Deir el-Medina, tomb of Senedjem, Nineteenth Dynasty.*
Below : *Young girl with a bunch of lotus flowers picked in a pond. Thebes, Tomb of Menna, Eighteenth Dynasty.*

Lotus Stem with Leaf and Rhizome

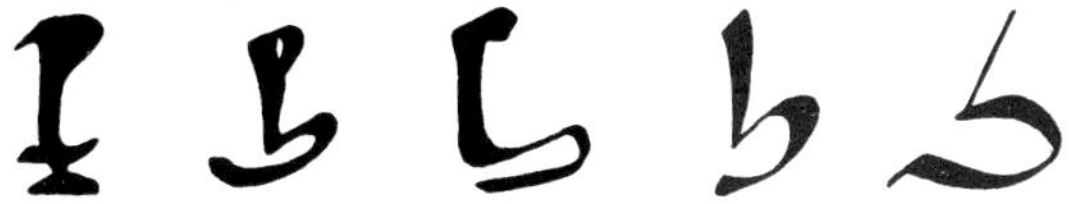

***Ideogram in* ḫ3*, part of the lotus flower, whence its phonetic value* ḫ3.**

This hieroglyph shows a leaf of the *Nymphaea* (lotus flower) with the stem and rhizome. The characteristic heart-shaped leaf of the lotus is easy to recognize. Conventional codification of the sign, already elaborated in the Old Kingdom, shows the leaf (according to the perspective rules of the Egyptians) floating on water. In some rarer variants it is shown vertically. There has been discussion as to the exact meaning of *ḫ3* in connection with the name of the lotus flower, from which the phonetic value for the sign is derived. Some believe it is the leaf of the lotus, which seems to be the most prominent part of the sign; others believe it is the rhizome. The former hypothesis seems preferable.

The sign was used as a numeric symbol to indicate ten thousand. In this capacity, it appears quite frequently in the offerings lists of funerary inscriptions, which proclaim that the deceased hopes to enjoy forever "tens of thousands (*ḫ3*) of good things, fowl, oxen," etc. In these lists, the hieroglyph is repeated in hopes of securing a more abundant offering, by invoking the sympathetic magic of the repetition.

Long-stemmed Lotus

Ideogram or determinative for* wdn, *"offer."

The flower-loving Egyptians considered long stems an attribute of beauty. In temple and tomb scenes, flower are never cut near the blossom: the sinuous young women who carry offerings have very long-stemmed lotus flowers in their hands; luxurious garlands are made by braiding them. The offerings heaped in front of the deceased rarely lack flowers, either laid across the food, with their long stems dangling along the table, or nicely wound around the wine amphoras. It is easy enough to understand why this hieroglyph became the ideogram for the verb *wdn*, "to offer."

As usual, the ancient documents show variations of this sign. Though the long and curvaceous stem remains a constant, it can rest in different positions; sometimes the flower is a long thin bud, while at other times it is a full blossom. The meaning of the hieroglyph stimulated one of the graphic puns so much loved by the Egyptians. The scribe replaced the flower with a goose's head, one of the favorite offering foods.

This sign's similarity to the hieroglyph representing the intestine caused many instances of confusion.

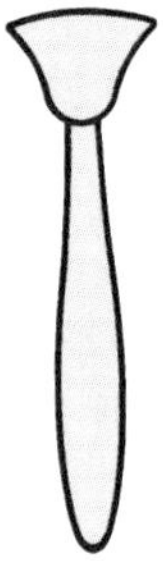

Papyrus Stem

***Ideogram in* w3ḏ, *"papyrus stem"; whence its phonetic value* w3ḏ, *and from the Middle Kingdom,* wḏ.**

This hieroglyph renders the stem of the papyrus *(Cyperus papyrus* L.) in a highly stylized manner. The flower is represented as a compact shape, not as the feathery tuft of the actual umbellar, which is composed of many thin filaments.

In archaic times, and sometimes even later, the sign incorporated the long, narrow outer leaves at the base of the flower, just as it sometimes included the tall sheath of leaves at the base of the stem. The bulging lines of the stem allude to its characteristic triangular section.

It was from the stem of the plant that the fibers to make sheets of writing material were taken. In addition, the strong stems were used in the construction of light, flexible boats, as well as woven mats, cages, sandals, and even clothing.

The swampy Delta, in particular, abounded with forests of the plant, which in Egypt reached a height of 2.25 feet (.83 meters). From the name of the green stem of the papyrus is derived the adjective "green," written with the same sign. From this (in an association which was obvious to the Egyptian who contrasted the verdant valley with the reddish tones of the desert), came a series of nouns and verbs related to the idea of well-being, prosperity, and youth. The hieroglyph *w3ḏ* lent its form to a highly regarded amulet in ancient Egypt, which was naturally realized in green material.

The color itself was generally thought to augur well, as does the proper name which is drawn from the adjectival form. The stem of the papyrus is the magic scepter of the goddesses and Wadjet ("The Green") is the name of the cobra-goddess of Buto.

Just as the solar divinities come from the flower, the gods come from the stem of the papyrus, lending them lunar symbolism.

Papyrus-shaped columns. Thebes tomb of Nakht (#52), Eighteenth Dynasty.

VARIANTS/COMBINATIONS

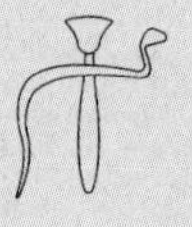

Combination of the sign *w3ḏ* with the cobra. The phonetic value is identical.

Clump of Papyrus

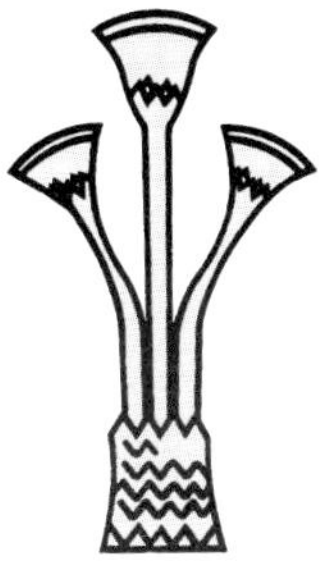

***Phonetic value:* ḥ3.**
Determinative and then ideogram for* t3-mḥw, *"the north country (the Delta)

Egyptian scribes were frequently fanciful in drawing this sign, sometimes dividing the umbellar by thin, curved lines to indicate its green filaments, or adding conventional wavy lines at the base to represent the water in which papyrus grows, or varying the delicate greens and blues used in its painting.
The hieroglyph is a nearly unvaried codification of an image common to reliefs and paintings: the thick growths of papyri into which boats ventured to hunt and fish. In the shade of the papyrus could be found insects, fish and small reptiles, nesting birds, and occasionally wild young cattle. Myth narrates that in the midst of these growths which covered the Delta (the "Land of the Papyri"), Isis and her young son Horus found refuge from the god Seth, brother and assassin of Osiris.
It is not clear where the phonetic value *ḥ3* comes from. The dictionaries do not give the word *ḥ3* with the meaning of "cluster of papyri" or anything similar. However, in the list of hieroglyph signs in the so-called Tanis Papyrus (named after the Delta site where it was found), the hieratic gloss to the sign says, "*ḥ3*: uppermost part of the papyrus (*ḏwf*)," suggesting that the sign, like the ideogram, indicates the papyrus flower.
Starting with the Middle Kingdom it was frequently mistaken for the hieroglyph of the papyrus flower with buds.

Left: *Wild ducks in flight over a cluster of papyrus. Royal palace of Tell el-Amarna. Eighteenth Dynasty. Cairo, Egyptian Museum.*
Right: *Relief from the mastaba of Nefer at Saqqara, Fifth Dynasty.*

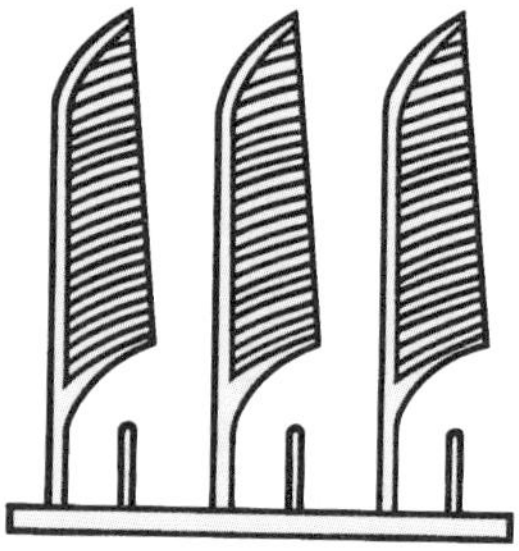

Country

I*deogram or determinative in* sḫt, *"country," and its derivatives. It sometimes has the phonetic value* sm.

While *š3* indicates the flooded land, the hieroglyph *sḫt* represents the land that emerges from the waters, damp and covered in black silt, which in no time turns green with grass and cane. These are shown by the triple repetition (another graphic indication of multiplicity) of the sign for flowering cane, *ỉ*, alternating with short vertical lines indicating the sprouting plants. The base of the sign is a flat area of ground, similar to that of the hieroglyph *t3*; *sḫt* is thus arable land, that which has "come out of the water and is good to work," as Anubis the farmer says to his younger brother Bata in *The Tales of Two Brothers*. The ideogram thereby assumes the sense of "cultivated land, fields," as the place of agricultural work rather than city or desert.

But *sḫt* is also swampy land—apparent from the canes—and here the borders between the ecological realities codified by *sḫt* and *š3* become confused. In many Old Kingdom tombs the hunting and fishing scenes in the swamps are introduced by the title "Watching the works in the *sḫt*," (referring to the deceased lord watching the activity of his servants). Here, *sḫt* is unequivocably that semi-aquatic swampy environment in which the ancient Egyptian moved with easy familiarity.

The "works" represented in these scenes are in fact "the wonderful things one does in the cane brakes," as the captions say: "capturing birds," "throwing the boomerang over the nests," "taking fish," "throwing the harpoon." Thus Sekhet is the name of the divinity of these places, shown with a wild duck in her hand.

The term incorporates both the double economy and the double rhythm that the flooding brought to the Nile Valley: it was a land of hunting and fishing when the terrain was covered with water, and a land of fields to be cultivated as soon as the waters retreated. The hybrid nature of reality to which the term alludes—simultaneously earth and water—is clearly indicated in the list of natural elements found in a Middle Kingdom religious text, wherein *sḫt* appears beside sky, earth, and water.

Temple walls often were decorated with a scene in which Pharaoh offers the hieroglyph *sḫt* to the gods, as symbol of the fertile earth with all its fruit.

Field with grain waving in the wind. From Tell el-Amarna, Eighteenth Dynasty, Schimmel Collection, no. 265.

VARIANTS/COMBINATIONS

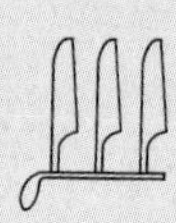

The ideogram in *sm*, "grass"; phonetic value *sm*.

Swt-Plant, Rush

***Ideogram in the name of the plant* swt, *phonetic value* sw.**

There have been various hypotheses about the identity of this plant, which long ago became the symbol of Upper Egypt. It looks quite similar to the sign commonly identified as "rush," except that it has a double row of leaves at its base, which in ancient examples are superimposed.

Much evidence suggests that this sign also represents the rush—it is used, among other things, in the construction of cane boats—but numerous examples from the Old Kingdom show it in arid semi-desert areas, while rushes are swamp plants par excellence.

A passage from Plutarch (*De Iside et Osiride*, chapter 36) favors an identification with rushes: he writes that the rush was drawn to indicate the south and its ruler. The name of the king in Upper Egypt—in historic times, part of the royal protocol—is derived from the ideogram *swt*: *nswt* is a contraction of *ny swt*, "he who belongs to the plant *swt*."

It has been noted that the Greek name used by Plutarch to indicate the plant may also indicate a type of cane (the *Typha*), which would seem to be better adapted to the Greek author's description. In any case, this cane is also a swamp plant, which conflicts with the desert related citations. Perhaps the true identity of the plant had already been forgotten by the time of the Graeco-Roman era.

According to another theory, the hieroglyph represents the *Ensete Muse* or *Ensete edule*, a type of wild banana considered by some to have been represented in predynastic art. In this case, it would have to be distinguished from the plant *šmʿ*, which is commonly thought to be the flowering version of the *swt* plant, which would then be identified instead as a type of *Ferula*, the *Silphium* of the ancients.

The swt-*plant in the "Calendar of the Seasons." Sun temple of Pharaoh Niusirra. Abusir, Fifth Dynasty.*

VARIANTS/COMBINATIONS

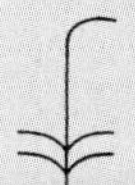

The *swt*-plant growing from the mouth, *r*: the sign for *rswt*, "south."

Symbolic Plant of Upper Egypt

***Ideogram in* šm‘w, *"Upper Egypt"; whence the phonetic value* šm‘.**

This sign appears to be a variant of the *swt*-plant, with bell-shaped, three-piece flowers. Beginning in the Middle Kingdom, it sometimes assumed the form of the lily, with two curving, lateral petals on the outside and a cob painted red-orange at the center. Representing the symbolic plant of Upper Egypt, this sign is very common in the iconography, appearing in the *sm3-t3wy* motif, or "the union of the two lands." It appears particularly on the sides of the thrones in royal statues; there, the *šm‘*-plant is tied together with the papyrus—the symbol of Lower Egypt—sometimes by two Hapi (fertility genii) to symbolize the unification of Upper and Lower Egypt which occurred under the kings of the predynastic era.

As for the *swt*-plant, which many have considered the non-flowering variant of the *šm‘*, there have been many pages written in discussion of its identity; but there is still no solution. The most credible theory speculates that the *šm‘*-plant is an example of the *Kaempferia aethiopica*, a Zingiberacea which today is found only in southern Sudan and Ethiopia, noted for its splendid purple flower (similar in shape to the lily) whose flowering precedes its leaf formation. The lack of leaves in the Egyptian drawings of Upper Egypt's emblem plant, along with the flower's reddish or orange internal coloring, seem to add credence to this last theory.

However, paleography shows that the three-part, bell-shaped blossom is a stylization of the New Kingdom. In older examples, only the three-part division of the flower is documented; its petals are more separate, and do not resemble the lily. This fact precludes finding its prototype in plants with a blossom like that of the lily or iris, even though confusion or willful substitutions may have taken place over time.

Above: *the plant in a hunting scene in the desert. Saqqara, Tomb of Ptahhotep II, end of the Fifth Dynasty.*

Left: *The Union of the Two Lands. Relief from the throne of Sesostris I, Twelfth Dynasty. Cairo, Egyptian Museum.*

VARIANTS/COMBINATIONS

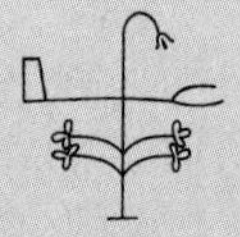

Combination of the *šm‘*-plant with the sign ‘, as a phonetic complement.

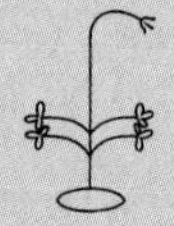

The *šm*<-plant over the sign for mouth, *r*. This is an erroneous way of writing the *swt*-sign over *r*.

Barley Kernels

Ideogram in* ìt, *"barley." Determinative of grains.

Three oblong kernels of ancient Egypt's most commonly used grain (used primarily for beer) were chosen as the determinative to represent every category of grain in the hieroglyphic system.
The choice may not have been casual: barley is known to have been one of the first grains to be domesticated and cultivated in the ancient world, including the Nile Valley.
Barley is, in sum, a "historic" grain. Wild barley (*Hordeum spontaneum*) was abundant in the Near East, from which it may have been introduced into Egypt, though recent archaeological discoveries show that very early experiments in cereal cultivation were conducted in African regions west of Egypt as well.
The spatial arrangement of the kernels in the hieroglyph may vary according to the needs of the page layout: they may be horizontal, vertical, or in a triangle with two of the kernels above the third.
The triplication of the sign of the single kernel, as in the case of liquids and granular materials, indicates enormous quantity.

Spelt Spike

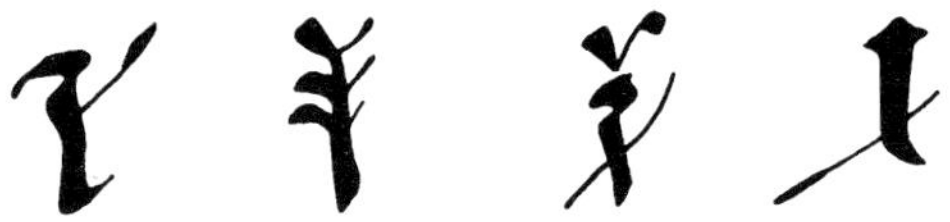

Ideogram or determinative in* bdt, *"spelt."

This sign represents a shaggy spike of spelt (*Triticum dicoccum*), the grain used by ancient Egyptians in bread, today almost unknown.
Together with barley, spelt was a fundamental part of the ancient Egyptian diet, which was largely based on bread and beer with the addition of vegetables, fresh fruit, and (less often) fish.
Egyptian texts list different types of spelt, distinguished by color: white, red, yellow, black, and still others.
These details find support in the scientific classification of this grain. The Egyptians' understanding and versatile usage of their natural environment allowed them to include spelt (as well as barley) in their pharmacopeia, usually in topical applications. In one case it was used to foresee a birth.
A charming vision of spikes of spelt waving in the wind appears in a bas-relief originally from Tell el-Amarna, the site of the capital founded by Amenophis IV. The bas-relief was later reused in buildings in Hermopolis Magna, where it was discovered.

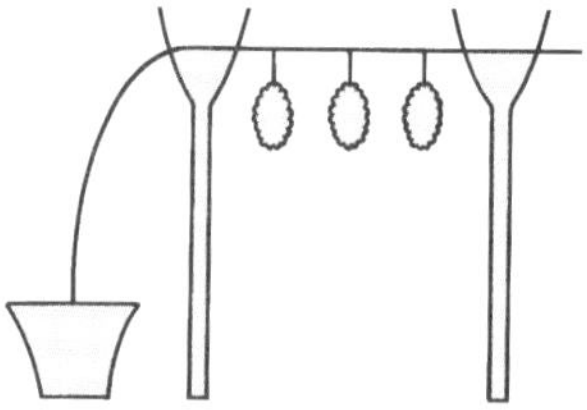

Grape Arbor

Determinative and occasional ideogram in words connected to "vineyard"* (ỉ3rrt), *"wine"* (ỉrp), *and sometimes "fruit" and "orchards."

This sign shows a grapevine with stylized clusters hanging on an arbor. The basket or vat beside the tree is missing in the oldest examples and does not appear prior to the Twelfth Dynasty, when it can be found as the determinative of the single word *ỉrp*, "wine," in a synthetic indication of the gathering of grapes. The vine has been cultivated in Egypt from predynastic times and is represented in many images from the Old Kingdom. It appears as part of the shady arbors, which no garden worthy of its name would be without, and as part of lively scenes of grape-harvesting. "The night comes, the grape is heavy with dew. Let us hurry and squash them and take them home to our master!" the pickers in the tomb of Petosiris at Tuna el-Gebel urge one another.

In the Egyptian cosmology, in which the sacred was always near, the sun-warmed grape and the thick wine that was made from it had divine significance. From time immemorial, they were offered in funeral rites as symbols of regeneration. Religious texts call the grape "the pupil of Horus's eye," while wine, like the perfumed resins from Arabia, is likened to the tears of his eye.

The Egyptians held wine in great esteem. The warehouses of temples and royal palaces have yielded countless labels for amphoras and terra cotta vases. With punctiliousness comparable to modern quality control, these labels registered each container's production year, the place, vineyard and proprietor, and notes on the quality: "Wine which is three times good, eight times good. . . ."

Reapers gather grapes from hanging vines. Thebes, tomb of Nakht, Eighteenth Dynasty.

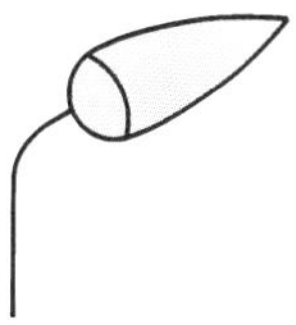

Lotus Bud

Determinative of the name of the lotus bud, *nḫbt*.

Bunch of Lotus with Buds

Determinative in names of swamps and bogs. Ideogram for the name of Lower Egypt, *t3-mḥw*. Phonetic value *3ḫ*.

Flowering Rush

Ideogram in *ỉ*, "rush," whence its phonetic value *ỉ*.

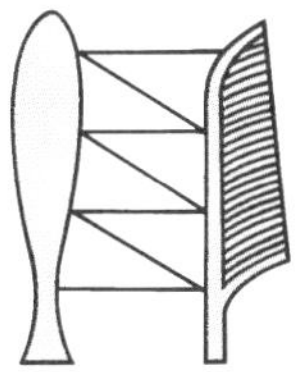

Piled-up Cone-shaped Sweets

Determinative and abbreviation for *ʿ3bt*, "stack of offerings."

Cane

Name of the plant *nḫbt*, whence its phonetic value *nḫb*.

Carob

Used as ideogram in the name of the tree *nḏm* and for *nḏm*, "sweet."

Date

Ideogram or determinative in *bnr*, "sweet."

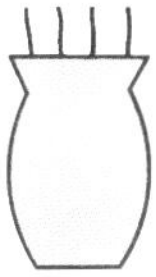

Lotus Rhizome

Determinative in *rd*, "grow."

Lotus Rhizome

Variant of the former.

Stack of Grain

Determinative in *ʿḥʿw*, "stack."

Bundle of Linen Flowers

Phonetic value *ḏr*. Determinative in *dm3*, "tie together."

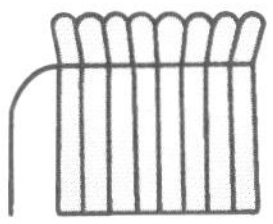

Bundle of Linen Flowers

Variant of the former.

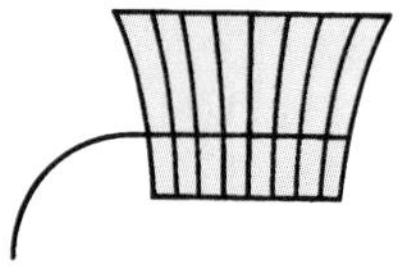

Variant of the Former
Determinative in *mḥ*, "linen."

Basket of Fruit
Determinative of "plant offerings."

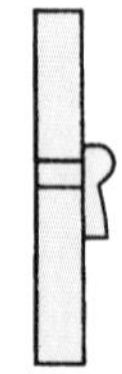

Rushes Tied Together
Ideogram in *ỉ*sw, "rushes," whence its phonetic value *ỉs*.

Trunk of Tree with Branches Cut Off
Determinative in names for wood.

Flower
Phonetic value *wn*.

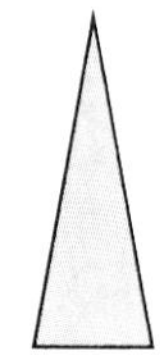

Thorn
Determinative in *srt*, "thorn"; ideogram or determinative in *spd*, "sharp, pointed," and related terms.

Sky, Earth, and Water

This section contains the hieroglyphs used by the Egyptians to describe and synthesize the celestial phenomena, landscape configurations, and aquatic elements (both natural and man-made) known to them. The categories into which these hieroglyphs are divided were already part of Egyptian thinking. The word-list known as the *Onomasticon of Amenope*, a sort of encyclopedic index listing everything a cultured Egyptian of the New Kingdom should know, describes its contents thus: "Beginning of teaching for clearing the mind, for instruction of the ignorant and for learning all things that exist: what Ptah created, what Thot copied down, heaven with its affairs, earth and what is in it, what the mountains belch forth, what is watered by the flood, all things upon which Ra has shone, all that is grown on the back of the earth, devised by the scribe of the sacred books in the House of the Life, Amenope son of Amenope" [translated by A. Gardiner, *Ancient Egyptian Onomastica*, Oxford, 1947].

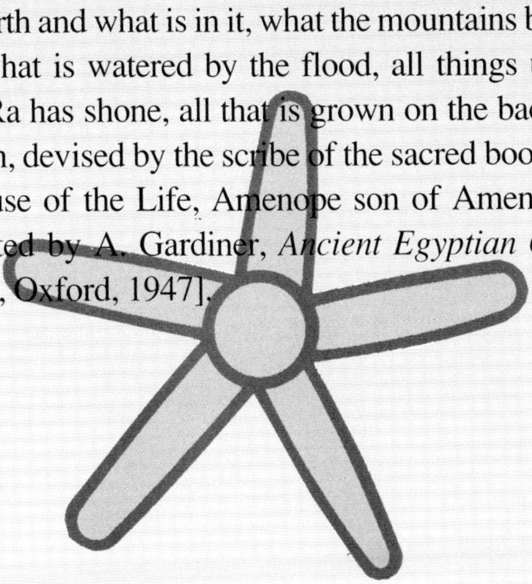

Sky

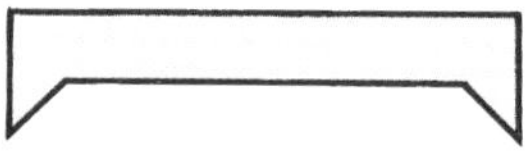

***Ideogram in* pt, *"sky." Determinative in the synonyms. From* ḥrt, *"sky," phonetic value* ḥry.**

Of all the ways of representing sky, the one chosen for this hieroglyph is exempt from any mythological implications. It represents the sky simply as a gigantic ceiling resting on four props, an image taken from architecture. This image is quite consonant with a concept well-rooted in Egyptian thinking, that of the world as a large building. The idea has its counterpart in the symbolism of sacred architecture, in which the temple is a microcosmic synthesis of the world and its parts mirror the cosmic elements. The ceiling represents the celestial vault and is decorated with astronomical figures. This sign, sometimes sprinkled with stars, sits atop scenes on Egyptian stelae and monuments in which they wished to emphasize the cosmic ambience. In mythological iconography or in the portrayals of solar circumnavigation, however, the sky more often appears as the celestial cow (the animal manifestation of the celestial goddess Nut) or the likeness of the goddess bent in an arc, her hands touching the earth; from her vulva the sun is born every morning, and her mouth swallows it again every evening. All these graphic symbols have the idea of the four supports in common: the four legs of the animal, the arms and legs of the goddess. The feminine element is another constant: *pt* and its synonyms are feminine words. For some, the oldest iconography is that of a female feline. In the myth of the goddess Nut, originally, she lay atop her companion Geb, the Earth, until their mythical union was broken by their son Shu, representing the air and dryness, who lifted his mother. From then on, the celestial goddess was known as *ḥrt*, "The Distant."

The sky goddess Nut, bent in a bow. Detail from the sarcophagus of Khonsumosis, Thebes, Twenty-First Dynasty. Turin, Egyptian Museum.

VARIANTS/COMBINATIONS

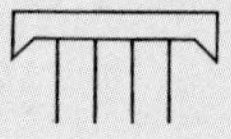

Water that descends from the sky: ideogram or determinative for *ỉꜣdt*, "dew," and *šnyt*, "rain."

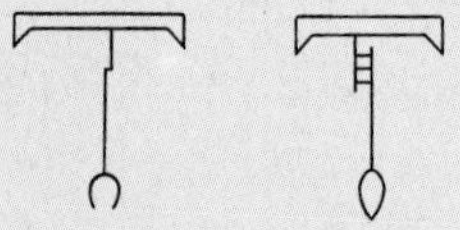

Sky with a broken scepter (in ancient examples it is an oar), as determinative for the words meaning "obscurity": *grḥ*, *wẖ*, "night"; *kkw*, "dark," etc.

Sun

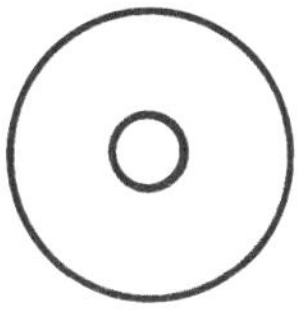

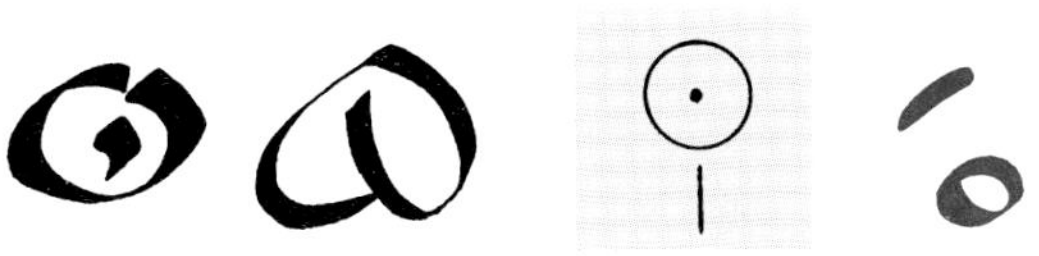

Ideogram in* r‘, *"sun"; in the name of the sun god Ra; and in hrw, "day." Determinative in words connected to the sun and phenomena related to it.

In the Egyptian universe, the sun was a dominating element. Its physical presence, as it reigned implacably over the sky, could never be ignored. It pervaded every aspect of Egyptian existence.

As a god, Ra was soon affirmed over the entire pantheon. The great national gods, who aspired to universality, could not avoid assuming a solar aspect eventually; thus were Amon-Ra, Montu-Ra, Khnum-Ra born, a significant theological recognition of the dependence of all creation on the sun.

Egyptians were always aware of this dependence. A sedentary and agricultural people, their existence depended on the light and warmth of the sun, just as it did on the fertile waters of the Nile. There are no references in the texts to the negative aspects of its burning, suffocating heat; instead, they celebrate the beneficial qualities of the sun. "You are beneficial to mankind when you rise; a rest for the cattle when you shine.... It is you who have created all things . . . you who produce the forage that feeds the herds and the fruit trees for man, who create that which feeds the fish in the current, give air to the embryo in its egg, nourish the small worms, create food for the mosquitoes, the serpents, and the flies, give what is necessry to the mice in their holes and feed the birds on every tree," says a papyrus in the Cairo Museum (p. Bulaq no. 17).

And here, in contrast, is a description of the night from the *Hymn to Aten* (the solar disc) by Amenophis IV: "When you rest on the western horizon, the earth is in the dark as though dead. [Men] sleep in their rooms, with their heads covered, and one eye cannot see the other . . . All the lions come out of their dens; all the serpents bite."

The sun is never represented in Egyptian art as a natural element (like the moon) but appears always and only in symbolic form, generally as a winged disc, above the scene.

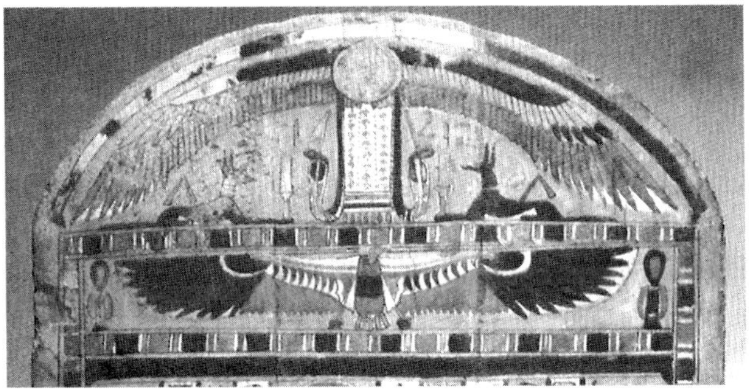

Upper part of a wooden stele (with a winged solar disc) dedicated to a god. Thebes, Late Period. Turin, Egyptian Museum.

VARIANTS/COMBINATIONS

Combination of the disc with the sign *ḫrw*, as an abbreviation of the expression *ḫrt-hrw*, "that which belongs to the day; the course of the day, daytime."

Sun with Rays

***D**eterminative or ideogram in nouns connected to the sun's shining:* **3ḫw**, *"light, splendor";* **psḏ**, *"shine" ;* **stwt**, *"rays." From* **wbn**, *"rise," comes the phonetic value* **wbn**. *The sign is also the ideogram (or phonogram) for* **ḥnmmt**, *the mysterious "people of the sun" in the Heliopolitan theology.*

In this hieroglyph of the solar disc, the focus is placed on the rays and the radiating capacity of the star. It is no accident that the symbol assumed sudden importance in the Amarnian era: it appears high up in bas-reliefs and on stelae, its rays ending in little hands with the sign of life (*ankh*), which beat on the figures of Pharaoh Amenophis IV-Akhenaton and his wife Nefertiti.

This anthropomorphic solar disc, thought of as a caring father, became increasingly identified with the pharaoh. Simultaneously, it became an expression of a new intimacy between king and god. In the fragmentary hieroglyphic "dictionary" in the Carlsberg papyrus number seven, the sign is explained as follows: "*ḥnmmt*, that is, the people of the god Atum." Atum is the Heliopolitan creator and solar god, identified with the disc at sundown in the solar cycle, and the *ḥnmmt* are certainly an invention of Heliopolitan thought.

References to the "people of the sun god" are quite ancient. The *ḥnmmt* are generally associated with the *pʿt* and the *rḫyt* as classes of humanity, even though the exact significance of this Egyptian concept eludes modern researchers. The Egyptologists Gardiner and Gunn have pointed out the significance of the "people the sun shines on" and their connection to the rising sun and the new king. The term seems to have been used to designate the Egyptians themselves, but with what specific connotation is still not certain.

Left: *Akhenaton and Nefertiti offer libations to Aton. Relief from Tell el-Amarna, Eighteenth Dynasty. Cairo, Egyptian Museum.*

Right: *Detail of the throne in the tomb of Tutankhamen (#62 in the Valley of the Kings). Cairo, Egyptian Museum.*

Crescent Moon

Ideogram or determinative in* i͗ꜥḥ*, "moon," and the name of the lunar god. In dates it stands for* 3bd*, "month."

The crescent moon is generally represented horizontally, as it appears in the Egyptian sky, but it can also be found in the vertical.

i͗ꜥḥ is a masculine noun; in keeping with this, the Egyptian gods (there were more than one) who were associated with the moon were also masculine. They took on the characteristics of the moon, and were connected to the telling of time and to the idea of cyclical regeneration.

Other hieroglyphs reprsented the moon in the different phases of its cycle (such as full, or new moon). Also quite common was the image of the lunar disc resting in the concavity of the horizontal crescent moon, a synthetic rendering of the complete cycle.

There were mythological explanations of the phases of the moon's cycle, connected to the complex myth of Horus's Eye. However, the Egyptians had at least one rational theory, written in the hieratic-demotic Carlsberg papyrus number one, according to which the invisibility of the moon was due to an increased proximity of the sun, whose brightness diminishes that of the stars nearby.

It is known that the Egyptian calendar was originally lunar. The observation of the heliacal rising of the star Sirius was used at first not to establish the first day of the new year, but to determine whether the new moon should be calculated in the old year or the new one. The year was divided into twelve months of thirty days each, with five days added at the end. The lunar origins of the Egyptian months are quite evident. The names of the days of the month—each day was named—are all related to the lunar cycle. They reveal the refined observations of the Egyptian astronomers, who were able to perceive characteristics and anomalies in the lunar cycle and related phenomena which were not readily visible.

For the Egyptians the month began on the morning the moon became invisible, or just before the new moon, and the phase of invisibility was part of the new month. This method of calculating is relatively rare; its only known parallel is among the Masai of eastern Africa.

Moon, crescent and disc, on the head of the baboon sacred to Thot, bronze. Turin, Egyptian Museum.

VARIANTS/COMBINATIONS

Variant of the sign with the same phonetic value.

Star

***Ideogram or determinative in the word* sb3, *"star"; whence its phonetic value* sb3. *Determines names of constellations and nouns connected to the measuring of time. Also phonetic value* dw3.**

It would seem that the iconographic model for this hieroglyph was the starfish, which was plentiful in the Red Sea. This is not surprising: the Egyptians conceived of the celestial world as an aquatic world, on whose blue breadth the sun god's boat sailed; from its deep liquid night the stars shone, perhaps like red starfish. In any case, the Egyptians considered the celestial movements of the stars to be real (and sometimes dangerous) navigations and the vocabulary employed in their connection frequently coincided with nautical terminology. In the Old Kingdom, *sb3* is the term which indicates a journey across water, and *sb3w* is the pilot who guides the ship and its crew with an expert and steady hand. Hence, probably, the name *sb3w* for choir-master, and, above all, *sb3* for the verb "instruct, teach," since the Egyptians knew well that instruction is dangerous navigation.
The star is always shown with five points, like the starfish. In the older examples it has rounded ends and is more massive; sometimes the center is neatly marked by a double concentric ring and the arms have small cross bars. The colors are the classic colors of the stars: yellow, golden, or red, and rarely blue.
In the most ancient times the inhabitants of the Nile Valley imagined that the stars were the souls of the dead. The term *dw3t*, written with the star, indicates both morning and the world beyond the tomb, where the sun navigates in the night and swarms of souls (in star form) follow in its wake.

The constellations on the ceiling of the tomb of Seti I, shown in human and animal form. Thebes, Nineteenth Dynasty.

The Otherworld

Ideogram in* dw3t, *"the otherworld."

A star (*dw3t*, morning, place where the sun is born) in a circle: this is the symbol for the otherworld. Initially, in the *Pyramid Texts*, this sign stood for the place in the sky where the sun and the stars reappeared after having been invisible; then it began to represent the otherworld, whether celestial or subterranean. The image of a subterranean otherworld is more recent in Egyptian culture; but at the same time it is closer to the ancient idea that no one but the king could expect more than a pale replica of life after they died. The deceased would be supplied in the tomb with offerings from devoted relatives, and the soul could come and go at will through a "false door."

When the destiny of the deceased began to be associated with the symbolic death of the god Osiris, the otherworld began to be envisioned as an underground space with an intricate and detailed geography. The dead moved through this subterranean otherworld with the help of funerary rites and the so-called "guides" to the otherworld (which sometimes took the form of real maps painted on the sarcophagi).

The blessed and the damned coexisted in this strange world, which provided an arboreal paradise (green with rushes and papyri, and running with water) only for the blessed, after they passed the crucial test of the "weighing of the soul."

Very early, it became necessary to harmonize the solar funerary beliefs with those regarding Osiris. The nocturnal solar voyage was thus set in the bowels of the earth, and the two theologies were melded in a unique mystery god, Ra-Osiris. This new god incorporated the principles of both day and night; Ra-Osiris meant not only life, but also a death that contained in it the germ of life. The circle of the Duat is a symbol of cyclical rebirth. Like other Egyptian metaphors for life in the afterworld, it is a closed internal space that is naturally associated with the image of the female womb, the point of departure and hoped-for destination.

The deceased in the Egyptian paradise. Aaner Papyrus, Twentieth Dynasty. Turin, Egyptian Museum.

Earth

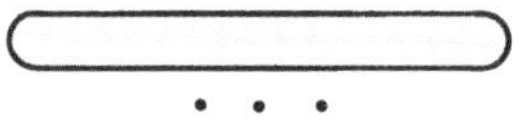

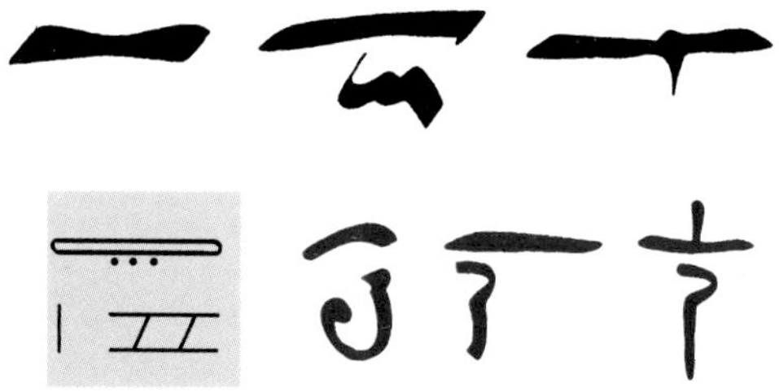

***I**deogram in* t3, *"earth." Rarely a phonogram. Determinative in the word* **ḏt**, *"estate," from which stems its improper use as phonetic determinative in the like-sounding words* **ḏt**, *"eternity," and* **ḏt**, *"servants."*

This is the flat flood plain of the valley, generally painted black, with three grains of sand underneath (sometimes missing) to evoke immensity. Strangely, the list of signs in the Papyrus of Tanis describes the three small circles of the hieroglyph as three "*ḳrrt*," a word meaning holes or caverns. Is this an erroneous interpretation in a period already distant from the origin of the hieroglyph, or does it signify that the word has another meaning still unknown to us? The symbol graphically portrays the idea of Egypt as a flood plain, the "gift of the Nile." But *t3* is also the hieroglyph for the earth in general, "world," seat of life and of men, as opposed to sky and water.

In the *Onomasticon of Amenope*, the largest part of the treatise is relative to "the earth and what is in it" and to "what grows on its surface," covering the diverse types of ground, various duties and functions, humanity in its various components, an ample ethno-geographic list, names of grains, names of bovines, cuts of meat, and so on. In the few known Egyptian illustrations of the earth, which date from the first millennium B.C., it is shown as a circle inscribed in a space surrounded by the arms and legs of the celestial goddess. Around it runs the waters of the primordial ocean, according to the iconography of the solar circuit.

The known world in the form of a globe circumscribed by the goddess Nut. Stone sarcophagus, Twentieth Dynasty. New York, The Metropolitan Museum of Art.

Island

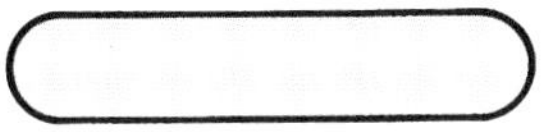

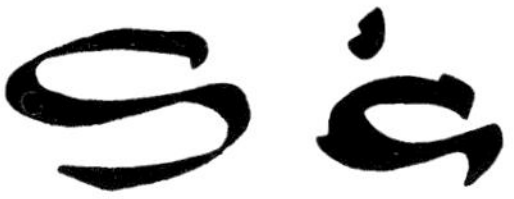

Ideogram in* iw, *"island." Sometimes determinative of foreign countries.

This sign appears as a narrow oval, painted a reddish yellow and sometimes accompanied by the points indicating sand. The oval (and rounded borders in general) distinguish natural spaces from man-made ones.

The ideogram may represent the sandy islands in the middle of the river Nile as well as the sandy hills that sometimes interrupt the flood plain, which the Arabs call *gezireh*, "islands."
The word *iw* can thus indicate not only islands in rivers and seas, but also the Delta's characteristic hilly formations on which cities were built.
In the continuous and unpredictable remodelling of the Nile landscape that came with each year's flood, *iw* was also the name given to the newly arable land deposited by the river, later known as *m3wt*. This synonym for island literally means "new land."

Irrigated land

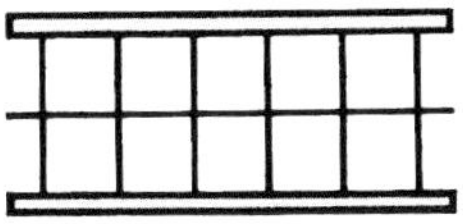

Ideogram or determinative in* sp3t, *"district, nomos." Determinative in names of provinces and regions and in the noun* ḥsp, *"garden, vegetable garden, orchard."

This hieroglyph represents a parcel of land furrowed by an orderly network of lines, which are painted black. These furrows have been interpreted as canals for irrigation, but the black coloring makes it more likely that they represent dikes built to contain the flood waters.
It is easy to understand how the sign came to represent the names of the administrative subdivisions of ancient Egypt. There was a strong correlation between the need for irrigation (the excavation and continual maintenance of the canals, the construction of dikes and sluices) and the need for a centralized administration, whose fiscal income was regulated by the exact value of the irrigated (and thus arable) land. The designation of the oldest nomarchs (the governors of the "nomos") was "he who digs the canals."
Thanks to their precise system, the inconstancy and capriciousness of the floods were controlled to allow agricultural production; the waters of the Nile were bridled and taken where they were needed. Political and hydrological anarchy were simply two faces of the same coin.

Hilly Terrain

Ideogram or determinative in* ḫ3st, *"hilly land, desert, foreign land." Determinative in names of desert places and foreign countries.

This hieroglyph represents the hilly areas outside the Nile Valley (which, on the contrary, is characterized as a flat, black terrain). "Outside the valley" covers the desert and semi-desert regions contiguous to the valley, as well as any foreign land. In the more detailed examples a green line runs along the bottom, illustrating the cultivated land of the valley and functioning as a spatial and conceptual border of the idea represented by the sign.

In opposition to the fertile black earth of the *t3* sign, the three hills of this sign have the yellow, pink, or reddish colors typical of sandy terrain, with scattered darker spots indicating the roughness of the area.

Once again, the hieroglyph is a mixture of naturalistic image and graphic convention: the idea of the asperity of the earth and its sandy, rocky nature also characterize the naturalistic portrayals of the desert in the hunting scenes that are so plentiful in Egyptian tombs. The image of the *gebel*'s endless sequence of valleys and hills is rendered by the three hills of the graphic code, using three yet again to indicate infinity.

The term *ḫ3st* and its ideogram thus bring together ancient Egypt's notion of "otherness"—geographical, above all, but also cultural. *ḫ3st* is the domain of the wild beasts (sometimes fabled) which, almost en masse, were associated by the Egyptians with evil forces. In particular, the gazelle, oryx, and wild ass were associated with Seth.

This area is also the region from whence the nomads came from time to time, invading the valley to procure food and other goods, or in not very well received attempts to integrate.

The increased difficulty of living in the areas surrounding the valley and in their increasing aridity (which started in the remote Pliocene era and ended in the third millennium B.C.) certainly conferred a negative connotation on a word which was originally more neutral.

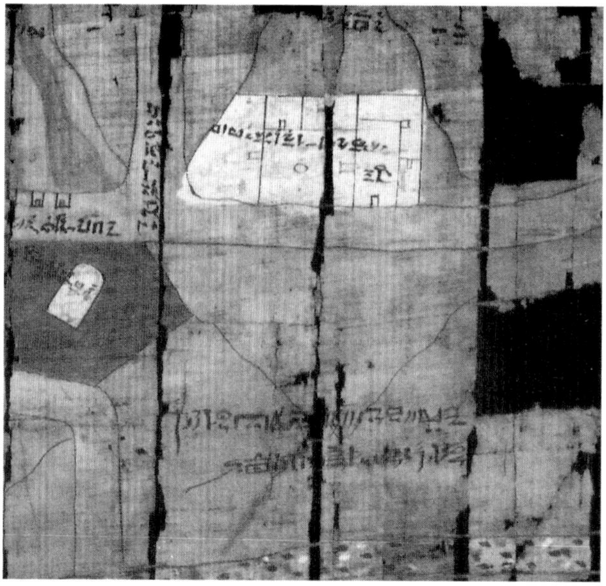

Map of the eastern desert, with mines and quarries indicated. Papyrus. Ramesside Period. Turin, Egyptian Museum.

Tongue of Earth, Cultivated Parcel

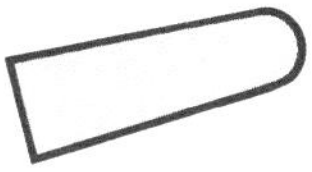

Ideogram or determinative in* ỉdb, *"riverbank." Determinative in names for earth, regions, etc.

In the traditional interpretation, this sign would have represented a sandbank which extended into a river or the sandy bank. In fact, the term *ỉdb* designates the bank of a river, while *ỉdbwy*, "The Two Banks," is a metaphor to indicate Egypt itself. *ỉdb* is, however, also the term indicating plots along the river bank, and there has been a recent suggestion by Annie Gasse that the hieroglyph should be interpreted to represent the "standard" cultivated plot.
The data from papyri show that farmed parcels were almost always the shape of an elongated irregular trapezoid, with the long sides parallel to the river's course. The surveyors who measured them for tax assessments reduced the irregular plans to simplified geometric shapes where possible, similar to that shown in the hieroglyph.
This would explain the habit, which became frequent beginning in the Eighteenth Dynasty, of using the hieroglyph as determinative in names of cultivated terrain or countryside, often replacing the sign for canal.

Mountain

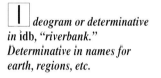

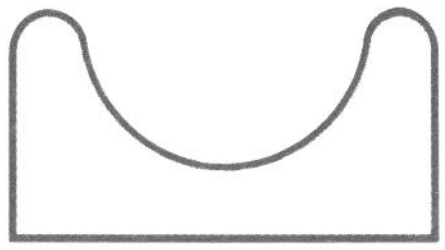

***Ideogram in* ḏw, *"mountain," whence the phonetic value* ḏw.**

Similar to the ideogram for *ḫ3st*, this sign represents the two hills that frame a *wadi*. Like the preceding sign, it is colored pink or yellow and has dark spots. Sometimes its base is marked with the black or green that indicates cultivated land. This too may be used as determinative of names of foreign countries. It is a part of numerous place-names.
The translation "mountain" does not render the meaning of the ideogram exactly; or, at least, the Egyptian conception of mountain did not coincide exactly with the modern idea. *ḏw* designates rocky sites, but of moderate altitude, like the islands scattered about the river at the level of the first cataract. The sign may be used to describe a desert highland, a single peak, or an entire mountain range.
In the later period, *ḏw* ended by slowly but surely absorbing all the meanings of *ḫ3st* and replacing it. The process is definitely completed in Coptic, which does not have any terms which descend from *ḫ3st*, but adds to the already known meanings of *ḏw* the new sense of "monastery, desert hermitage."

Canal

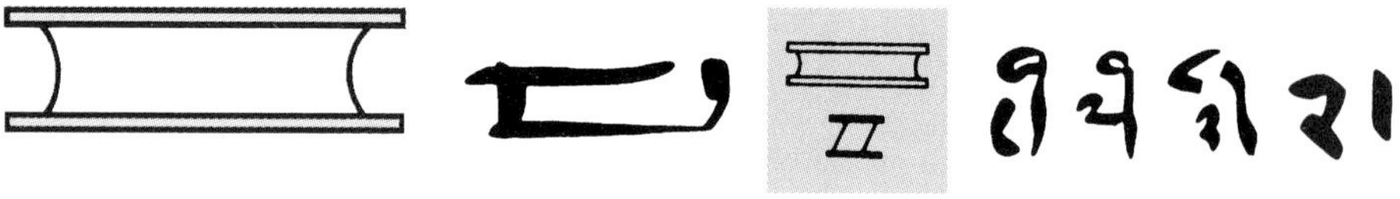

Ideogram in* mr, *"canal," "body of water"; whence phonetically* mr. *Determinative of courses and bodies of water.

This sign represents a body of water bordered by banks or dikes. It may portray an artificial canal or a natural body of water: the ideogram *mr* indicates both terms. As a determinative, the sign is found with names of canals, rivers, lakes, and even the sea, *w3ḏ-wr* ("the Most Green"). In the more detailed examples, which come from the Old Kingdom, the water between the two borders is clearly indicated by the usual undulating lines. The two vertical strokes (sometimes rounded) that enclose it indicate, according to the Egyptian graphic convention, that the hieroglyph illustrates only a part of the whole. In some cases, the line for the banks is curved, an effective portrayal of the sinuousity of many Egyptian canal banks.
The whole of the *mr* constituted a significant part of the by-ways of ancient Egypt: on their waters traveled the greater part of traffic between city and province. Following is the description, in the words of an Egyptian woman in love thirty-five hundred years ago, of a boat which took her along the canals to her loved one: "I descended the waters of the Prince's Canal, and into those of Ra, because my heart's desire was to raise my tent on the highlands in view of the Ity canal. While I ran, my heart thought of Ra, I thought that I would be able to see my love" (Harris Papyrys 500, 2, 13-15.).
Maintenence of these canals and dikes, including the cleaning and dragging of the bed to permit a regular flow of water, were tasks of fundamental importance, for both irrigation and navigation purposes. It is not unusual to see inscriptions about nomarchs or other high functionaries that list among their accomplishments the excavation or repair of a silted-in canal.

Agricultural scenes in the mythical "Fields of Iaru." Deir el-Medina, tomb of Senedjem, Nineteenth Dynasty.

Hill Illuminated by the Sun

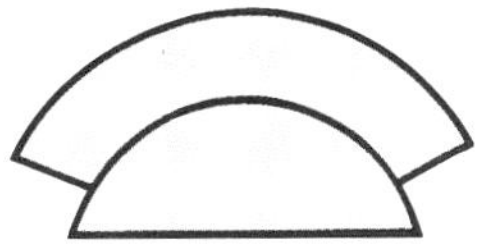

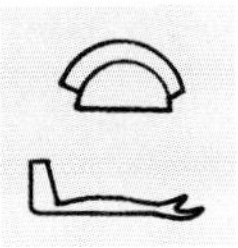

Ideogram in ḫʿ, "hill over which the sun rises (?)," and ḫʿi, "appear, rise"; whence the phonetic value ḫʿ.

Examples from the Old Kingdom show a semicircular figure with four bands of diverse colors—blues, greens, and reds—with a sort of halo of rays above. This might seem to be a plausible rendering of a rainbow, with the upper band as a schematic image of the sun's rays. But there is no other evidence to support this hypothesis, although the significance of the ideogram *ḫʿ* is uncertain. It occurs in the *Pyramid Texts* in the complex expression *ḫʿn t3*, which is usually translated "place of the sun's appearance over earth." It appears in formulas relating to the celestial ascendance of a dead king, which use many images like that of a ladder on which the king climbs towards heaven. It would not be out of place, in this context, to interpret *ḫʿ* as the Egyptian word for "rainbow," which is unknown to date.

Mountain with the Rising Sun

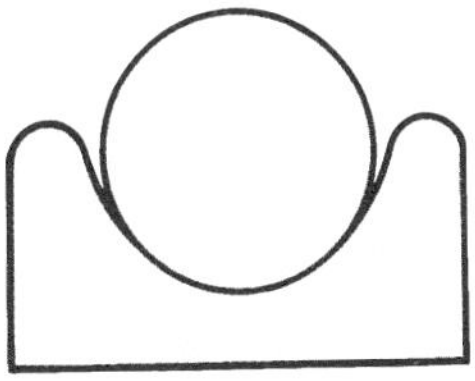

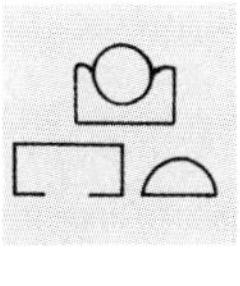

Ideogram in 3ḫt, "horizon."

The sign *3ḫt*, born of the union of the disk and the hieroglyph for mountain, is rather inappropriately translated as "horizon," associating it with a modern notion which is foreign to Egyptian thinking.

The sign is a relatively recent creation of Egyptian writing, unknown in the *Pyramid Texts*, in which the sign that determines the word *3ḫt* is the hieroglyph of a sandy island. The earliest known documentation of the sign is from the Fifth Dynasty, an epoch that saw the official affirmation of the solar cult. Thus the hieroglyph represents the point where the sun appears above the earth at daybreak and where it touches the earth again at sunset. This is the proper meaning of the ideogram, connected to the root *3ḫ*, "to shine."

The dualistic nature of the sign is made clear by the symbolic portrayal in which two human or mummified figures are placed on the two slopes of the sign.

Road

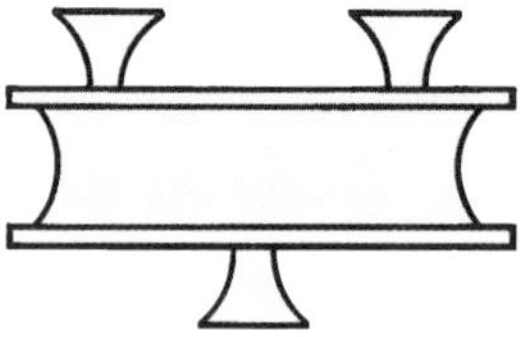

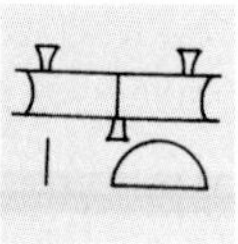

***Ideogram or determinative in* w3t, *"road" and similar words. From* ḥrt, *"road," is derived the phonetic value* ḥr.**

This sign shows a road flanked by very stylized shrubs. Older versions, as usual, show a greater adherence to more naturalistic rendering; they portray a typical winding Egyptian path which follows the higher terrain above the flood plain. The change from the original undulating line into a straight line, part of the graphic schematicizing process, took place rather early.

Little is shown about the road systems of ancient Egypt. In the towns, roads were no more than twisting alleys between houses, with the exception of the processional way leading from the inevitable temple, along which wound the sacred processions for the local divinity. Naturally, the capitals had two or three large streets to which all alleys led. The roadways outside, leading from town to country, could not have been much better once one left the desert for the thick mosaic of fields, canals, and dikes of the Valley. The roads almost always followed the uneven banks of the canals, if they did not just use the dikes themselves as the roadway.

A famous text from the First Intermediate Period, the tale of *The Eloquent Peasant,* tells of a poor inhabitant of the oasis who came into Egypt to sell his products, only to be treacherously relieved of his merchandise by a local lord. The instrument of the injustice is a road along a dike, which the peasant must traverse in order to reach the city. It was, the story tells, "so narrow that it was indeed no broader than a piece of fabric. One of its sides was under water, the other under grass." To pass along it without stepping on the clothes stretched out there—on purpose—by the lord, or the field of barley on the other side, was indeed impossible. From this event the story develops.

An intricate network of alleyways and houses in the ancient workers' ruins in the village of the Valley of the Kings. Deir el-Medina.

Water Surface with Waves

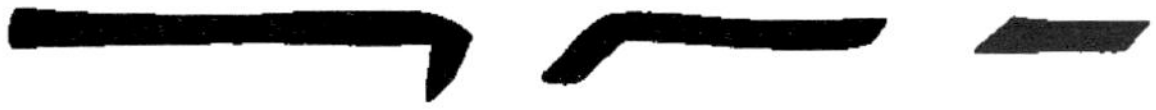

***Phonetic value* n.**

The undulating line, colored black or gray in the oldest examples, represents waves on a watery surface. However, this was not the ancient Egyptian sign for water, nor is it ever determinative in aquatic terms; it is used only as an alphabetic sign for the phonetic value *n*.

The derivation of this phonogram is not certain: it has not been found used as an ideogram to designate water or anything similar. A derivation from the word *nt*, "water," has been hypothesized, but there are no examples older than the Middle Kingdom. An alternative could be *nwi͗t*, which indicates water as early as the *Pyramid Texts*; its root is also connected to the word *nwn*, "the primordial Ocean."

In more hurried samples of the hieroglyph, influenced by hieratic writing, the undulations of the line are often omitted, and the sign is rendered by a single horizontal line that sometimes rises at the end. This frequently caused confusion with other similar signs, above all the hieroglyph for *t3*, "earth."

Three Wavy Water Lines

Ideogram in* mw, *"water," whence the phonetic value* mw. *Determinative for liquids and actions connected to water.

The Egyptians felt that triple repetition, generally used to indicate the plural, was the best way to represent a mass of water. The same stylized undulation is also used in naturalistic depictions. Here the conventions of the graphic code have influenced art. The Egyptians knew that water is an essential element for life and creation: there is hardly an Egyptian cosmogony which does not place the origins of life in water. The idea was influenced by the image of the earth reborn with vivacious life and vegetation as the Nile's waters retreated after each flood.

Together with the other elements—light, fire, earth, and air—water was a manifestation (or *ba*) of the supreme god. But it was also an ambiguous element, at once inside and outside creation. The created world and life were an island, a space surrounded by an infinity of water, the primordial Ocean, whose liquid chaos pressed eternally on the portals of the Ordered World.

Lake, Basin, Pool

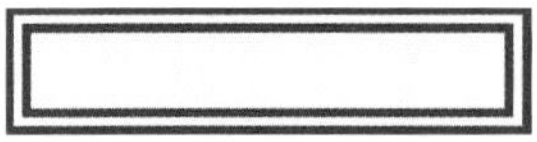

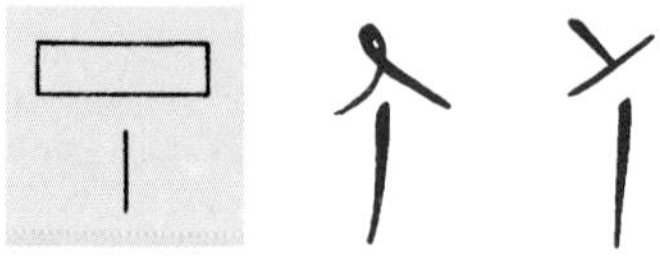

Ideogram in š, "lake, basin, pool," whence the phonetic value š. Sometimes determinative for irrigated land.

This sign represents a closed body of water, natural or artificial. In its more stylized form it is a simple rectangle, but sometimes there are green or blue wavy lines inside it indicating water.

Because the ancient Egyptians loved water, they routed it frequently into their landscape: they engineered a thick network of canals to carry the Nile water into the desert, and created hundreds of lakes and basins so they could look out across broad expanses of natural waters. The sign *š* represented not only the great lake of Fayum, but also the innumerable basins dug by the Pharaohs to beautify their palaces and cities, the sacred lakes at the temples, and the tree-ringed garden pools dug by those who could afford them (and dreamily portrayed in tombs). Sycamore trees, palms, and figs shaded the banks; ducks and fish swam in the water; water-lilies and aquatic plants floated gently. For those who knew that eternal life in the hot and inhospitable desert of the necropolis awaited them, there was nothing more attractive than the blue freshness of those waters: "That they [the gods] let me . . . enter and leave my tomb, cool myself in its shade, drink from my pool every day . . . , every day without ceasing, to walk along its banks. . . ." is the dream expressed on many funerary stelae of the New Kingdom.

The artificial pool in the garden of the noble Nebamon. Wall painting from the tomb of Nebamon at Thebes, Eighteenth Dynasty. London, British Museum.

VARIANTS/COMBINATIONS

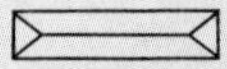

Pool with sloping sides.

Ingot, Crucible

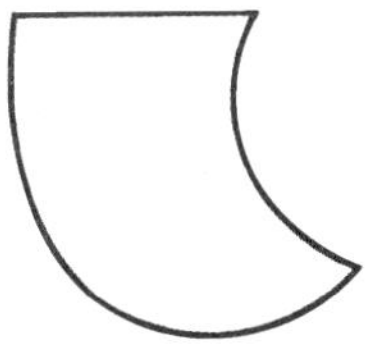

***As an ideogram this may be read as* bi͗3 *or* ḥmt, *designations of iron and copper (respectively). Determinative in names of metal objects and in the word* bḏ, *"crucible," from which arises the rare phonetic value* bḏ.**

Gardiner interprets this sign as "an ingot of metal" but the scenes of metalworking in the tombs beginning in the Old Kingdom show that it is unquestionably a crucible for melting metals: men crouching near the foundary oven blow through long pipes onto crucibles of a shape identical to this hieroglyph. Furthermore, various original examples of these crucibles, in terra cotta, have been found in different places in Egypt. In the Old Kingdom this hieroglyph had not yet come to be used as a symbol for copper. Instead, it was indicated by the ideogram for the foundary oven or, alternatively, schematic images of masses of molten copper—obviously of very different shapes, but with the same phonetic value, *bi͗3*. In a variant of the latter sign, dating from the First Intermediate Period, the copper ingot takes on the shape of the crucible for the first time. This shape finally affirms itself in the Eighteenth Dynasty.

Well, Hole Full of Water

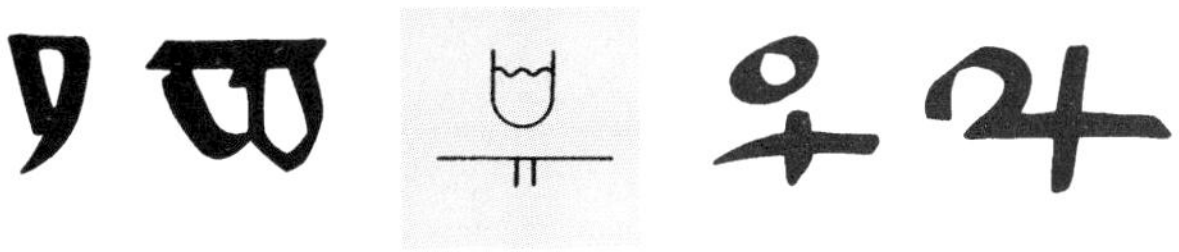

***Phonetic value* ḥmt, bi͗3.**

This sign is a rather realistic representation of a hole full of water, especially in more precise samples which incorporate the conventional undulations of the water's surface.

Its phonetic values, however, do not lead back to any word signifying "hole with water" or "well": in this sense, it functions only as a determinative for words such as *ḥnmt*, "spring, well," and *pḥw*, "swampy land," etc. The phonetic values *ḥm* and *bi͗3* come to the hieroglyph from two other signs, which had limited use. These two other signs had no relationship to this hieroglyph except for a graphic similarity which was likely to cause confusion. One represents the uterus, with a phonetic value of *ḥm* (connected to various words, including *ḥmt*, "woman"), and was avoided in writing. The value *bi͗3* comes from contamination with variants of the symbol for copper. Because of this complicated derivation, the sign when pronounced *ḥmt* came to designate the uterus and copper; when pronounced *bi͗3*, it entered an important class of words connected to the idea of the marvelous, from the term for "miracle" to the names for mines and precious minerals.

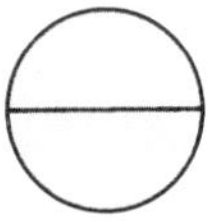

Moon with its lower half darkened
Ideogram or determinative in *psḏn*, "feast of the new moon," whence phonetically *psḏ*.

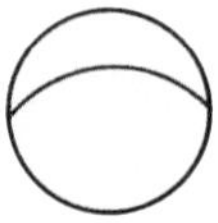

Partially darkened moon
Variant of the former.

Star with a half-crescent moon
Phonetic value unknown. Mid-month feast.

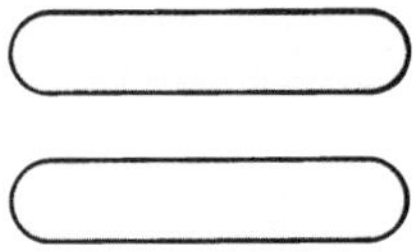

Two islands, one over the other
False dual for the adjective *3ḫty*, from *3ḫt*, "horizon," in the name of the god Horus of the Horizon.

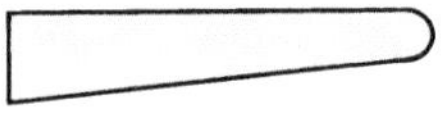

Tongue of earth
Determinative in *wḏb*, "riverbank, beach," whence the phonetic value *wḏb*.

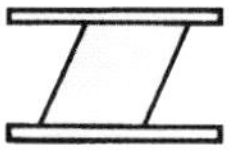

Irrigation canal
Used as the sign *mr* for canal.

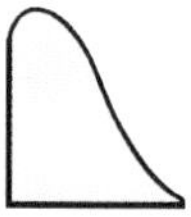

Slope of a hill
From *ḳ33*, "hill, height": phonetically *ḳ*.

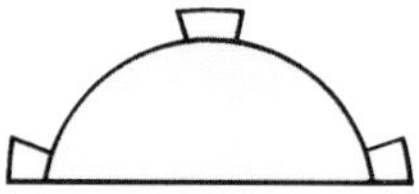

Hill emerged from the flood, with shrubs
Ideogram for *ỉ3t*, "primordial hill."

Clump of clay
Often mistaken for the sign for excrement, and used as determinative in its place.

Grain of sand
Determinative in *šˁ*, "sand"; tripled it represents an indefinite number, determinative of mineral or granular substances.

The House

The house, with all the dense symbolism it carries in modern cultures, was perhaps a concept foreign to the ancient Egyptian. His social and emotional reference point was his family or extended social group (such as a tribe, village, or nation), rather than the complex of spatial and affective elements that make up a house. In a land blessed with a mild climate in which storms were rare, his life was lived primarily outside—in courtyards, on the streets, or in the fields. The simplicity of domestic architecture is witness to its elementary function, fundamentally that of nocturnal defense and protection.

Naturally, the homes of the wealthy were different, sometimes consisting of dozens of rooms, shady patios, and luminous rooms with walls painted in gay colors. The nobles loved to have their tombs painted with scenes of their busy servants' coming and going, filling the cellars and storerooms. Even so, they preferred to be portrayed sitting in the cool shade of their gardens.

House

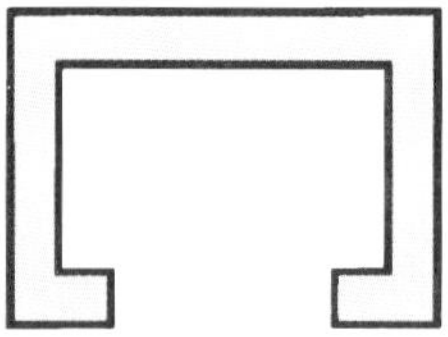

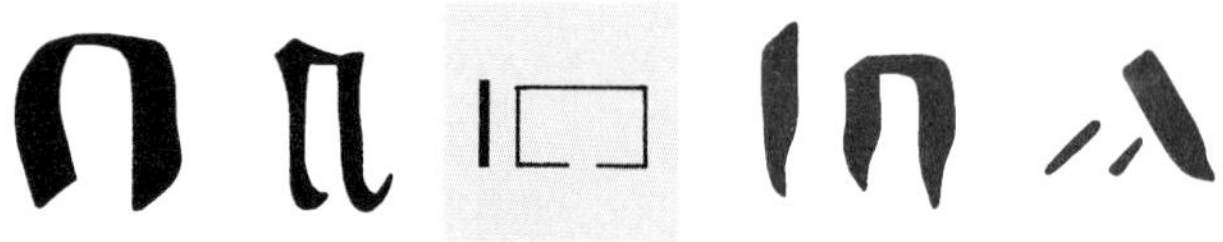

Ideogram in* pr*, "house," whence the phonetic value* pr*; determinative for buildings and connected words.

A simple drawing of the walls, painted black to indicate the color of the dried mud bricks, and an opening in the front: thus the Egyptians represented the abstract concept of the house. Some believe that this more likely indicates the walls of the courtyard, but no evidence favors either interpretation.

A nation of admirable builders, the Egyptians must have become familiar with the horizontal projection of constructions very early in their history. One prehistoric house found on the site of Hierakonpolis, dating from about 3,700–3,600 B.C., is very similar to the simple plan in the hieroglyph *pr*, which was certainly made close to this epoch itself. The Hierakonpolis house consists of a rectangular room measuring not much more than twelve square meters, set somewhat into the ground, with a roof frame of wood and cane around which clay was modeled. It is this very ancient type of house which serves as the model for the hieroglyph *pr*, not the luxurious multi-storied houses found in the excavations in Tell el-Amarna, nor the more modest but nonetheless large houses of the artisans at Deir el-Medina.

Clay model of a house with a walled court. From Gebelein. Turin, Egyptian Museum.

VARIANTS/COMBINATIONS

Pr with the phoneme *-ḥḏ*, *pr-ḥḏ* (literally "the white house") was the designation of the safe or storeroom.

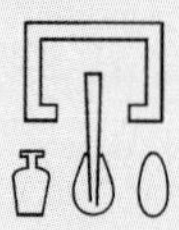

The house with *ḫrw*, "voice," a pitcher and bread: *prt-ḫrw*, literally "the coming out to the voice." This was the name of the invocation to the dead which accompanied offerings.

Door

Ideogram or determinative in ʿ3, "door"; determinative in verbs signifying "open."

Normally, each sign had a given position in space, which the Egyptians tended to respect. But as the purely pictographic phase of writing ended and the phonetic phase began, the traditional placement of each sign was overlooked in favor of other considerations, such as the harmony of the signs' reciprocal positions within the framework of the writing. Thus the hieroglyph representing a door or door-frame, which we would expect to be vertical, is almost always horizontal in classical writing. As a matter of fact, because of its phonetic value *ʿ3*, it was generally accompanied by the like-sounding hieroglyph *ʿ3*, written with a wooden column in the horizontal (in these cases, the frame functioned as determinative). The *Pyramid Texts* seem to show a functional differentiation between the ideographic use of the sign to indicate the frame, and the determinative use in verbs meaning open, like *wn*: in this case, the sign was placed on the horizontal. Even in the stylized form, the sign illustrates the bronze flashing to be found on one side of the wooden panel, where two cylindrical bronze pins turned in the hinge.

Bolt

***Ideogram in* s*, "bolt"; whence the phonetic value* s.**

Illustrated representations and excavated specimens of bolts have allowed us to identify this hieroglyph, which is relatively faithful to the actual models despite the restrictions of the graphic code. The bolt represented in the hieroglyph is the type that was used to close the double doors of the temple tabernacles where the statues of the gods were kept. It was designed to secure the door from the outside: on one half of the door were fixed two bronze rings, through which the bolt could run, while on the other half was fixed a third ring (the central enlargement limited the bolt's movement between the two rings on the one side).
Once the bolt was pushed beyond the third ring, the door was blocked. The name *s* means "loop." In single doors a type of wall bolt, fixed in the masonry, was used.

VARIANTS/COMBINATIONS

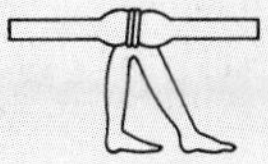

s with legs: ideogram or determinative in verbs of motion.

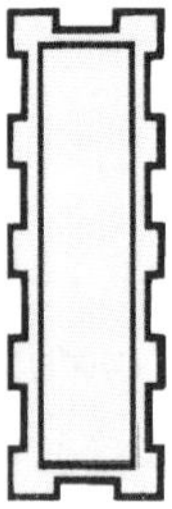

Wall

Ideogram or determinative in* ỉnb*, "wall"; determinative in associated words.

The hieroglyph that serves as ideogram for *ỉnb*, "wall" did not originally represent a wall in elevation, but rather the plan of a fortified enclosure with its buttresses. This significance was lost very early. It is probable that the true model for the sign is to be found in the imposing predynastic and protodynastic dried-brick buildings—primarily tombs—which are characterized by their so-called "paneled façades." Their decoration repeated a single motif without interruption: the great ceremonial gate of the royal palace, framed by high towers. The result was a surface of alternating projections and recesses which was reproduced in stone during the Third Dynasty for King Djoser's funerary complex at Saqqara. This type of architecture finds its precise counterpart in the slightly earlier or contemporary buildings at Uruk, in Mesopotamia, a parallel that raises the possibilty of contact between the Nile Valley and Mesopotamia in very ancient times.

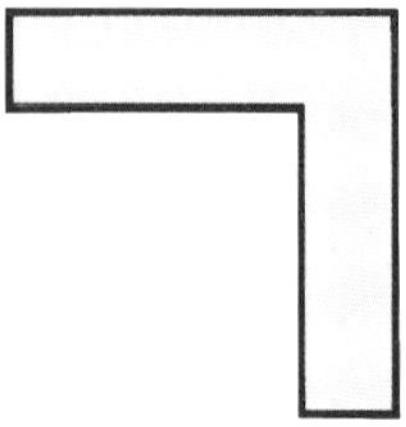

Corner

Determinative in* ḳnbt*, "corner," and connected terms.

While this hieroglyph clearly represents a right angle, the term *ḳnbt* had a more generic usage. It could designate the corner of a building or pool (presumably rectangular), or the winding curves of a road, as indicated by its use as determinative in the word *mrrt*, "road." Etymologically, the sign is connected to the verb *ḳnb*, "to curve, bend," whose proper meaning would seem to be "bend (oneself) at a right angle."

Egyptian monuments were usually constructed with precise right angles, not difficult to achieve when the dimensions were not too great. It was enough to simply make a square, a simple method with a slight margin of error. It is not at all certain that this method could give accurate results in larger constructions like pyramids, temples, and cities. Many Egyptologists speculate that as early as the Old Kingdom the Egyptians were capable of applying the method of the "sacred triangle," better known as the Pythagorean Theorem.

Block of Stone or Brick

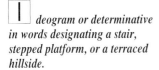

Ideogram or determinative in* ỉnr, *"stone, block"; determinative in names of building stones and minerals and in* ḏbt, *"brick."

This sign shows the squared form of cut stone blocks or sun-dried mud bricks of various size. As we know, the Egyptians always used rectangular blocks in their constructions, even though the blocks could vary greatly in dimension (as in the case of stone structures).
In order to form the mud bricks, a mud and straw mixture was pressed into rectangular wooden frames to dry.
Limestone and sandstone were the types of stone most frequently used for building in ancient Egypt. The best quarries were generally located on the east bank of the Nile. Every sovereign was bound to undertake expeditions into the desert to obtain beautiful semi-precious stones for statues of pharaohs and gods, an expensive activity.
The sign *ỉnr* was the generic term for building stone, while *ʿ3t* was more specifically used for precious stones. Both were determined by the same grapheme.

Stair

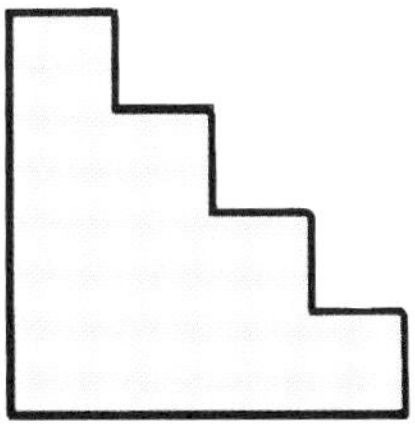

Ideogram or determinative in words designating a stair, stepped platform, or a terraced hillside.

The number of steps in this hieroglyph is conventionally fixed at five. It may represent the stairs to the roof of a house, to the upper floors (*rwd*) of larger habitations, or the stairs of the throne or a ceremonial pedestal.
The name *ḫtyw* designated the stepped platform on which the god Min stood, and it also evoked the exotic and almost fabulous "terraces" of myrrh in Punt, of turquoise in Sinai, and of the tall and perfumed evergreens in Lebanon and Anatolia.
Some scholars think that the term *ḫtyw* also designated a port or commercial emporium, thus supposing in ancient Egyptian the same etymological nexus tying the ancient Italian maritime term "scalo" (stopping place) and the French "escale" to the noun "scala" (step; French: escalier)."
In religious iconography the stair is a lunar symbol. Often portrayed with fourteen steps, it represents the days of the lunar cycle's ascendant phase.

Country Shelter

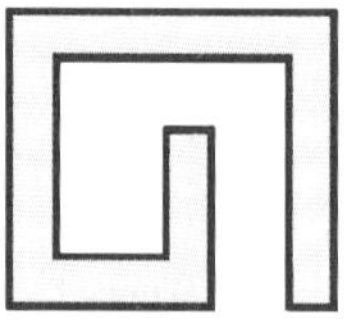

***Ideogram in* h*, a building or part of a building, whence the phonetic value* h.**

The building represented in the hieroglyph *h* has not been precisely identified: it seems to be a dwelling-place which was entered by way of an L-shaped corridor. This prevented outsiders from looking in, and insured a minimum of privacy.
The same ground-plan has been found in a type of straw Sudanese hut in village outskirts, which the farmers use as shelters and places for short stays during the summer's agricultural labor. The outside is open to view, is used for social purposes, and is identified by the Arabic word *diwan*. The smaller inside, called *harim*, is usually reserved for the women.
This type of hut must have had very ancient ancestors in Egypt. Excavations at Hierakonpolis—a city in Upper Egypt that shows the clearest traces of the making of the Egyptian state in the fourth millenium B.C.—a house whose plan is very similar to the hieroglyph *h* was found in the strata dating from the beginnings of the Old Kingdom. It has a long narrow corridor which opens on one side to a walled courtyard, which houses the working area. A wall separates the working area from a small area with a low dry-mud bench on one wall, which was the true living space.
The origin of this hieroglyph, like so many others, is buried in the depth of Egyptian antiquity, and has become obscure even to the inhabitants of the Nile Valley. In the fragmentary hieroglyphic dictionary at Copenhagen (P. Carlsberg VII), *h* is the fourth item (in the late Egyptian alphabet, in fact, the alphabetic sequence began with the consonant *h*).
The dictionary explains that the sign represents a hen-house (but the term is partially in lacuna) or a house in the fields (*pr n sḫt*); it could also be interpreted, the papyrus adds, as "field-house of the nomads." In any case, the old dictionary seems to interpret it as a rather rudimentary or temporary structure.

Clay model of a country house from El Amrah, second half of the fourth millennium B.C. London, British Museum.

Threshing area

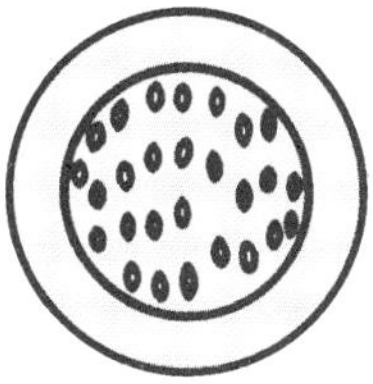

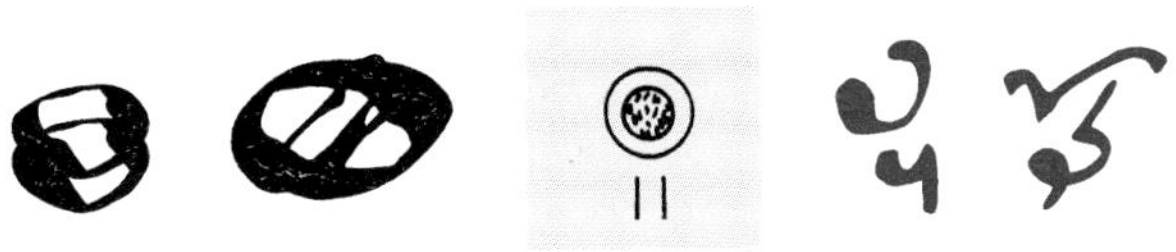

Determinative in* spt, *"threshing area", whence the phonetic value* sp, *in the word* sp *"time," and related expressions.

At times this sign is only a circle surrounded by an outer ring; at other times there are recognizable oblong kernels of grain in the internal area, and the external ring has green markings. The contexts in which the grapheme appear have made it easy to interpret. It is the area for threshing the grain that has been reaped. Prehistoric archaeology has given us illuminating examples: four circular depressions, four meters wide and not very deep, were found at Merimde Beni Salame, one of the largest and oldest neolithic villages discovered in Egypt, situated in the western Delta. The depressions were close to a series of enormous earthenware jars and baskets set into the sand, which have been identified as silos for the grain. The bottom of the threshing ground was covered with a cane mat woven in a spiral pattern, and there were still kernels of grain on it. Junker, the German archaeologist who first excavated at Merimde, hypothesized that the depressions were in fact the common threshing areas of the village. He was the first to associate them with the hieroglyph *spt*.

Granary

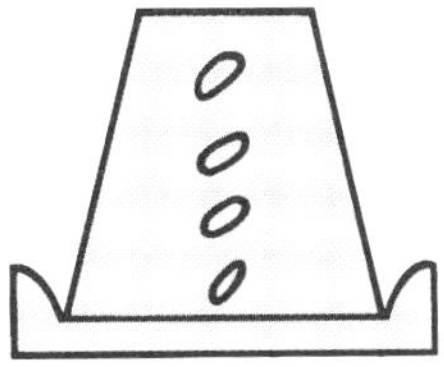

Ideogram or determinative in* šnwt, *"granary."

Just exactly what this hieroglyph represents has been the object of debate: the kernels drawn inside the trapezoidal structure clearly show that it contained, or was composed of, grain. The base on which it stands has been seen as a raised pavement of dried mud. Some perceive it as the filled up granary, as the significance of the word that it determines or represents would indicate. However, others have noted that in reaping and threshing scenes, the storage of the grain takes place in a structure different from that of the hieroglyph, which is generally covered by an arched roof. However, these scenes show constructions in the form of truncated pyramids near the edges of the threshing ground or in the fields. It seems that they represent (depending on the case) piles of chopped straw meant to be stored this way, or small granaries of dried mud, which were perhaps used for temporary storage of the grain before its removal to the large arched-roof silos.

Stool

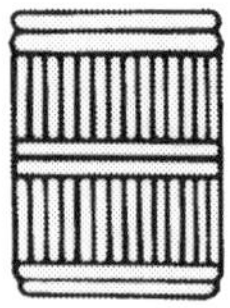

Ideogram in **p*, "mat," "stool," "socle," whence the phonetic value*** **p.**

Initially this sign represented a mat: it is surely in this sense that the word *p* occurs in an ancient formula in the Coffin Texts. It is possible that similar mats were used to cover stools and chairs and that in this way the word came to take on the meaning of "stool" or "chair" and could even designate socles and supports. However, one can not exclude the possibility that the first chairs called *p* were really made of cane or woven reeds, and that this is the reason they are called by the same name as mats. The oldest variants show in rich detail the weave of the reeds, which in the hieroglyph was a brilliant green.
Stools (along with baskets or chests) were among the most common of the practical furnishings in Egyptian houses. Collections worldwide have many examples of various kinds and sizes of stools, made of various sorts of wood. They have in common the simplicity of their shape, which is either cubic or trapezoidal in cross section.

Headrest

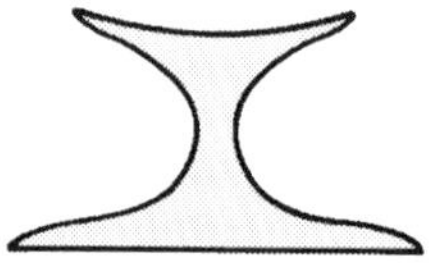

Determinative in **wrs*, "headrest."***

Though it looks uncomfortable to our eyes, headrests like this one are still commonly in use in various African cultures. It was intended as a support for the side of the head as one slept on one's flank. Generally, it was made of wood: the examples in ivory, alabaster, semi-precious stone, clay, and even faïence were only for funeral use. Certainly those meant for daily use must have been made more comfortable with a fabric covering or the like.
This hieroglyph represents one of the simpler and more common type of headrest, with its curved "cushion" supported by a flared column and pedestal, which could be rectangular or elipse-shaped. It appears in this form in images from as early as the Third Dynasty. The function of the headrest connected it with the disquieting nocturnal world. It was designed to support the head, which was more vulnerable than other parts of the body to attack by the forces of evil, and thus was in greater need of protection. For this reason the object was often decorated with images of the apotropaic gods traditionally associated with sleep and benevolent watchfulness over the sleeper: most importantly, the dwarf Bes and the hippotamus goddess Thoeris.

Chest

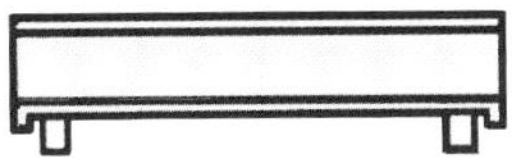

D *eterminative in names of chests and similar containers.*

Chests, boxes, and baskets took the place of our wardrobes and bureaus in the scantily furnished Egyptian home. Depending on their size, material, and appearance, these were used for storing linen, pots of ointments and cosmetics, or clothing. They came into the house with the bride as part of her personal effects, or were ordered from artisans as the family grew.

The tombs have given us hundreds of these containers, some with lids inlaid with precious ivory and blue faïence in the shapes of papyrus flowers, like the graceful linen chest in Turin which dates from the Old Kingdom. Others were made of brightly painted wood with the lozenge and rosette motifs typical of cheerful woven mats, alternating with floral themes. The cover could be flat or peaked, and was closed by means of sealed cords. Often a knob allowed easy lifting of the lid.

The depictions of funerary processions found in tombs have confirmed and enriched archaeologists' understanding of these chests.

Brazier

D ***eterminative in words connected to the flame* (ḫt, sḏt, nsr) *and to heat* (rkḥ, t3).**

The brazier with its lively flames was chosen as the graphic code for fire and related things. The sign is used as determinative for the various words meaning flame, heat in all its gradations, and many activities that use fire or heat. The object itself was called *ʿḫ*: by the Egyptians: the texts of the Old Kingdom determine the word "brazier" by a great variety of signs that reflect the different types, from the large grills for roasting ritual offerings of goose and choice cuts of beef, to the concave charcoal stove, to the most rudimentary flared clay containers for everyday use. This hieroglyph illustrates a particular type of four-lobed ritual portable grill which was used essentially for funeral offerings. The rear lobe is not shown in this hieroglyph, as if it were hidden by the flame, but it is quite clear in those writings of the word *ʿḫ* that use only the container without the flame as determinative. The lobes were essential to the portable nature of the grill: it was possible to lift it without burning oneself by using one of its lobes as a handle.

Gold

Ideogram in* nbw, *"gold," and determinative in names of precious metals.

The hieroglyph *nbw*, "gold," like many other graphemes in ancient Egypt, probably has its roots in quite ancient times. It is generally agreed that it portrays a type of archaic necklace composed of threads of assorted grains in the shape of droplets in its lower part, with two long side elements that were tied behind the head. In many Old Kingdom tombs the goldsmithing scenes show goldsmith dwarfs, responsible for these works of art, engaged in "stringing the pearls of gold" of a *nbỉt*-necklace: this is the name that the Egyptians gave to the type of necklace drawn in the hieroglyph. Examples of this same necklace are shown, with the same name, among the objects of the funeral provisions painted on the sides of wooden sarcophagi of the Middle Kingdom.
The interpretation of the sign given by Ippolito Rosellini (the Pisan Egyptologist who accompanied Champollion in leading the Franco-Tuscan Expedition into Egypt) was quite different and fascinating. According to him the sign was a long sack or an intricately folded sheet, with the extremities hanging, used for washing gold: the droplets shown in the lower part would have been the filtered water.
Bloody military campaigns, terrible desert expeditions, and inhuman work in the mines were the high price the Egyptians paid in all epochs to obtain this shining metal. The people of the ancient world associated it very closely with Egypt: *Nwbt* "the City of Gold," was the name of one of the oldest and most powerful cities of prehistoric Egypt which was a departure point for caravans going to the mines, soon exhausted, in the eastern Egyptian desert. "In Egypt, there is more gold than there is dust," say the letters of ancient Near Eastern princes, found in the archives of the palace of Tell el-Amarna. They ask gold of the Pharaoh, reminding him of how much their predecessors had received: "You sent him ingots of gold as if it were copper."
Shiny and unchanging, it was the perfect divine metal; the limbs of the gods were gold, and gold itself contained divine nature and could confer divinity: the gilt mummy could be identified with the solar god Ra (the golden god by definition), and insure itself a destiny of eternal rebirth.

The goddess Isis kneeling on the gold symbol. Detail from the sarcophagus of Hatshepsut, Eighteenth Dynasty. Cairo, Egyptian Museum.

VARIANTS/COMBINATIONS

The sign for gold with the sceptre-*ḏ'm*: writing for *ḏ'm*, "electrum," an ancient alloy of gold and silver.

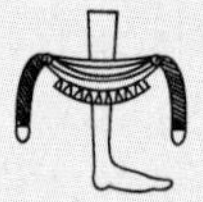

Combination of the gold sign with *b* for *nbỉ*, "gild," "gilt."

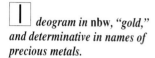

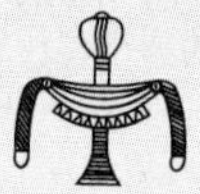

Combination of the gold sign with the mace *ḥḏ*: writing for *ḥḏ*, "silver."

Necklace with Counterpoise

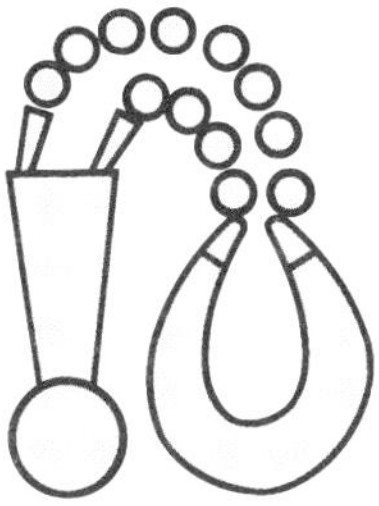

I ***deogram or determinative in mnit, "necklace of menat-pearls."***

T he necklace known as *menat* was originally a jewel composed of some strands of little pearls gathered together, strung through two or more circular pieces, and tied behind the neck. The type shown in the hieroglyph does not seem to have been common before the New Kingdom: in this age the *menat*-necklace added, as a characteristic element, the long and thin piece that ended by broadening into a circular or rounded shape, which functioned as a counterpoise for the heavy jewel. This characteristic element was often decorated with scenes of the birth and infancy of Horus and the goddess Hathor in her role as nurturer of the god-child. It was really the stylization of a unique type of object: the so-called "dolls," crude figures carved in the wood, the bodies cut off below the pubic area and their female sexual nature strongly marked. The bottom of the body was rounded, to indicate the sloping of the sides and pelvis. These "dolls" were fertility symbols and the counterweight of the *menat*-necklace inherited this significance.

From the beginning, the *menat* was associated with Hathor's cult and with the rites accompanying birth, rebirth, and every critical phase of passage.

When the protagonist of one of the most beautiful works of Egyptian literature, the fugitive Sinuhe, returns to Egypt after long years of wandering in foreign lands and is received at court, princes and princesses perform for him the ritual of the "offering of the *menat* and of the sistrum": Sinuhe, whom foreign habits have made "barbarous," must in fact be "reborn" to Egyptian culture and life. Some scenes in Theban tombs show how these rites must have been carried out: the singers or priestesses of Hathor held in one hand a *menat*-necklace, and in the other a sistrum, which they raised and lowered alternately and rhythmically: like the sistrum, the *menat* thus rhythmically agitated produced a sound from its metallic parts.

The goddess Sekhmet with the menat-necklace around her neck, funerary temple of Seti I, Abydos, Nineteenth Dynasty.

Ornamental Belt

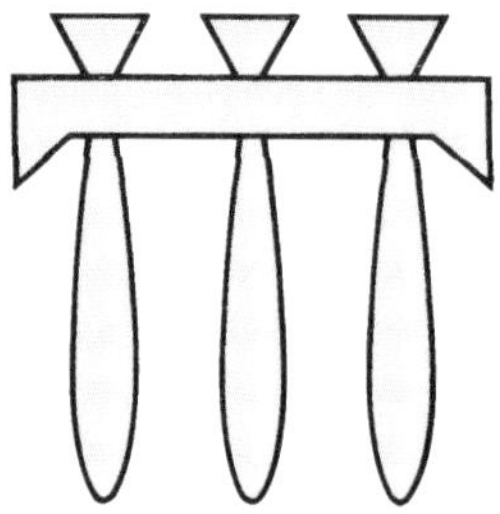

Ideogram or determinative in* tḥnt, *literally "the brilliant," name given to faïence (from the verb* tḥn, *"to be brilliant").

The Old Kingdom version of this hieroglyph was slightly different and more detailed, representing an ornamental apron—a belt from which hung numerous strings of small pearls of glazed frit, which the graphic code indicated by showing three elements. A similar ornament is still traditionally worn by the Bedouins of the eastern desert and the Sinai.

It is probable that the evolution of this hieroglyph, which transformed the line of the belt into a sign very similar to that for the sky, played allusively on the relation between the splendid turquoise color of the material (called, in fact, *tḥnt*, "the brilliant") and the luminosity of the vault of the sky, whose colors reflected the various artificial and natural substances that carried the name *tḥnt*. In texts, this name may designate not only glazed frit or faïence but also a natural material that was extracted from mines, but whose exact identity is still under debate.

Folded Fabric

Phonetic value* s. *Abbreviation for* snb *in the augural formula which follows the name of the king.

This grapheme shows a fabric which falls softly, just as Old Kingdom scenes pictured cloth coming from the loom to be given by the weavers to their supervisors. The mysterious cylindrical object that hangs on one side (held in dignitaries' hands in paintings or statues) is a handkerchief. Court etiquette considered it a necessary accessory for the upper class of the period. These representations show it in lively colors, red or yellow, and the hieroglyph maintains the chromatic convention.

The derivation of the phonetic value *s* is still undiscovered. It is possible that the sign is an abbreviation of one of the numerous terms which begin with *s* and designated various types of fabric.

VARIANTS/COMBINATIONS

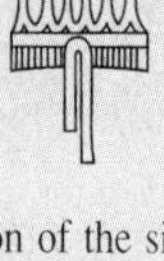

Combination of the sign s with a fringed fabric. Determinative in *ḥbs*, "cover, cloth," "piece of clothing," and connected terms.

Sandal

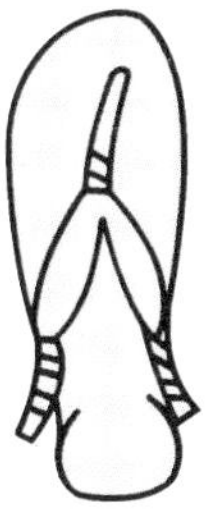

Ideogram or determinative in ṯbt, "sandal"; phonetically ṯb.

This hieroglyph represents a very simple form of sandal: a sole with two strips of leather or other material to keep the foot in place. They are present in tombs from as early as the First Dynasty at Abydos (the beginning of the third millennium B.C.). At the same time, this is the longest lasting style, still to be found today in millions of leather, plastic, and rubber examples. The Egyptians began to make them long ago, not only of leather but also of papyrus or other vegetable fibers, and even of painted wood. The cosmetic palette of King Narmer, dating from the end of the fourth millennium B.C., shows a high functionary (perhaps even a vizier) immediately behind the king, carrying the king's sandals. Shoes at this time were a status symbol: the wearing of sandals was an unequivocable indication of rank. In the Old Kingdom, sandals were still the prerogative of kings, priests, and high dignitaries: everyone else walked unshod. In his *Admonitions*, the wiseman Ipuwer, who lived in the turbulent period following the collapse of the Old Kingdom and witnessed much social disorder, laments that "he who could not afford sandals owns riches."

The carrier of the sandals of King Narmer. Narmer's Palette, from Hierakonpolis. End of the fourth millenium B.C. Cairo, Egyptian Museum.

During the Middle Kingdom, sandals became quite common: for example, they were given to the members of expeditions about to cross the desert. They grew even more widespread in the New Kingdom, when traditional dress began to undergo various changes. It is then that decorations begin to appear on the soles: lotus flowers, or (in the case of the king) the profile of a sworn enemy, which the royal foot could thus step on at all times. Royal mummies show that the kings also wore precious sandals of gold and silver. The strange sandals with points turned back were also a royal prerogative. *ṯb* originally derived from *kb*, the term for the sole of the foot. Later, as the Egyptian language evolved, it transformed first into tb and then into *twt*/*twỉ*.

Parasol

Ideogram in* šwt, *"shade" and in* sryt, *"military standard."

The parasol was a useful object for protecting oneself from the relentless Egyptian sun. The one represented in the hieroglyph was the simplest and lightest, made for carrying on strolls like the obsolete little umbrellas of times closer to ours. It was a necessary element in ceremonies, in which it protected the king and statues of the gods carried in processions. The scenes illustrating these spectacular occasions show very luxurious parasols made of ostrich feathers mounted on splendidly decorated bases.
The images on Egyptian monuments show us other types, heavy and broad, adapted for use in a fixed location. These were perhaps the ones that protected farmers and others from the pitiless rays of the sun in the marketplaces, as they sold their crops and wares. The Egyptologist Montet maintained that the word for merchant—*šwty*—derived from these umbrellas' name. However, the texts show that this second type of parasol was in fact called *sb3*, "star" (probably from the shape of the crossed ribs that supported the fabric). Furthermore, there is no documentation of the word *šwty*, "merchant," before the New Kingdom.

Wick

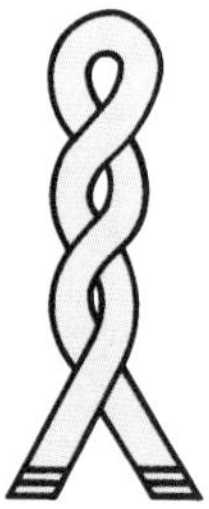

Phonetic value* ḥ, *probably from* ḥꜥt, *"wick."

Torches and wicks are well known from scenes on the walls of temples and tombs of the New Kingdom. The daily cult of the temple included a series of rituals that involved the lighting of torches, later to be doused, with the recitation of appropriate formulas. The ritual called for the torches to be extinguished by plunging them into basins full of milk which were prepared for the purpose. The paintings clearly illustrate the shape of the wick, identical to the hieroglyph, and the formulas specify that it must be made "with new fat and washed linen," or with perfectly clean material, soaked in unused fat. Archaeology has found real examples, such as those found among the funerary provisions in Tutankhamen's tomb. The wicks were generally made of a folded strip of fabric which was twisted tightly and then soaked in resinous fat.
Naturally, torches and wicks were not used only by the cult, but were widely used in everyday life–dipped into lanterns, to lay on the bottom in the oil or fat that aided their burning.

Cord

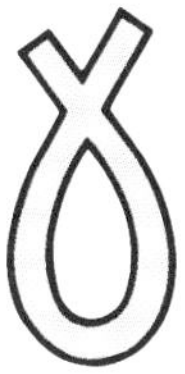

Ideogram or determinative in* šs, *"cord," whence the phonetic value* šs. *Determinative in names of fabrics and verbs of "tying, knotting."

The cord is shown folded with its two ends crossed, as in the first steps of making a knot. Ropes and cords were widely used in ancient Egypt: to tie, lead, and hobble animals; to moor boats or manage sails; and to create nets for hunting, fishing, or carrying.

The Egyptians made cord by weaving grasses, the fibers of palm, papyrus, or even leather. Techniques for the manufacture of cords and objects differ from modern ones. For example, the Egyptians did not make long rolls of cord to be cut as needed, but instead made short pieces tailored for the task at hand. This was not an efficient method, from our point of view, but it permitted the cord to be made appropriately for specific projects, which is impossible with prefabricated products.

Bolt with Cord

***Ideogram in* sṯ3 *(then* st3*), "pull, drag," whence the phonetic value* sṯ3.**

The commonly accepted interpretation of this hieroglyph is that it represents a cord passing around a bolt in such a way that, by pulling it, the door could be opened from the outside. New Kingdom versions of the sign support this interpretation as well: examples from this era clearly show the cord wrapped around the channeling of the bolt. The meaning of the verb *sṯ3*, the grapheme of which is the ideogram, seems to confirm this interpretation. The Egyptologist Graefe, however, has demonstrated that this system of opening could not work without another cord, which the hieroglyph does not show. The systems for opening and closing which we can reconstruct indicate other procedures. Moreover, the oldest variants of the sign in Old Kingdom tombs show a very different object, which looks more like a stick or board with a cord. A scene in a tomb of El Bersheh shows a similar instrument apparently intended as a yoke for oxen, a function which would nicely explain the sign's ideogrammatic use as the verb "pull, drag."

Basket

I ***deogram in* nbt, *"basket," whence the phonetic value* nb.**

This sign has been found in predynastic inscriptions, and even in that early era it had become a phoneme. The art of weaving baskets is one of the oldest Egyptian crafts: Neolithic settlements have given us numerous samples of baskets and containers for grains. They were made of local plants and fibers, using rushes, ribs of palm leaves, and the thicker and harder grasses for bases, and using whole palm leaves and stems of "halfa" (a strong grass common in Egypt) to tie the whole basket together. The most common technique was a continuous spiral, with strips whipstitched together.

Hieroglyph variants from the Old Kingdom show this type of construction. The signs were colored green or yellow to simulate the colors of fresh or dried plants, and inside the baskets a series of horizontal lines were drawn to represent the turning spirals of the twisted fibers. New Kingdom scribes and artists amused themselves by decorating the hieroglyph with the details that made baskets the gayest and most colorful articles of daily life: the most common of the lively and elaborate patterns were checked and multicolored. Naturally, the portrayal of baskets in tomb scenes outdid hieroglyphs in their beauty of pattern and color. An eloquent demonstration of this is to be found in the painting of the storerooms in Amon's temple, in the tomb of the visir Rekhmire at Thebes: on shelves, on the ground, or on chests rest baskets and containers of all types of woven fibers, with or without lids; the patterns alternate from geometric mosaics and undulating zig-zags to stylized drawings of human figures. There is real evidence of the color sense which is still intact in present-day Nubian basket production.

Nb was the obsequious Egyptian term of address for "lord," king, god, or any superior. The hieroglyph of the basket served to write this word and for the same purely phonetic reason it was often found under the grapheme which indicates a god. With the signs of the cobra-goddess Wadjet and the vulture-goddess Nekhbet it was used in writing the *nebty*-name, part of royal protocol which designated the king in respect to the two tutelary goddesses of Upper and Lower Egypt.

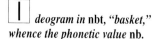

Baskets with juniper berries and cumin from the tomb of Kha, Deir el-Medina, Nineteenth Dynasty. Turin, Egyptian Museum.

Linen Bag

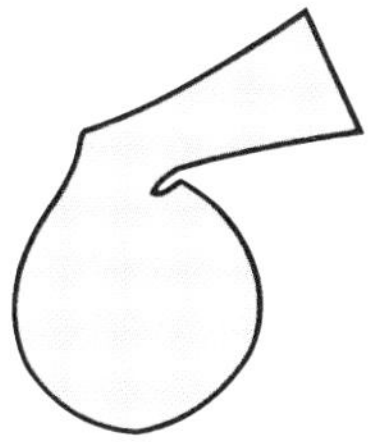

Ideogram or determinative in* ssr, *"linen, fabric," whence the phonetic value* ssr; *it has the phonetic value of* gbt *in the name of the city* Gbtw, *Coptos—today's Quft.

This hieroglyph represents a sack made of fabric, probably a handkerchief tied by its corners to make it into a container. The writings of the Old Kingdom—and sometimes of later periods—show many variations: the tied ends may be thicker, and the sack itself is sometimes triangular with a convex bottom. The graphic and phonetic affinity with the sign for a cord with its ends crossed (*šs*) caused the two to be confused quite frequently.

The fact that the linen bag appears in the writing of the city of Coptos offers scope for interesting speculation: Coptos was the city where caravans to and from the eastern desert roads arrived and departed, transporting things to the Red Sea or to the mines (of gold, emerald, and other precious stones) that lay between the Nile Valley and the sea. The hieroglyphic texts cite "gold from Coptos," evidence of ancient mines situated in the eastern desert more or less on the same latitude as the city, but these were soon exhausted. Gold, however, had made the area rich during the predynastic era. The city of Ombos (from the Egyptian word *Nwbt*, "City of Gold"), not far from Coptos, owed its name to its power in controlling the access roads. Many scholars agree that the name *Gbtw* or *Gbtiw* came to Coptos from an ancient word no longer found in historic times, *gbt*, designating the small sack in which gold-hunters kept the precious dust.

The most precious products of every age, valued first by the Egyptians and then by the Mediterranean world, traveled the roads of the eastern desert. These included not just gold, emeralds, and beryls, but also galena, antimony, and the entire range of aromatic resins from the trees of southern Arabia or the Somalian coast, the incense and myrrh which gladdened the hearts and nostrils of gods and men. With the Late Period's opening of commerce with India and Far East, the roads that lead to Coptos began to carry spices and resins whose wasteful use was so censured by Pliny the Elder.

The bag represented a container of precious stones and of resins: as a result, we find a variant from the Eighteenth Dynasty that functions as ideogram for the word *sty*, "perfume."

Large baskets with bags full of the gold for the Nubian tribute. Thebes, tomb of Rekhmire, TT 100, Sheikh Abd el-Qurna, Eighteenth Dynasty.

Jug for Beer

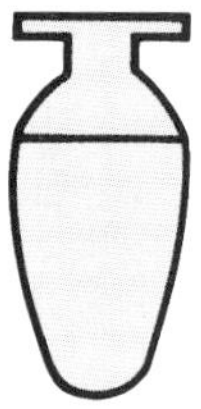

Ideogram or determinative in* ḥnḳt, *"beer." Determinative for pots, liquid measures, and related actions.

The small jug represented by this hieroglyph—often painted red on its bulging lower part and blue on its narrower upper part—was one of the most common liquid containers. The extensive use of beer at the Egyptian table explains why the jug came to determine the beverage's name. *ḥnḳt* derives from the verb *ḥnḳ*, "to run, flow," and the beer in ancient Egypt did indeed "run" in rivers: beer and bread were the basic elements of the Egyptian diet. The state workers received both staples as part of their salaries. It would have been unthinkable to deprive the poor or the dead: whoever wished to seem pious and generous affirmed in his autobiography to have given "bread to the hungry and beer to the thirsty." The well-liked drink could not be lacking in funeral offerings, to the point that the jar itself functioned as determinative for the word designating an offering. The brewing of beer was associated with breadmaking: both were prepared from barley and spelt flour and the methods of mixing and cooking were analogous.

Spherical Pot

Phonetic value* nw*; sometimes determinative in* ḳd, *"construct," "mold."

The simple spherical pot presents more than one obscure facet to close analysis—not in its incarnation as an actual pot, which is well known from even the most remote times, but specifically as a hieroglyph. The origin of the phoneme escapes us; whether the globular pot was called *nw* is not known. Our ignorance of phonetics in the oldest phases of Egyptian prevents us from grasping in full the oscillations of the sign between the phonetic value *nw* and *nnw* or *nwnw*.

A triple repetition of the pot seems to be associated with the last value above. It is found, for example, in the written name of the primordial ocean—three pots above the sign for sky determined by the sign for water, which apparently should be read as *nwn*. There are numerous other words that unexpectedly contain the hieroglyph, without clear explanation.

Lastly, the sign has a playful use: a pot drawn on the sign for water, to indicate *m-ẖnw*, "inside of." This can be explained as the rebus for *m(w)* (water), *ẖ(r)* (under), and *nw* (the pot): "the water that is under the pot."

Bread

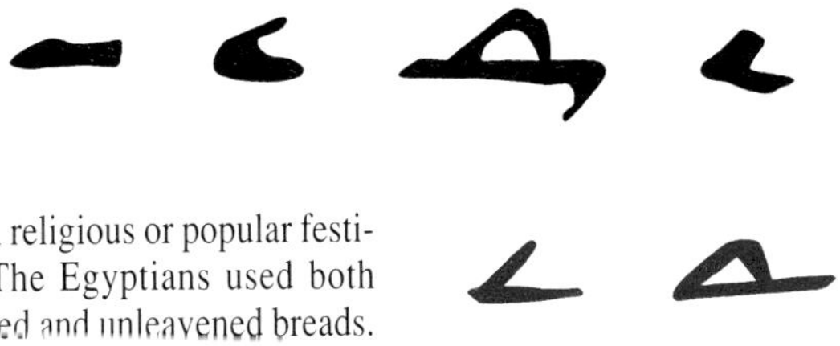

***Ideogram in* t, *"bread," whence phonetically* t.**

This sign represents a common loaf of semicircular form, samples of which have been found in Tutankhamen's tomb (Eighteenth Dynasty). Loaves could come in many shapes, however. The offering scenes show them as oval, triangular, and even in animal or human shapes for special religious or popular festivals. The Egyptians used both leavened and unleavened breads. The analysis of samples found in archaeological digs prove that from at least the middle of the second millennium B.C. a pure form of yeast was known, probably the product of beer fermentation. Before this time it is very likely that some of the mixture was left to acidify during the night, to be used as yeast in the next day's breadmaking.

Unleavened bread was equally common. It is pictured in tombs—and found in digs—in circular shapes, like that which is still eaten in Egypt today.

Cone-shaped Loaf

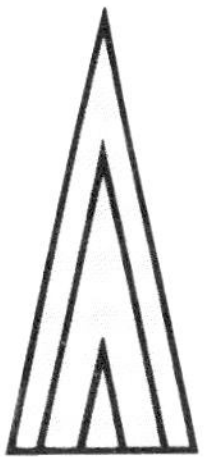

Ideogram in* rdì/dì, *"to give."

In the ancient *Pyramid Texts* this sign occurs as the imperative of the archaic verb *ìmì*, "to give." Its use was then extended to all forms of the verb, but by the time of the Middle Kingdom it was frequently replaced by the sign for an arm offering the hieroglyph on its palm, indicating for the same verb *rdì*, "give." There is no sure proof that this indeed represented a loaf of bread, but the fact that it occurs in both verbs with the same meaning renders it probable.

The loaf was presumably a ritual loaf, to be offered in the course of the rites. The custom of baking bread in clay forms was quite common in ancient Egypt.

The most common forms were in fact the conical ones, and the hieroglyph *dì* may represent an extreme stylization of long conical loaves.

The scenes of breadmaking and pastry-making also show triangular loaves, a sort of sweet bread (or slice of one?) on which a confection of honey and dates could be spread. The pastry-makers are shown mixing the confection in a large pan on a stove.

Wooden column

Phonogram *ʿȝ*.

Supporting pole

Ideogram or determinative in *sḫnt*, "support."

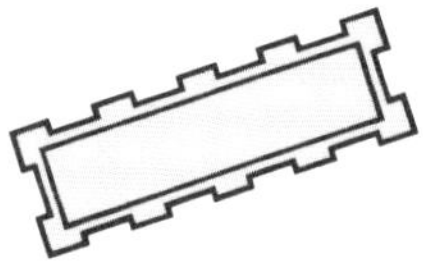

Collapsing wall

Determinative for "knock down": *wḥn*, "overwhelm," and *sḫnn*, "demolish."

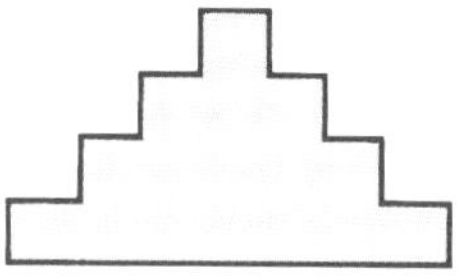

Double stair

Determinative in *ḳȝỉ*, "elevated place"; *ỉȝr*, "climb."

Strip of fabric to be worn as a hair ribbon

Ideogram or determinative in *wȝḥw*, "diadem," and *mḏḥ*, "ribbon"; whence the phonetic value *mḏḥ*.

Multi-string necklace with falcon-head clasp

Ideogram or determinative in *wsḫ*, "the wide necklace." Occasionally used as phonogram in *wsḫ*, "to be broad."

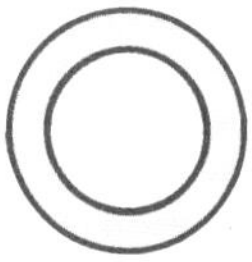

Ring

Determinative in *ỉwʿw*, "ring."

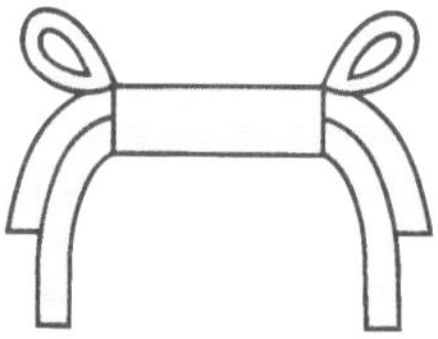

Knot to keep suspenders together on the shoulder

Phonetic value *sṯ*. Ideogram or determinative in *tȝ-wr*, "larboard."

Belt knot

Ideogram in *ṯst*, "knot," "vertebra," and similar words.

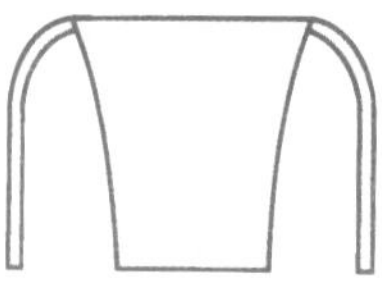

Item of clothing

Phonetic value *ỉʿȝ* in *ỉʿȝw*, "interpreter."

Apron

Ideogram or determinative in *šndyt*, "apron."

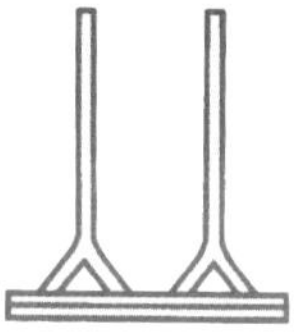

Fringed fabric

Ideogram or determinative in *mnḫt*, "item of clothing."

Fringed fabric
Ideogram or determinative in *sỉ3t*, "cloth, fabric"; whence the phonetic value *sỉ3* in *sỉ3*, "recognize, perceive."

Fan
Ideogram or determinative in *ḫw*, "fan."

Walking stick, cane
Ideogram in *mdw*, "walking stick"; whence the phonetic value *md*.

Mortar and pestle
Determinative of *sḥm*, "pounding," and *smn*, "push"—hence the phonogram in *ḥsmn*, "natron" (embalming fluid). Determinative in *ḥm3t*, "salt" and in words expressing heaviness: *dns*, *wdn*.

Pestle
Ideogram in *tỉt*, "pestle"; whence the phonetic value *tỉ*.

Cord
Determinative of cord and activities connected with it. From *šnw*, "net," the phonetic value *šn*.

Knotted cord
Determinative in *snṯ*, "plan," "found," and derivates.

Cord being knotted with the ends pointing down
Phonogram *šn*.

As before, from a different point of view
Determinative in "tie, knot."

Cord wound around a small staff
Phonogram in *wḏ*.

Rag or broom of twisted fibers
Determinative in *sḳ*, "to clean," "dust"; whence the phonetic value *sḳ*.
It also has the phonetic value *w3ḥ*.

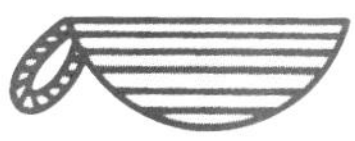

Basket with handle
Phonogram *k*.

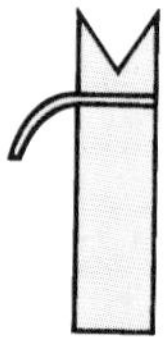

Container
Phonogram *ḥn*.

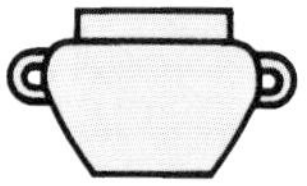

Type of pot
Determinative in *wḥt*, "cauldron."

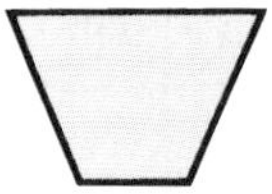

Cup
Determinative in various nouns meaning "cup"; whence the phonetic values *ỉʿb*, *wsḫ*, *ḥnt*.

Support for jars
Ideogram or determinative in *nst*, "throne," and *dšrt*, "pot of red terracotta." Phonogram g.

Object of red terracotta
Ideogram or determinative in *dšrt*, its own name .

Milk pitcher with carrying net
Determinative in *mhr*, "pitcher of milk." Phonogram *mr* and *mỉ*.

Pair of wine vats
Determinative in *ỉrp*, "wine."

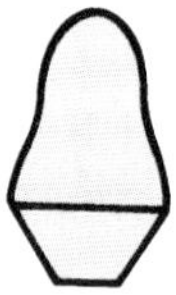

Bun, small loaf
Determinative of bread and other foods. May be used as writing for the name of the god Thot.

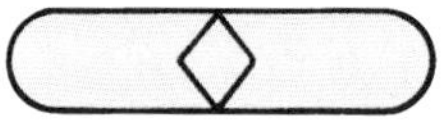

Bun, small loaf
Determinative of bread and other foods. From snw, "food offering," the phonetic value sn.

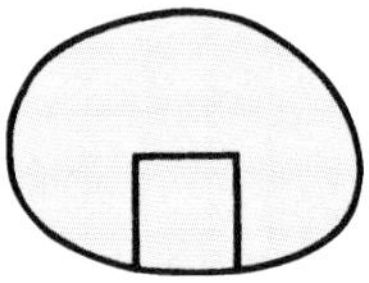

Small loaf with decorations pressed on before baking
Determinative in the name of the loaf *p3t*; whence the phonetic value *p3*.

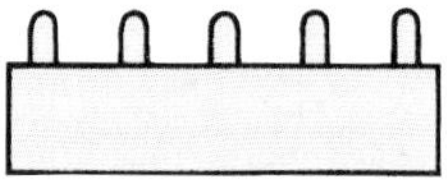

Chessboard or wall
Phonogram *mn*.

Pawn of the Egyptian chess game [senet]
Ideogram or determinative in *ỉb3*, "pawn"; phonetic value *ỉb3*.

City, Palace, and Temple

The hieroglyphic system was formed in an epoch when god and king, palace and temple were superimposed, and often interchangeable. During the formation of the Egyptian state, an ideology of power grew around the idea of divine kingship–thus their unification in one section of this book. Many of the hieroglyphs illustrated in this section belong to the primitive framework of symbols around which the entire dynastic culture coagulated and expanded: the royal palace, the emblem of divinity, the symmetrical symbols of the two sanctuaries of Upper and Lower Egypt, the *djed*-pilaster, the symbol of life—all images heavy with cultural meaning for anyone familiar with that ancient and fascinating world. In addition to the hieroglyphs which had an important symbolic role are those that illustrate the life of the cult and daily rituals. These include the processional boat, libation vessels, containers of ointments for the divine statues, and small braziers for burning incense of all kinds, loved by both men and the gods.

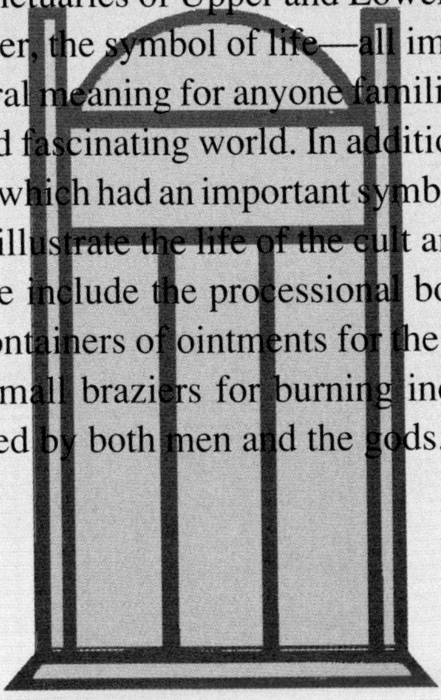

City Plan

I deogram in nìwt, *"city"*; *determinative in names of inhabited places.*

The sign *nìwt* represents a round settlement, walled and divided by a network of roads. This sign is a very simplified version, reduced to the two principal axes. Even in this form it is documented as one of the oldest hieroglyphs. Excavations have revealed settlements like this in Upper Egypt, dating from the oldest epochs of urbanization. On predynastic palettes, the cities conquered or founded by the pharaohs are illustrated as rounded squares or ovals, with outlines showing characteristic buttresses that clearly indicate fortified settlements. The fact that inside these signs, in an approximately round form, are protohieroglyphs—evidently designating the name of each city—shows that the images are not purely pictorial but are actual graphemes, from which the more regular *nìwt* would later develop. The constant presence of the city wall, together with the emphasis that art of the period placed on war and violence, reveals the turbulent nature of the era in which the the Egyptian state began.

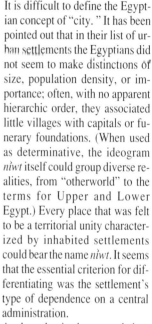

The walled predynastic settlements. Detail of the "Libya Palette," from Abydos, end of the fourth millennium B.C. Cairo, Egyptian Museum.

It is difficult to define the Egyptian concept of "city." It has been pointed out that in their list of urban settlements the Egyptians did not seem to make distinctions of size, population density, or importance; often, with no apparent hierarchic order, they associated little villages with capitals or funerary foundations. (When used as determinative, the ideogram *nìwt* itself could group diverse realities, from "otherworld" to the terms for Upper and Lower Egypt.) Every place that was felt to be a territorial unity characterized by inhabited settlements could bear the name *nìwt*. It seems that the essential criterion for differentiating was the settlement's type of dependence on a central administration.

Archaeological research has shown that, even before the unification and the beginning of the historic period, Egypt possessed real "cities" with concentrated populations, functional differentiation (living zones, industrial zones, holy areas, etc.), and a marked social stratification.

Palace

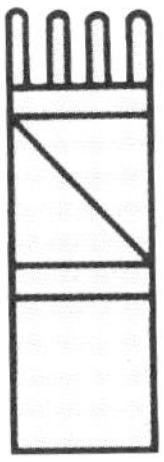

Ideogram in ʿḥ, "palace."

The hieroglyph *ʿḥ* shows the rectangular section of the earliest kings' ancient palaces: a fortified tower, topped by stylized crenelations. The oldest and most detailed examples of this sign show that originally the crenelations were formed by a line of *khekher*, a very common frieze in ceiling and other architectural decorations, representing an upside-down alabaster vase (a sort of cheval-de-frise). Often enough this residential tower was included in hieroglyphs representing walls or fortified courtyards.

The ruins of archaic palaces have been found on the sites of ancient Memphis, Abydos, and at Hierakonpolis; whether these had more than one floor, however, is not known. Much better known are the royal palaces of later eras, naturally. The Pharaohs usually had more than one residence. Their palaces were actually complexes of palaces, rather than a single royal habitation. The walls surrounded the residence proper, the harem, kitchens, baths, gardens, temples, storerooms, and various administrative buildings, not to mention workshops and laboratories of all sorts.

The magnificent remains of the palaces constructed by Amenophis III at Malqata, on the banks facing Luxor, or by his son Amenophis IV-Akhenaten at Tell el-Amarna, show the Egyptians' ability to combine the magnificence and imposing quality proper to the residence of a demigod king, with the lightness and gaiety of a life-affirming art. Wall paintings of extraordinary freshness, which drew from a repertory of natural landscapes (thick clumps of papyrus, delicate lotus, brightly colored birds, and wild animals), adorned the walls and even the floors. Airy colonnades and patios connected the buildings; in the gardens, now buried in desert sand, artificial lakes allowed the ladies of the court to amuse themselves in boats.

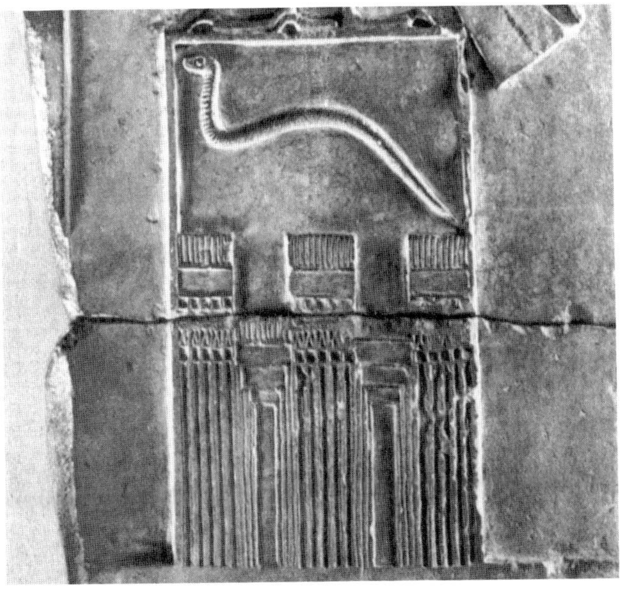

The serekh *that surrounds the name of the King Serpent. From Abydos, beginning of the third millennium B.C. Paris, Louvre Museum.*

VARIANTS/COMBINATIONS

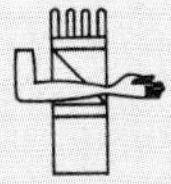

Variant of the above, which combines the hieroglyph for palace with the arm ʿ, as phonetic complement.

Walled Rectangular Settlement

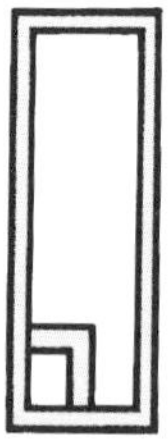

Ideogram in* ḥwt, *"palace," "temple," "tomb."

The sign *ḥwt* is the counterpart—or, more accurately, the alternative—of *nỉwt*: a rectangular wall, with a door indicated in one of the lower corners. According to another interpretation, which sees the hieroglyph as the plan of a walled habitation, the small interior rectangle portrays the roofed area that served as the real living quarters. *ḥwt* is the sign for palace, the urban and multifunctional nucleus of the ancient Near East—and, in Egypt, in a broader sense, the foundation of royalty and an administrative center. It can also designate the temple (the palace of god) or the tomb. *ḥwt-k3-Ptḥ*, "the palace of the ka of Ptah," was the name of the god's temple at Memphis, from which the Greeks drew "Aiguptos," a name then given to all of Egypt. The external walls of the *ḥwt*, perhaps originally made of cane, were in eariest times made of crude brick. We can easily imagine this on the basis of the large tombs of the first dynasties, which imitated the model of the palace, with its walls alternating in and out. They are examples of what is known as "niche architecture," which seems to have originated in Mesopotamia.

Hall with Columns

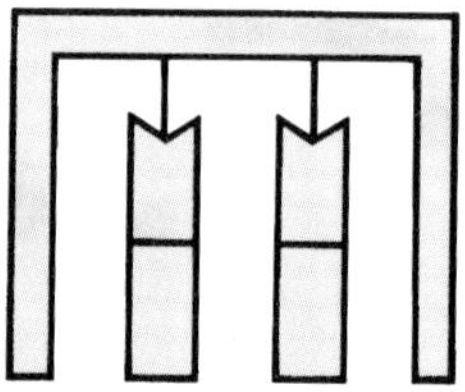

***Determinative in names that designate rooms with columns. From* ẖ3, *"office" ; thus determined, sometimes the phonetic value* ẖ3.**

The large atrium with columns is the place where the king usually held audience. Even when designated with diverse names (*w3ẖy* and *ḏ 3dw* are the most common), it was determined by this same hieroglyph. The shape of the columns, with a tenon on top fixed to the room's covering, suggests that at first the structure must have been light, a sort of pavilion with wooden columns. The name *w3ẖy* literally signifies "atrium of the flood"—an allusion to the type of column, papyrus- or lotus-shaped, holding up the ceiling. The literary autobiography of Sinuhe provides a description of what must have been the audience room of the Twelfth Dynasty, preceded by a wide portal with niches, in front of which were enthroned stone sphinxes in the king's likeness. In a niche and under a canopy entirely covered with electrum (the alloy of silver and gold so well loved by the Egyptians) was the throne. The funerary temples of the kings of the New Kingdom have the same sort of room, with columns that imitate vegetation and a throne in a niche.

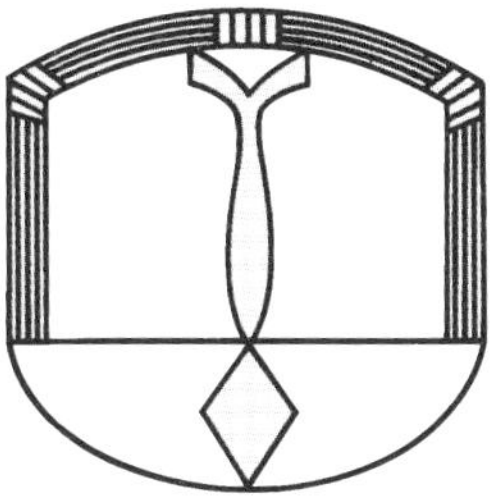

Festival Pavilion

Ideogram or determinative in* ḥb, *"holiday."

This hieroglyph is a combination of the hieroglyph *sḥ* (a tent or similar light structure held up by a pole) and the alabaster basin used in ritual purification, itself already the ideogram for "holiday" with the phonetic value *ḥb*. On holidays, tents or canopies were put up to house the king, the statue of the god to be celebrated, or his ceremonial boat, and in their discreet shade the rituals took place. The festivals were of great cultural importance in ancient Egypt: the year was sprinkled with holidays, some tied to the calendar (the new year or the beginnings of seasons), some to the agricultural cycle (planting, reaping, or flood), some to the events of royal life.

Besides the coronation, one of the most imposing festivals was the jubilee, or "*sed*-festival" (*ḥb-sd*), which was celebrated after the first thirty years of a reign. Consisting of a series of very ancient regeneration rituals for the magic-religious powers of the pharaoh, it was perhaps a remnant and sublimation of what was originally a ritual sacrifice of the king. The funerary context surrounding the stepped pyramid of Djoser, king of the Third Dynasty, is a translation into stone of the tents and booths built for that feast, and the implied ideology of its marvelous construction should be read in the light of those rites.

Predominating the interminable sequence of ceremonies were the religious feasts, both national and regional. The more important ones, like the feast of Amon at Thebes, could last as long as a month, similar to the noisy and joyous gatherings of pilgrims (as many as 700,000!) observed by Greek historian Herodotus at Bubastis in the fifth century B.C. By then, however, many of the minor feasts which had been celebrated with show and display of means in the second millennium (much loved were the processions in which the god or goddess crossed the river or the city to visit the god with whom they were associated), had become much quieter. The feasts of the dead, however, remained joyous occasions for the ancient Egyptians over the millennia. These celebrations were for the living to meet their dead and eat with them, for which they even organized real country outings in the necropolises.

Stone chapel replicating the festival pavilion. Funerary complex of Pharaoh Djoser, Saqqara, ca. 2,630 B.C.

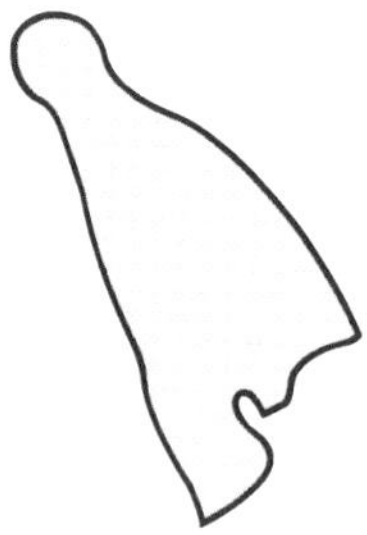

White Crown

Ideogram or determinative in* ḥḏt*, "the white crown."

From the most ancient of times, this crown was worn by the rulers of Upper Egypt, before the unification of the Two Lands. Images of this headdress are well known, but like all the crowns worn by the kings, queens, and gods, we lack any archaeological evidence. Because of this, it is difficult to imagine precisely its materials and dimensions. It had the form of a tall mitre, perhaps made of cloth or felt, with a sort of knob at the top. In historical times, the pharaohs were portrayed with the white crown when they wished to emphasize their association with Upper Egypt. Normally, however, this crown was associated with the red crown of Lower Egypt, and in this form was called by the Greeks (and even now, by Egyptologists) *pschent*, from the Egyptian *p3 sḫmty*, "the crown of the two powers."

VARIANTS/COMBINATIONS

Variant of the former, combined with the sign *nb*.

Red Crown

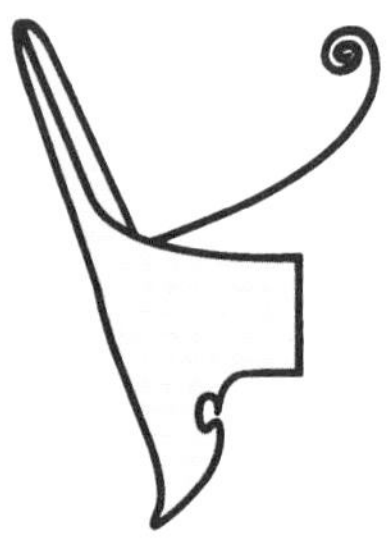

Ideogram or determinative in* dšrt*, "the red crown."

Of a more distinctive design than its sister from Upper Egypt, the red crown had a high crest in the back, and a long rigid line that curled up at the end in front. It is the oldest hieroglyph known, appearing on a pot dating from the middle of the fourth millennium; but it is hard to say whether it already had a value as a code or whether it was simply a drawing of the object. Even though there is no proof that a real prehistoric kingdom existed in Lower Egypt (as there was in Upper Egypt), it is certain that in very ancient times the red crown represented the power of the local sovereigns. Beginning in the New Kingdom the reading of the sign was affirmed as *nt* (thus the common usage of the sign "to write" *n*) and the crown was related to the goddess Neith, tutelary god of the city of Sais in Lower Egypt.

VARIANTS/COMBINATIONS

Variant of the former, combined with the sign *nb*.

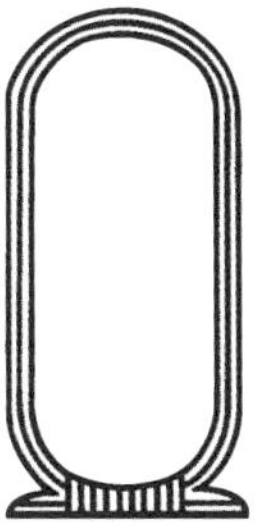

Cartouche

Determinative in* šn, *"circuit" or "ring" ; and later in* rn, *"name."

This sign clearly represents a cord knotted at the ends and forming an oval; in the earliest period, however, it was definitely circular. Its meaning is clearly amuletic: it is the ring that magically isolates and protects that which is inside it. Rings and ties—both positive and negative—are a recurring image in the practice and ideology of universal magic. In pictures from as early as the First Dynasty the gods hold the magic ring, still empty, out to the king. But quite soon—between the end of the Second Dynasty and the beginning of the Third—it became common to write the profane name of the king (given at birth, not at coronation) inside the ring. The transformation of the original circular form into an oval, squashed on the sides, can be explained by the difficulty of writing the hieroglyphs of royal names in a circular area, and by the need for more space. In Egyptian symbolism the *šn*-ring also represents the cosmos: "that which the sun circumnavigates" in its circuit.

This complied with the royal Egyptian theology, which closely associated the pharaoh and the solar cult. With the canonization of royal protocol in historical times, two names used to be written inside the cartouche: the personal name and the so-called *nswt-bỉty* name, which qualified the king as sovereign of Upper and Lower Egypt.

For Egyptologists, the cartouche (like a modern highlighting pen) emphasized and made immediately recognizable the names of kings.

They served as a starting point for the decoding of hieroglyphic writing: once cartouches' function was understood, it was possible to compare the hieroglyphs written inside them with the Greek letters that made up royal names on the famous Rosetta Stone. On this cornerstone Jean François Champollion constructed the decodification of hieroglyphic writing.

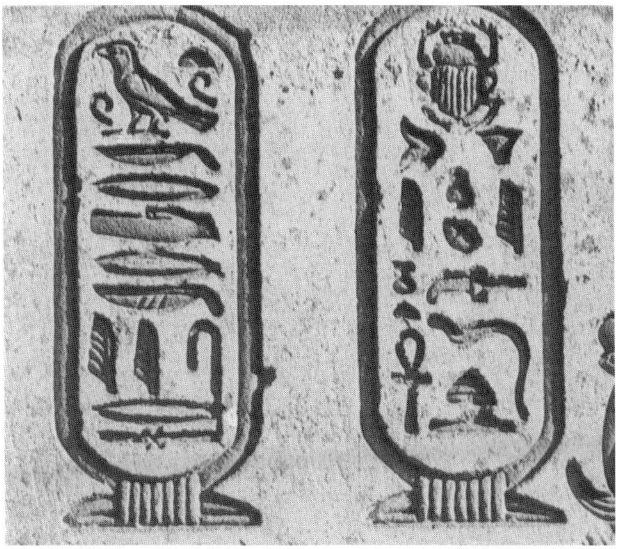

Cartouch of Emperor Trajan, from the temple of Hathor at Dendera.

VARIANTS/COMBINATIONS

Cartouche cut in half, determinative for actions and nouns connected to the idea of dividing, excluding.

Throne

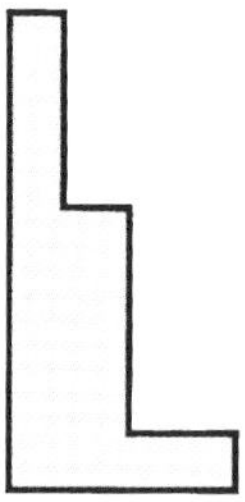

***Ideogram in* st, *"throne," "seat," "place"; whence the phonetic value* st.**

For a people that usually portrays itself seated on the ground, to be seated on a chair is in itself a sign of power. In this hieroglyph, the throne is a tall seat with a backrest, set on a pedestal. This form represents the final point of a long evolution, reached (judging from the earliest examples of the hieroglyph) in the Second Dynasty. In the archaic era, the grapheme for this symbol of power was a stepped platform: power and elevation are inextricably connected in ancient cultures. In both epigraphic and sculptural variants, very often the side panel of the throne was shaped as the hieroglyph *ḥwt*, a walled rectangle representing a royal palace or temple, with a carved square in the lower corner. A variant is the "palace façade" motif. Both of these decorations underline the sublime ambience—royalty or divinity—to which the tall seat belongs. Specifically connected to sovereignty is a decoration found in representations of the throne, the motif called the "Union of the Two Lands." In this sign, two divine personages together tie the symbol-plants of Lower and Upper Egypt to the hieroglyph for "unite," *sm3*.

An important element in the furnishing of a palace, the throne usually took one of two forms: the older, which nonetheless persisted until the late period, was a simple cube with a low backrest; the other "leonine" style appeared as early as the Fourth Dynasty and joined the large group of furniture with leonine legs or busts (armchairs, beds, etc.).

The throne appears in the name of the two greatest and most popular gods of ancient Egypt, the pair Isis and Osiris. In Isis's case, the writing of the name of the goddess itself coincides with the hieroglyph of the throne. Many scholars consider that Isis was originally the divine personification of the throne, but this hypothesis is not unanimously accepted. The name of the god *Wsỉr* (*ws*/*wst* being the ancient phonetic value of throne) associates the throne with the sign for eye, *ỉr*. The explanations proposed for this writing are multiple, and oscillate between sustaining the ideographic value of the two hieroglyphs (and thus the connection between the eye and the throne) and denying this ideographic value, preferring instead phonetic interpretations; but the question is far from being resolved.

Statue of Hathor, enthroned. Dendera, temple of Hathor, south crypt #1. Graeco-Roman period.

Seal

Ideogram or determinative in* ḫtm, sḏ3t, ḏbʿt, *synonyms for "seal" and connected words.

This sign and its variants portray the oldest type of seal found in Egypt, the cylindrical seal. This small cylinder of stone, clay, or other material bears a short inscription on its convex surface, and has a hole drilled so that a cord or chain can be passed through it in order to wear it around the neck. The small inscribed cylinder could then be rolled over a soft or malleable surface so that the carved inscription would be impressed on it: it was, in sum, a forerunner of the invention of printing.

Its role in ancient civilization was no less revolutionary. The operation required a certain skill—the ability to apply constant pressure and even motion to the small object. Sometimes, in order to render it easier to use, the seal was mounted on a metal bar that extended on either end: this permitted the small seal to be held more firmly between the thumb and index finger, while the bar itself—being the axis—made it easier to regulate its movement and pressure. The bar sometimes had a loop on its end so that it could be hung on a necklace or a cord.

The quantity of seals and imprints from seals found in Egypt is enormous, and is also witness to their use in very ancient times. Besides documenting the first hieroglyphic writing, they testify to its fundamental importance in the everyday life of ancient civilizations. This was a way of marking private property, transmitting and delegating power, verifying the integrity of that which was sealed, and protecting against unpleasant surprises in authenticated documents.

Perhaps seals had their origin in the intent to mark property. More likely, they began with the birth of the great centralized administrations, based on a redistributive economy. Seals were initially the prerogative of the highest dignitaries, whether in the private or the administrative world. Between the First Intermediate Period and the Middle Kingdom they began to have a broader range of diffusion. In the Middle Kingdom, the ancient cylindrical seal of Mesopotamian origin was abandoned in favor of a button-shaped seal and, most of all, the typical scarab.

Cylindrical seal bearing the name of the King Merira-Pepi I, Sixth Dynasty.

VARIANTS/COMBINATIONS

Variant of the former, more commonly used in the title *sḏ3wty*, "chancellor," "treasurer."

Emblem of Divinity

Ideogram in* nṯr*, "god," and phonogram.

From as early as archaic times this symbol was chosen to express the concept of divinity, but it is not easy to say exactly what object it represented. The more detailed variants indicate that it represented strips of fabric (the dominant color is yellow, alternating with blue and green) wrapped around a support, with the upper part uncovered. It has been hypothesized that the object is a fetish, carefully wound and hidden by the fabric; in this case, the sign owes its role as a divine ideogram to the holy nature of the mysterious object. Today it seems plausible that the cloth covered a simple staff and, in the manner of a flag, indicated the presence of a god wherever it was placed, with its upper part flapping joyfully in the breeze.
In the hieroglyphic papyrus of Tanis (the list of hieroglyphs drawn up in the Roman period, accompanied by an explanation in hieratic), of the sign *nṯr*: was described as "that which is placed in the tomb (*ḳrs*)." The explanation should perhaps not be understood in relation to the objective representation of the hieroglyph but to that which was in the late period a common meaning of the word *nṯr*:, as designation of the deceased (god in that he was assimilated to Osiris). It is, however, possible that later speculation had elaborated an explanation of the hieroglyph as being the deceased wrapped in bandages: the determinative of the verb *ḳrs*, used in the Tanis Papyrus, is that of the bandage.

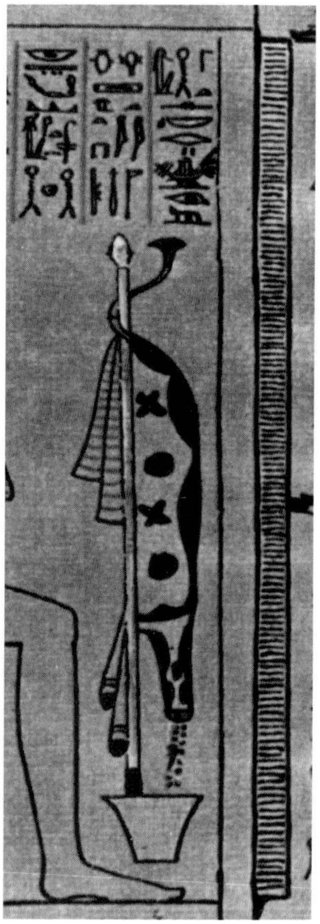

Nor can one exclude that the theory elaborated by the sages of late Egypt was closer to reality than is commonly believed. A scholar of Egyptian religion, the Egyptologist Wolfhart Westendorf, considers that the divine emblem was a stylization of the sudarium known as *ỉmy-wt*, which was originally the skin of an animal in which the king's body was wrapped, and which, with the appropriate funeral rites, aided his rebirth. In this case the emblem would be tied at the beginning to the divine kingship and, in particular, to the dead king, a theory that merits consideration: these were, in effect, the poles around which the most significant part of ancient Egyptian religious thought was elaborated and solidified.

The imi-ut *pictured in a scene from the Anhai Papurus, Twentieth Dynasty. London, British Museum.*

VARIANTS/COMBINATIONS

Combination of *nṯr*: with *ẖr=ẖrt-nṯr* : "necropolis."

Sanctuary of Lower Egypt

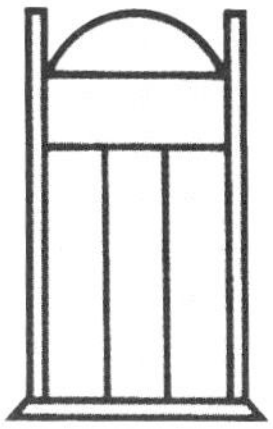

Determinative in "sanctuary" (*ỉtrt, ḫm*), and in names of the specific sanctuaries of Lower Egypt (*pr-nw, pr-nsr*).

Two types of sacred buildings are frequently portrayed in ancient Egypt, sometimes in cult scenes, but most often in the archaic documents, sometimes transposed into hieroglyphic form. These are the *pr-nw* and *pr-wr*, respectively the names of the national sanctuaries of Lower Egypt and Upper Egypt. The *pr-nw* was originally the sanctuary of the cobra-goddess Wadjet, tutelary divinity of Lower Egypt, whose cult seat was the city of Buto in the Delta.

Whether indeed the hieroglyph derives from an archaic building is still being debated. The shape appears to be that of a brick structure with a vaulted roof and high walls which extend beyond the roofline.

Recent archaeological research at the predynastic levels of ancient Buto has shown the common existence of brick buildings, but we still lack evidence of the ability to construct large, round, vaulted roofs in this era. On the other hand, the green color of the hieroglyph would suggest a wooden and cane structure.

Sanctuary of Upper Egypt

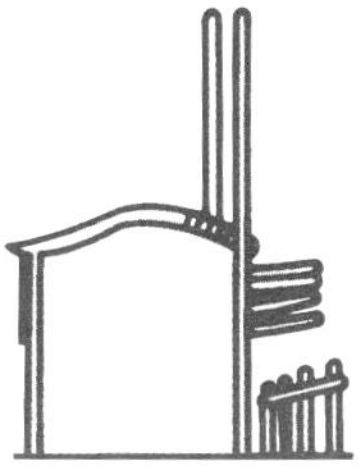

Determinative in* pr-wr, *name of the archaic sanctuary of Hierakonpolis, and in* ỉtrt šmꜥw, *"sanctuary of Upper Egypt."

This hieroglyph originally represented the sanctuary of the tutelary god of Upper Egypt, the vulture goddess Nekheb, known as *pr-wr*, which was in ancient Nekheb (today's el-Kab), site of the goddess' cult. There was, however, another sanctuary attributed to the goddess in ancient Nekhen, which functioned as the sanctuary of the crown. The two buildings, at first distinct, melded into the unified concept of the national sanctuary of Upper Egypt, and into the same graphic sign. Today it is agreed that *pr-wr* was the architectonic transfiguration (probably made of mats, skins, and wooden supports) of an animal—perhaps an elephant or rhinoceros. The oldest versions of the sign clearly show the humpy spine of the animal, which became the stylized "hump-backed" covering characteristic of chapels; the tusks, fixed into the upper part of the façade of the building (which the hieroglyph views from the side); and the tail. It is probable that this unique theriomorphic architecture was associated with the funeral rites for the rebirth of the king.

Chapel, Tabernacle

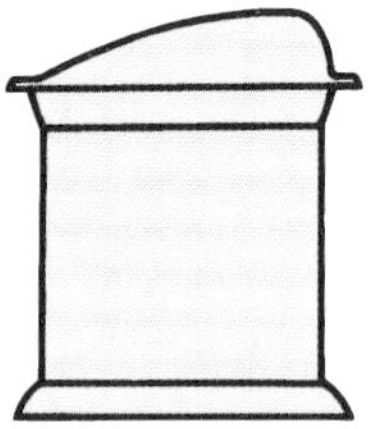

Ideogram or determinative in* k3r*, "chapel," "tabernacle."

This tabernacle is where the statue of the god was kept, at the very back of the temple, to be approached only by the elect few. In processional boats, this is the cabin which covers the god's image. The form shown in the hieroglyph—a rectangle on a pedestal, with a rounded lid, as viewed from the side—is one of the most common shapes. Its "hump-backed" covering seems to reproduce the shape of archaic sanctuaries, in particular the *pr-wr*, the typical sanctuary of Upper Egypt. There were also *naos*—as these tabernacles are commonly called—with flat covers bearing the "cavetto cornice," a curved molding composed of leaf-shaped elements. Another possible variant was a pyramid covering. The front of the *naos* was closed by a double door. The *naos* could be made of wood, semi-precious stone, or even precious materials; they were not generally taller than a man, even though the *naos* of Mendes in the Delta was seven meters in height by four meters wide.

Column, Pilaster

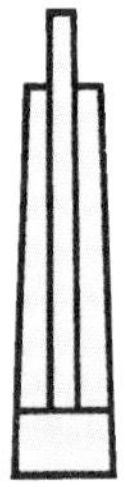

***Ideogram in* ìwn*, "column," and in the name of the sacred pilaster of Heliopolis,* ìwn.**

In the oldest texts, this hieroglyph is often shown as a bunched column, slightly narrowing towards the top. It lacked the characteristic notched top until the Sixth Dynasty. In contrast to the obelisk, which appears only in religious architecture and as a symbol, the *ìwn*-column does not belong only to the sacred environment. It is probable that quite early on it indicated a generically architectonic support. It is quite difficult to sort out its complex relations with the world of the pilaster-fetishes, which were venerated in various sites, from Heliopolis to Dendera, Armant, and Esna. It is possible that it was originally interpreted as something other than the tenon which the Egyptians themselves later saw in it. According to some interpretations, it could have represented the holy *benben*-stone, a cult object at Heliopolis which was erected on a pilaster representing the primordial hill. Heliopolis itself, the On of biblical texts, took its Egyptian name from its sacred pilaster.

Obelisk

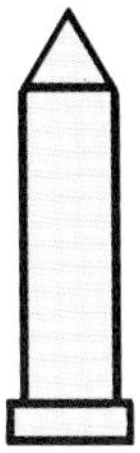

Ideogram or determinative in* tḫn, *"obelisk."

Among the most famous and characteristic symbols of ancient Egypt, the obelisk had its prototype in that stone monument which appeared for the first time in the solar temples of the Fifth Dynasty. Archaeological remains tell us that at that time the obelisk was made of white limestone covered in pink granite, the color with which it is generally associated. From its very first appearance it was clearly connected to the doctrine elaborated by the theologians of the great religious center of Heliopolis, which revolved around the cult of the sun god Ra. It is a grand synthesis which ties together the ideology of the monarchy and solar theology. According to one interpretation of the symbol, it represented in fact the translation into solid stone of the mutual rapport between god and king. It is more usual to perceive in the obelisk the image of the primordial hill from which rose the creator-god (Atum in the Heliopolitan doctrine), or better yet, the stylization of the sacred stone venerated in the oldest times at Heliopolis, the *benben*.

The hieroglyphic writings show that the *benben* was, like the later obelisk, erected on a truncated pyramid, representing the primordial hill. For others, it represents one or more solar rays, as Pliny the Elder sustained (Historia naturalis, XXXVI, 14, 64).

Other theories, also based on ample documentation, emphasize its connections with the idea of fertility and the reproductive power of the sun god. On this basis the obelisk could be considered a phallic symbol, developed from the interpretation of the *benben* as the petrified sperm emitted by the demiurge at the beginning of creation. The connections between sexual potency and procreativity (seen as the perfect manifestation of the vital force) and Egyptian religion are too extensive and deep to reject or underestimate this aspect of the hieroglyph's symbolism.

Obelisk of Tuthmosis I.
Karnak, temple of Amon-Ra,
Eighteenth Dynasty.

Boat with naos

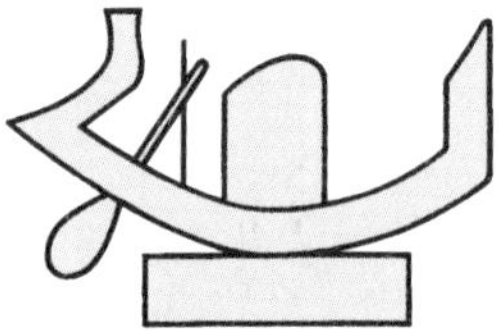

Ideogram or determinative in wỉ3, "cult boat"; determinative in the names of many sacred boats.

That the gods should have moved in boats, like the men of the Nile Valley, is not surprising in a civilization in which the Nile and navigation were vital. Since prehistoric times, crude graffiti on desert roads evoked an obsessive nostalgia for the world of boats and river travel, and in some graffiti boats already bear the sacred standards and symbols. Other boats—especially in predynastic documents—have a curtain supported by poles, the embryonic form of the later *naos*, and carry a statue or hieratic figure. This could allude to the last voyage of a dead king: real boats were buried alongside the royal tomb as early as the first dynasties so that the sovereign could reach the aquatic celestial regions.
The solar god, who traveled these regions by day and by night, never left his boats: in the daytime he sailed on the *mʿnḏt*, the daytime boat, and at night he was pulled by jackals over the sands of the underworld in his *msktt*, the nocturnal boat. The earthly gods who lived in the temples used boats only on certain occasions: to visit other gods during the many solemn feast-days of the Egyptian calendar year, or to visit their domains or participate in processions of various kinds, some of which took place inside the temple complex.
The strangest of these, from the modern point of view, were the oracular processions: carried by lines of porters who were chosen from among the temple's personnel, the god's boat followed a fixed route, stopping to utter the oracle. The statue was alternately open to view, or covered and closed in its *naos*-cabin. It seems that a question properly phrased could be answered by the god with either a yes or a no. The god answered "yes" by an oscillating forward movement of the boat, "no" by complete immobility.
There were two distinct types of sacred boats. Real boats could navigate the river and were used in the great ceremonies in which the statue of the god traveled to another cult site. Portable boats were small models of the former which could be carried on the priests' shoulders.
Sacred boats of various gods were differentiated by their specific insignias and sometimes by their shapes.

Boat of Amon-Re in procession. Karnak, temple of Amon-Re, Eighteenth Dynasty.

Stele

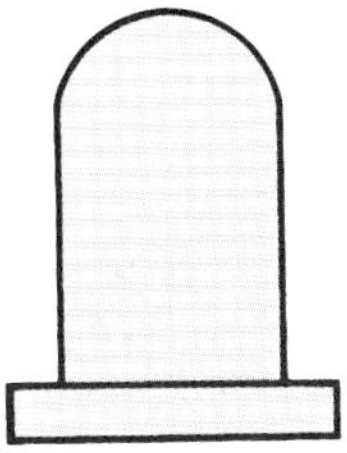

Ideogram or determinative in* wḏ, *"stele"; determinative in* ʿḥʿw, *"station (of a procession),"* *"stele."

The Egyptian stelae were monolithic slabs of stone meant to be erected as self-standing monuments or, more often, leant against or built into a wall. They were covered by inscriptions, usually carved, and often had images as well. The round-topped shape represented in the hieroglyph is one of the most common, but not the only one: a typical alternative is the stele framed on top by a "cavetto cornice." If the latter is in imitation of architectonic forms, the former is based on cosmic symbolism: the lunette is the microcosmic representation of the sky's vault in which the solar circuit is described. Its function as divine space is underlined by the types of images that appear on it, almost always taken from the symbolic repertory (eye of Horus, Anubis, jackals, winged scarabs, solar boats, etc.), or inspired by scenes of adoration and offering before the gods.

The stele's origin is funerary. At least, the earliest known stelae are funerary, contemporary with the First Dynasty. They have been found in the tombs of high functionaries of the time, inscribed with their names and titles. Even though the funerary use is the most documented—thousands of these stelae are preserved in collections around the world—it is not representative of the broad range of functions covered by this typical monument. We know of votive stelae, erected in gratitude for and commemoration of favors received; legal stelae, which document donations of land, divisions of property, or wills; stelae dedicated to one god or another, as simple manifestations of personal piety; and lastly, magic stelae, abounding with formulas against the bites of serpents and other poisonous animals. One particular category of funerary stele, which developed in the course of the Old Kingdom, is the "false-door" stele, in the back (western) wall of the mastaba tombs of the Old Kingdom: they were intended as real doors of communication between the worlds of the dead and the living. And last come the magnificent royal stelae—often imposing in their dimensions and the severe clarity of the semiprecious stone used (shiny black basalt, red granites and porphyry)—which bear precious inscriptions of historic events, eulogies for the reigning pharaoh, and royal decrees.

Lunette of the painted sandstone stele of Nakhy. Deir el-Medina, late Eighteenth or early Nineteenth Dynasty.

Sistrum

I ***deogram in*** **sššt,** ***"sistrum," and*** **sḫm,** ***another name for the instrument. Determinative in*** **sššt.**

The sistrum was a type of rattle used as musical accompaniment to some rites. In this function, it was often paired with the *menat*-necklace. From the beginning it was an instrument tied to the cult and symbolism of the goddess Hathor, and was used in religious ceremonies honoring her. It consisted of a handle and a frame to which cross elements were fixed. Sometimes these elements bore rattles. Agitated vigorously and rhythmically, it produced a tinkling sound from which is onomatopeically derived one of the names of the instrument: *sššt*, which imitates its characteristic strident noise. The Egyptians maintained that this noise, similar to the rustling of clumps of papyrus, had the power to evoke the goddess and, if necessary, to placate her. Thus its archaic sound was given the duty of exorcising the wild and negative aspects of femininity which were incarnate in the various lioness-goddesses. Erotic connotations were not extraneous to its symbolism.
The hieroglyph reproduced here shows one of the two known types: the so-called "*naos*-sistrum," characterized by a small sacred building (*naos*), erected on a papyrus stem handle and crossed by blades with rattles. This type was widespread from the beginning of the Old Kingdom; examples have been found with the name of the Pharaoh Teti and in scenes from the mastaba tombs. In the course of the second millennium, this archaic sistrum was combined with the symbol of the cow goddess Bat. It finally assumed its characteristic and definitive form with the head of Hathor-Bat framed by volutes and topped by *naos*, or better yet, the image of the monumental portal.
The second type, which was very common outside of Egypt in the Graeco-Roman era, is known as the "bowed sistrum." This is a later manifestation, with the first examples dating from the Eighteenth Dynasty. Its form, as reproduced in later hieroglyphic variants, is quite simple compared to the older one: the handle is surmounted by a simple bowed structure with holes, through which pass the cross pieces that emit the characteristic sound.
Sistra were generally made of metal, but there are also examples in faïence.
In combination with other hieroglyphic signs, the sistrum often served to create ideograms or determinative words denoting a rapport with music.

Bronze sistrum combining the two known types of sistrum. Graeco-Roman period.

Incense Burner

***Ideogram or determinative in* snṯr*, term for an aromatic resin, probably incense. It is often used in place of the hieroglyph representing the small* b3w*-container, assuming in this case the phonetic value* b3.**

The aseptic environments of modern civilization have forgotten the tyranny that odors—and bad odors—exercised in the ancient world. In days when the narrow alleys emanated the odors of open sewers and piles of waste left to rot (frequently thrown from windows directly into the streets, together with the contents of chamber-pots), the intense aroma of incense, sometimes acrid and purifying, were not just a divine pleasure but an outright necessity. The Egyptians drew heavily on the aromatic resources of their own land and their neighbors'. They made use of the perfumed resins of pines and Lebanese and Syrian evergreens, as well as the sublime secretions of the trees of "God's Land," as they called the producers of myrrh and incense, located from Arabia to Eritrea and Somalia.

The earth from which the valued aromas came was considered divine. Thus "making divine" was the Egyptian name for one of these aromas (*snṯr* = that renders divine), which was burned before the statues of the gods in the daily cult, offered to the dead as an aerial means of communication with the afterworld, and as a necessary accompaniment to funeral rites. The precise nature of the aromatic product is still the subject of lively debate, divided between those who sustain its identification with the resin of the terebinth and those who prefer real incense (gum-resin of the *Boswellia*). The hieroglyph used to write the name represents a brazier of the commonest sort, from which a thin spiral of smoke rises. It tells us clearly that *snṯr* was used essentially as an aroma to be burned, in contrast to myrrh, for example, which was used in the making of many ointments and perfumes. The simple container shown in the sign finds ample archaeological confirmation: it was a small flared bowl of crude clay, in which the perfumed grains were placed for burning. Incense burners of all sorts (some much more refined) were used for the cult, as can be seen in temple scenes: stylized imitations of a long arm, with an incense bowl held in the curved palm of the hand; or long-stemmed cups, to be held in the hand.

Offering scene with incense burner for the deceased in the form of the ba*-bird. Detail of a wooden stele of the Roman period (second century A.D.). Turin, Egyptian Museum.*

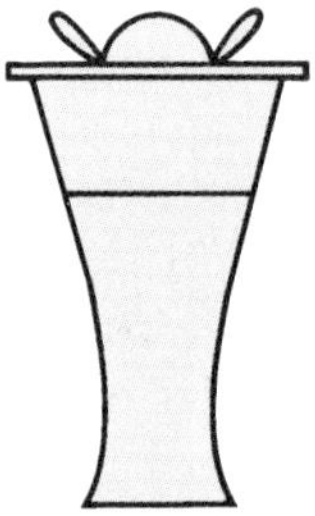

Container for Ointments

Determinative of oils and ointments: mrḥt, "fat, oil"; mḏt, "ointment."

The large container in the hieroglyph, narrow at the base and flaring out towards the top, was a particularly apt container for storing and conserving oils and ointments. The wide mouth with its flat edge was well adapted to being covered and sealed (the cord and seal are quite visible in the hieroglyph), and so were the materials of which it was made: primarily alabaster, white and translucent (from which the name "alabastron" for this type of container is derived), but also diorite (especially in the Old Kingdom), basalt, and anhydrite . This was the traditional shape for the containers of the seven sacred oils used in the divine and funerary cult, cited in the inscriptions that list the ritual offerings to the deceased. The ritual function made this cylindrical vase the favored type of votive object to be placed in deep holes dug at the corners of a new building, known as "foundation deposits." These vases were often inscribed with cartouches with names of kings. Some samples have been found outside Egypt—remnants of gifts and exchanges between kings, or, in some cases, of sackings in the turbulent late period.

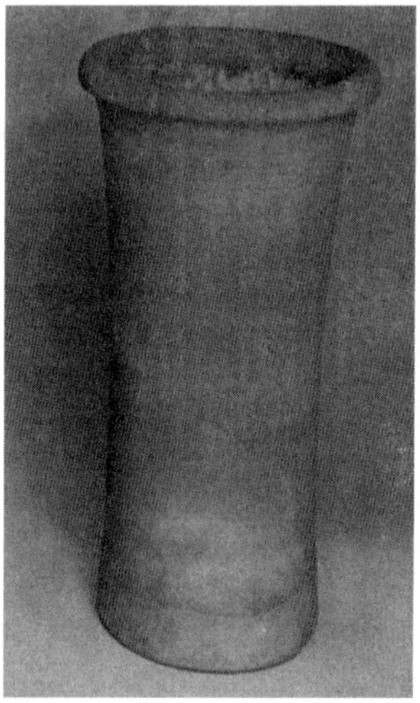

Above: *Alabaster vase for ointments. Beginning of third millennium B.C. Turin, Egyptian Museum.*
Below: *Ointment vase behind the chair of Meru. Detail from his stele from Abydos, Eleventh Dynasty. Turin, Egyptian Museum.*

Oils and ointments were widely used in Egypt, both in medicine and in caring for the body: cleanliness and outward appearance were very important to the Egyptians, and the dry climate required constant hydration of the skin to prevent its premature aging. Animal and vegetable fats were also the indispensable basis of the durable perfumes so enjoyed by the people, whether obtained from the most delicate of floral fragrances or from the dense balsamic extracts of the bark of certain trees. The cosmetic industry in ancient Egypt, even in the early eras, was an important and valued activity; and as late as the Graeco-Roman era, Alexandria was among the most famous centers of perfume production. The temples of the Graeco-Roman period have given us numerous recipes for ointments and perfumed oils made for the divine cult, but they are not easy to reconstruct, because of the difficulty of identifying all the ingredients named.

VARIANTS/COMBINATIONS

The same container, without its tie. Determinative in the name of the container *b3s*.

Container for Libations

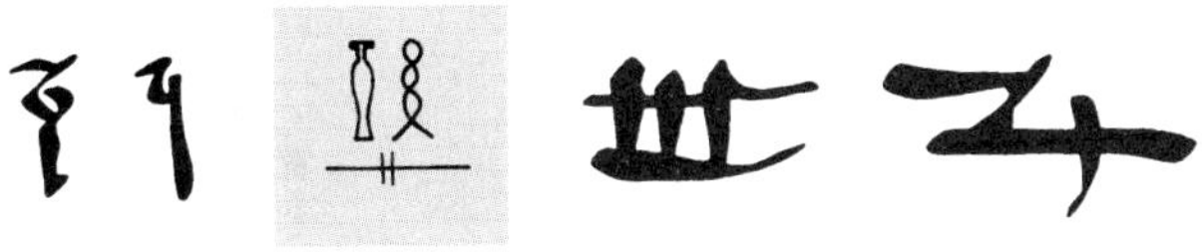

***Ideogram or determinative in* ḥst, *"ritual pot for water," whence the phonetic value* ḥs.**

The tall and elegant vase called *hes* belongs to a typology which was not common in daily life but was well known and often pictured in scenes of cleansing and libations or in funeral offerings. It could contain the purifying waters with which to sprinkle people in purification rites, or the liquids (water and wine) to pour in libations. Fresh water was likened to the primordial waters and possessed all its regenerative and life-giving powers. The gesture of pouring water on the offering table or on an altar recapitulated in the ritual the whole of the offering service, guaranteeing the same benefits. Very often these vases were made of metal, even precious metals, like the fine samples with spouts found in the royal tombs of Tanis. There are also less precious but no less beautiful examples, like those of clay with blue decorations from the New Kingdom.
Bands decorated with imitation lotus-flowers often bore inscriptions of exactly what sort of wine was contained therein: wines from the oases, or wines sweetened with dates, which the deceased carried with him in the tomb to cheer his eternal sojourn.

Loaf of Bread on a Mat

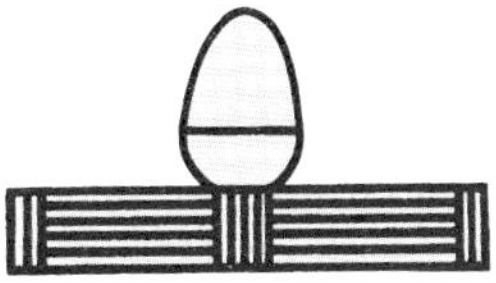

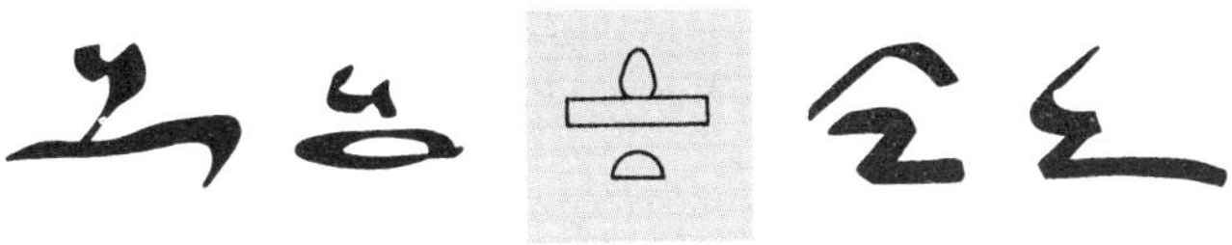

***Ideogram in* ḥtp, *"altar"; phonetic value "altar,"* ḥtp.**

The first altars were simple cane mats or woven rushes on which an offering of bread could be placed. The ideogram *ḥtp*, which in the oldest phase of the Egyptian language recurred with the sense of "altar," later fell into disuse.
Still, the notion of "altar" or "offering table" remained connected to the meanings associated with the root *ḥtp*, the keystone of the ritual and religious thought of ancient Egypt. *ḥtpw* are the offerings to the dead and to the gods; *ḥtp* is the verb "satisfy, to be satisfied," intimately involved in the act of offering, which pleases and satisfies the god; and lastly, in the final passage, *ḥtp* means to "rest oneself, to be at peace," thus designating sunset, the act with which the sun god goes to rest on his boat, a metaphor for the night and the underworld. The verb *sḥtp*, "pacify," gives the name to the important rites of pacification of a god, intended to placate anger or anxiety. More than a phonogram, *ḥtp* in the above cited cases is still an ideogram, even though it became an increasingly abstract and metaphoric sign.

Support for Statues of Gods

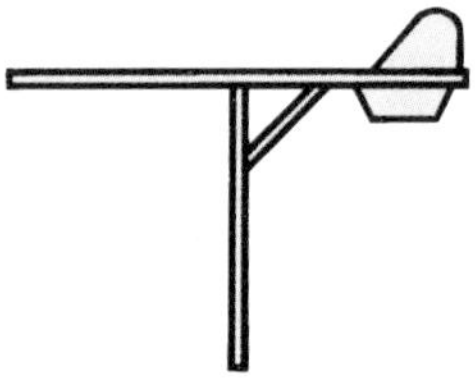

Determinative in* ỉ3t, *"support for statues and religious symbols."

This sign shows a standard for the transportation of statues or cult objects in religious processions, decorated with ribbons and with a cross-bar at the top. The god's image (generally in animal form), the insignias of gods, or even the hieroglyphs which served to write his name, were fixed to the cross-bar.

For the ancient Egyptians, the very fact that an object or a sign was transported or represented on one of these supports was enough to project it into the divine sphere, a fact that the writing exploited with its usual synthetic capacity: many names and determinatives of gods were created by drawing a hieroglyph above the *iat*-support. For example, the common falcon represented on this insignia-carrier becomes determinative of names of gods. The sign of two extended arms, representing the element of the human personality known as the *ka*, when thus elevated indicates the divine substance that exists in each person. Many fetishes or divine symbols, when placed on the divine support, indicate the name of the god itself, as occurred for Min, Wepwawet, Ha, Thot as Ibis, etc.

The origin of the insignia-carrier and its relative hieroglyph is very remote. Its image appeared with symbols of the gods, insignia of the Egyptian provinces (*nomoi*), and other undeciferable emblems as early as the late prehistoric era, on holy books, ceramics, fabric, in wall paintings, or in crude desert inscriptions. They became full-fledged elements of the hieroglyphic graphic code in the earliest inscribed palettes, like the famous one of Narmer, in which they are carried in procession just behind the victorious pharaoh.

In the late period, this insignia-carrier continued to be a recognition sign for a god and outward manifestation of his presence in chapels, temples, and religious ceremonies.

The sound of this sign is similar to that of the hieroglyph for the primordial hill *ỉ3t*. They had another more substantial affinity as well, in that they were both places where the god appeared and were both raised areas. Especially in religious texts, these similarities encouraged frequent graphic puns between the two signs.

Carriers of god insignias on the palette of King Narmer. From Hierakonpolis, end of the fourth millennium B.C. Cairo, Egyptian Museum.

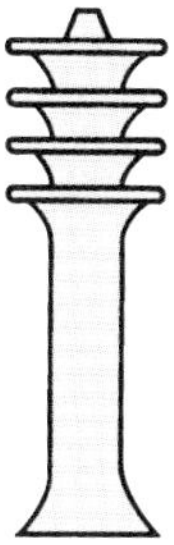

Pilaster-djed

Ideogram in* ḏd*, name of the fetish sacred to Osiris. From this it draws the phonetic value* ḏd *in the verb* ḏdỉ*, "to be stable, last."

The hieroglyph represents the *djed*-fetish, which as a symbol played a large role in Egyptian religion. It also assumed the form of an amulet, which became very commonly worn because of the idea of longevity and stability which the homophone verb *ḏdỉ* brought to it. The sign's exact nature is debated, but its antiquity has been proven by an ivory pilaster discovered in an archaic tomb at Heluan (near Cairo).

The most ancient interpretations saw it as a column imitating a group of stalks cut and tied together, or a trimmed plant. A more recent variant on the first hypothesis, proposed by the German Egyptologist Helck, sees it as a stack of grain in which the short spikes were tied in different parallel levels. According to this theory, the fetish was connected to agricultural rites, attempting to capture the favor of the mysterious powers that presided over the growth of grain.

However, this hypothesis does not agree with the color of the signs in the examples from the Old Kingdom; the upper part of the *djed* is generally green or red, while the body can be black, white, yellow, or red and sometimes even green. This chromatic convention suggests that the upper part of the fetish represented the branches of a deciduous tree tied together or the stems of canes. One thing is sure, however: from the beginning, the sign's meaning is to be found in the realm of religious symbolism. As a fetish, its cult rose at Memphis and was soon associated with an important ceremony known by the name "erection of the *djed*." It was celebrated in the course of the feasts honoring the god Ptah-Sokar, in allusion to his triumphal resurrection. Very early on, the precocious assimilation of the Memphite necropolis's god of the dead with the god Osiris brought the ceremony into the Osirian ritual, where it was interpreted as the triumph of the god over his enemies. The association with Osiris progressively covered and absorbed the original connection with Ptah and Sokar, and finally became predominant. Beginning in the the New Kingdom, the *djed* was commonly interpreted as the backbone of Osiris, and was venerated as one of the god's relics.

The sarcophagi of the New Kingdom often show a *djed*-pilaster painted in the lower part, just where the back of the deceased would rest. Because of its symbolic value, the hieroglyph appears often in scenes and texts associated with the knot of Isis or with the sign of the *uas*-scepter, signifying the undying stability of power.

A djed-*amulet found in Nefertari's tomb. West Thebes, Valley of the Queens, Twentieth Dynasty. Turin, Egyptian Museum.*

Seshat's Emblem

Ideogram or determinative in the name of the goddess* sš3t, *"Seshat."

In classical times, this hieroglyph was interpreted as a kind of flower or rosette with seven petals at the top of a long stem, surmounted by a pair of horns. In fact, it represented the inseparable instrument of an ancient deity, the goddess Seshat, connected from the beginning with writing and perhaps with astronomical calculations. Her name was itself probably none other than a feminine version of the title *sẖ*, "scribe." The exact meaning of the mysterious utensil and its precise function still remain doubful, but one may hypothesize that in the period of the Egyptian civilization's formation it was connected to the newborn and powerful technique of writing and to the observation of the stars. The sign became the emblem of the goddess, which she carried on her head in the classical period as the hieroglyph of her name. In the oldest examples, the horns were replaced with a sickle-shaped sign topped by two falcon feathers.

Neith's Emblem

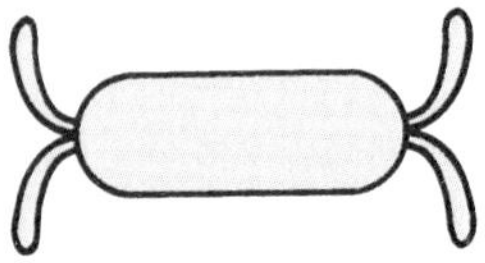

***Ideogram or determinative in the name of the goddess Neith,* Nt.**

There is general agreement about the interpretation of the hieroglyph used to write the name of the ancient warrior goddess of Sais in the Delta, Neith. The sign represented her emblem, two bows tied together in their case. The iconography of the goddess and the writing of her name move together and interchange: representations of the goddess quite often show her with this symbol as a headcovering, placed on the vertical or on the horizontal. The characterization of the goddess as an archer is in fact quite clear and continues through time, explaining why the sign of the two bows tied together is frequently replaced with two crossed arrows, sometimes resting on a shield; the grapheme changes but not the substance, in this instance the bellicose nature of the goddess of the Delta. The evidence suggests that this latter variant is the oldest, while hieratic and demotic prefer to write the name of the goddess in phonetic writing. Others have suggested that the emblem could be a bobbin, which seems to be rather similar in some weaving scenes from the Old Kingdom. If this were the case, Neith was probably considered the initiator of the art of weaving.

Min's Emblem

***Ideogram in the god Min's name,* Mnw*; and, with phonetic value* ẖm*, in the name of the city* ẖm *(the Greek Letopolis, today's Ausim in the Delta); whence the use as the phonogram* ẖm.**

This mysterious emblem first appeared in the very beginning of Egyptian writing: it was used to write the name of the god whom the Greeks called Min on a cosmetic palette from the second half of the fourth millennium B.C., found in a tomb of El Amrah, near Abydos in Upper Egypt. A formula in the *Pyramid Texts* (Pyr. 424b), in which the god is called *Mnw* (the only phonetic writing that we have of his name), shows that the Greek rendering of the name was correct. No doubt remains about the phonetic value of the enigmatic insignia of the god of Coptos, but there are still many veils obscuring its significance. On the archaic statues of the god found at Coptos the emblem occurs in association with two objects, which the Egyptologists, following the great English archaeologist W. Flinders Petrie, have identified as the bony appendix of a sawfish and two shells of the Pterocera species. The two marine attributes seem to confirm the god's origin in the Eritrean areas bordering on the Red Sea, the fabulous Punt that Egyptian texts often associated with the god. A different interpretation was proposed by Budge, based on one of the multiple variants of the sign, in which the sign cuts across a kind of curved staff. He preferred to see it as symbolic of sexual relations, in which the curved staff represents the male sexual organ while the emblem itself represents the female. This interpretation was naturally connected to the ithyphallic nature of the god, which is closely related to the cults of fertility and sexual potency. An original but substantially unverifiable hypothesis was advanced by Wainwright in 1931; in his opinion the sign represented a thunderbolt, an interpretation that would place Min in the circle of storm gods, quite common in the ancient Near East and in the Hittite world. The frequent association of Min with the Asiatic gods introduced into Egypt in a later period would confirm this hypothesis. Notwithstanding the attractiveness of this nicely argued theory, the world of atmospheric turbulence seems to be too marginal and unimportant a reality for the Egyptians for us to suppose that it could have produced a god, and such an antique and adored one. The question is far from being solved; for now, the emblem keeps its enigma intact.

Min's emblem on a cosmetic palette. From El Amrah, middle of the fourth millennium B.C. London, British Museum.

Emblem of the West

Ideogram for* ỉmnt, *"west," and associated words (for example,* wnmy, *"right").

This sign is generally interpreted as a simplification of the original emblem, used until the Twelfth Dynasty and shown here as a variant. This one did not appear before the Sixth Dynasty, but then replaced the original sign with increasing frequency, finally taking its place altogether. It kept the distinctive feather of the original, frequently connected to representations of the west and western people (for example, the Libyans), who wore it in their headdresses.
In the Egyptian enumeration of the cardinal points, the west preceded the east and followed the north. The Egyptians oriented themselves beginning with the south; thus the west coincided with the right side, the "good" side. The west was the region where the dead were buried in order to be reborn and join eternal life, and the Egyptian texts called it "the beautiful west."

VARIANTS/COMBINATIONS

Variant of the sign.

Emblem of the East

Ideogram in* ỉ3bt, *"east" and connected words (for example,* ỉ3by, *"left").

The significance of this emblem is still substantially obscure. In classical times, it is represented as a lance with the ornaments typical of emblems, but the oldest variants clearly indicate that it was originally a double feather. The symbolism of the east was always ambiguous in ancient Egypt. On one hand, it was contrasted with the west—the right and good side—and thus automatically assumed a negative connotation, the inverse and hostile side (think of the analogous negative aura of the left side in our own cultures). On the other hand, it was the cardinal point where the sun rose. With the imperious affirmation of the solar cult, the symbolism of the east became charged with positive values. Just as the emblem of the west came to symbolize the most western province of the Delta (the third nomos of Lower Egypt), that of the east designated the fourteenth nomos of the Delta, which in the Graeco-Roman period was called "Arabia."

Symbol of Life

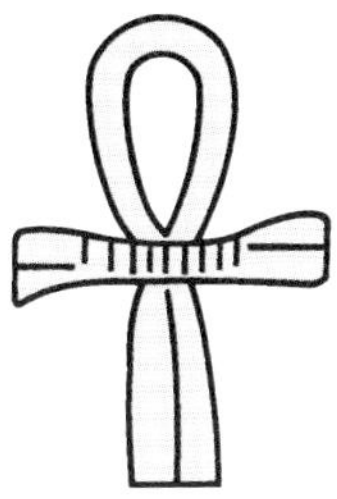

P ***honetic value*** **ʿnḫ.**

E gyptologists are not yet in agreement as to the interpretation of the object represented in this hieroglyph. Gardiner proposed a sandal strap, and although this interpretation does not seem valid, many hieroglyphic lists still follow it. An attractive hypothesis was put forward by Westendorf, who thought of a sort of belt, similar in origin to the so-called "knot of Isis." Still another theory compares the *ankh*-sign to the hieroglyph *šn*, which shows a knot, proposing that the two signs should be seen in relation to the magic ring of twisted cord that surrounded the name.

As a hieroglyph with the phonetic value *ʿnḫ*, the sign was common from the beginning of Egyptian writing in all periods: *ʿnḫ* is the verb "to live" and the noun "life." Above all, it was this meaning that determined the symbolism of the sign, whether or not it was connected to the original ideogram. In religious images the gods hold a magic object in one hand or they hold it out to the king: it is "the breath of life" that the god transmits to the king, and the king in turn to his subjects, an image of the air by which men live.

But life lies also in the beneficial power of the sun and water. From this derive the famous Amarnian images, in which the rays of the Disk terminate in the *ankh*-sign, and the scenes of libation and purification of the king, in which the gods pour a rain of *ankh*-signs over the king's head.

The idea of food as a vital principle for the living and the dead—for the latter in the form of funerary offerings—is expressed in the pure beauty of the stone in an offering tray in *ankh* form, which is in the Metropolitan Museum of Art.

Life on earth, and eternal life in the afterworld comprise the double meaning of this symbol. Because of its formal similarity with the cross, the sign of life was adopted by the Egyptian Christian world, surviving the extinction of the Egyptian religion in the image of the Coptic cross which is common all over Egypt.

Stone plate with the ka-*arms holding an* ankh-*symbol. Protodynastic Period (end of the fourth millennium B.C.). New York, The Metropolitan Museum of Art.*

Winding wall

Ideogram or determinative in *nmỉ*, "to cross" (in the nautical sense) and associated words. Determinative in *mrrt*, "road"; whence the phonetic value *mr*.

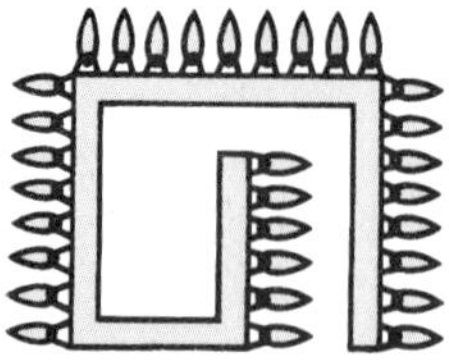

Walled enclosure protected on top by khekheru

Determinative in *sbẖt* "door, portal" and in the related verb *sbḫ*, "surround by walls."

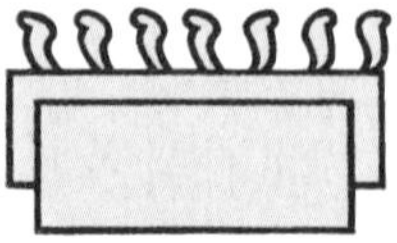

Door surmounted by a line of protective ureai

Ideogram or determinative in *t3*, a word of uncertain meaning: "curtain (of fabric)," "entrance."

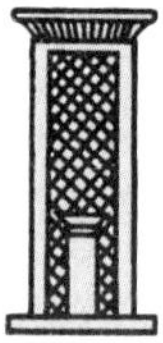

Chapel, front view

Ideogram or determinative in *sḥ-nṯr*, name of the tabernacle that housed the god's statue.

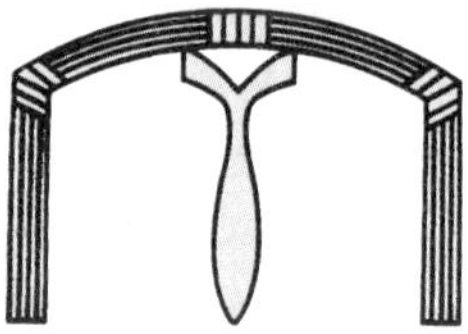

Curtain held up by poles

Ideogram or determinative in *sḥ*, with the same meaning as the former sign..

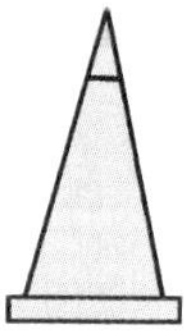

Pyramid

Determinative in *mr*, "pyramid" and in the names of cities near them.

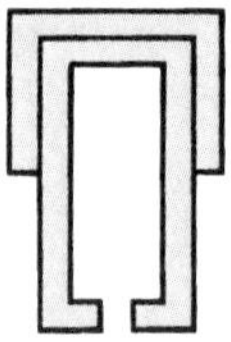

Door

Ideogram or determinative in *sb3*, "door, portal."

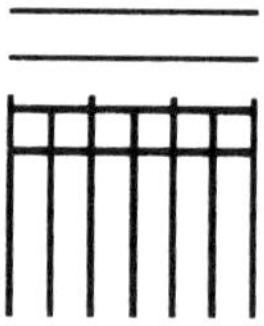

Façade of the royal palace

Determinative in *srḫ*, "palace façade," name of the rectangle decorated in this way in which was inscribed the "name of Horus" of the king.

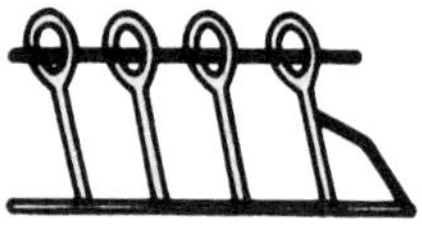

Fence surrounding the primitive sanctuary of Upper Egypt

Phonetic value *šsp* in *šsp*, "to receive"; *sšp* in *sšp*, "light."

Fetish of the temple of Min

Ideogram or determinative in *ỉ3wt*, "post, office."

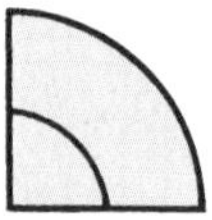

Building with vaulted covering

Ideogram or determinative in *ỉpt*, "harem," "part (of the building) for the women."

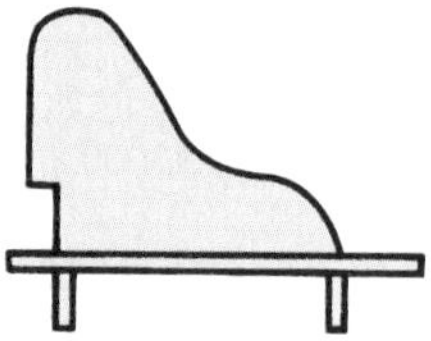

Portable chair

ideogram in *st*, "chair, seat." As phoneme *ws* in *wsỉr*, name of Osiris.

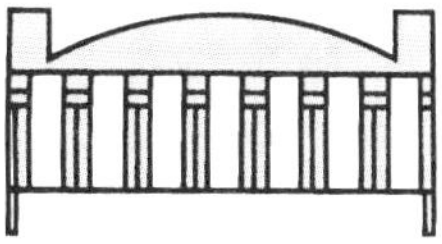

Sarcofagus

Ideogram or determinative in *ḳrsw*, "sarcophagus."

Table with offerings

Ideogram or determinative in *ḫ3wt*, "offering table."

Small table with offerings

Ideogram or determinative in w*ḏḥ*w, "offering."

Incense burner

Ideogram or determinative in *k3p*, "incense, to make smoke." Phonetic value *kp*.

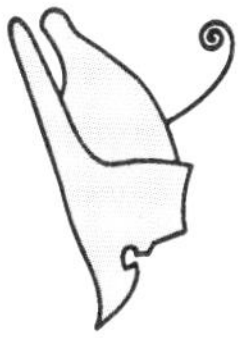

Crown formed of the white crown and the red crown together

Determinative in *sḫmtỉ*, "the two powerful ones."

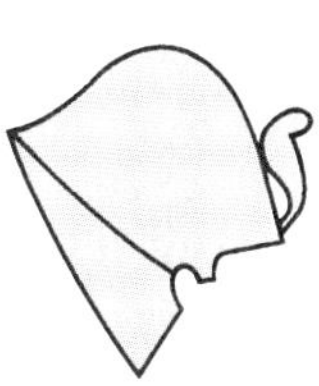

Blue helmeted crown

Ideogram or determinative in *ḫrpš*, name of the so-called "blue crown."

Composite crown with double feather and ram's horns

Ideogram or determinative in *3tf*, name of this type of crown.

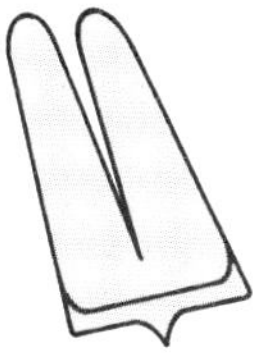

Two feathers

Ideogram or determinative in *šwtỉ*, name of the "double-feathered" crown.

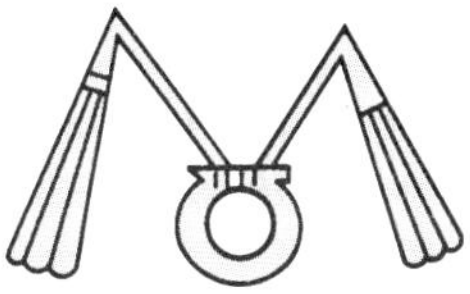

Two whips with the šnw-ring

Erroneous interpretation of the original sign, a necklace with hanging ends and an amulet suspended in front. Ideogram or determinative in *dmḏ*, "to unite."

Staff with curved handle

Ideogram or determinative in *ḥḳ3t*, "scepter"; phonetic value *ḥḳ*.

Sceptre with Seth's head on the handle

Ideogram or determinative in *w3s*, name of the scepter, and *ḏ‘m*, name of a similar scepter.

Variant of the former

Ideogram specific to the *ḏ‘m*-scepter.

Scepter

Ideogram or determinative in the name of the *ʿb3*-scepter and the *sḫm*-scepter. Phonetic value: *ʿb3*, *sḫm*. Ideogram or determinative in *ḫrp*, "lead, be at the head."

Whip, fan, or fly-whisk

Ideogram or determinative in *nḫ(3)ḫ(3)*, "flagellum, whip."

Ring of woven cord

Original sign for the royal cartouche. Determinative in *šnw*, "cartouche."

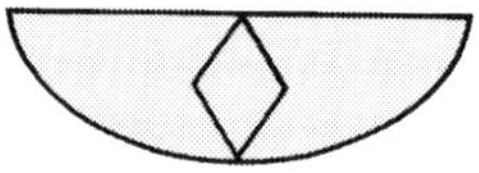

Basin of semi-precious stone

Determinative in *sš*, alabaster and in *ḥb*, "holiday."

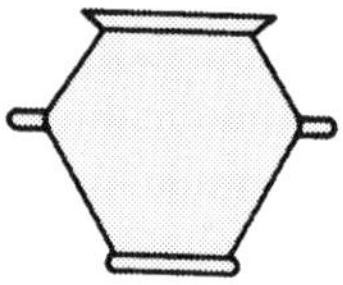

Granite vase

Determinative in *m3ṯ*, "red granite" and in *3bw*, "elephantine." Phonetic value: *3b*.

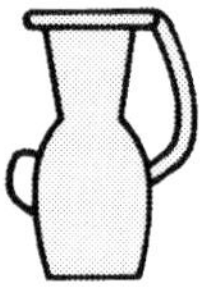

Pitcher with handle, for ritual use

Determinative in the name of the *nḫnm*-vase, container of one of the ritual oils. Phonetic value: *ḫnm*.

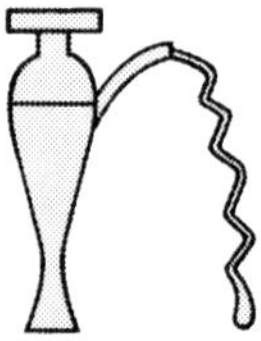

Libation vase, pouring water

Determinative in *ḳbḥ*, "libate"; *ḳbb*, "to be fresh."

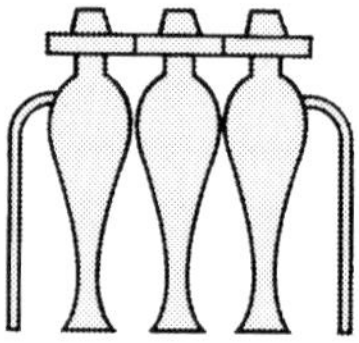

Water jugs in a stand

Ideogram in *ḫnt*, "stand (for vases)," whence the phonetic value *ḫnt*.

Arts and Trades

Hunting, fishing, farming, making war, goldsmithing, making pots of stone or clay: there is no ancient activity undertaken by mankind in the Nile Valley that is not documented by the hieroglyphs of this section. The variegated world of the trades was great fodder for the hieroglyphic system, contributing dozens and dozens of detailed graphemes to the collection, and providing Egyptologists with a very lively documentation of the material culture of that ancient civilization. In more than one case, paleography and archaeology have helped one another: the discovery of an object in a well-defined context, found during an archaeological dig, can clarify the meaning of a long-unexplained hieroglyph; or reciprocally, a grapheme whose meaning is known may explain the function and use of a mysterious ancient object. Frequently the hieroglyph gives us the archaic form of a tool that has evolved over the years, furnishing the basis for an "industrial archaeology" of the third and fourth millenniums B.C.

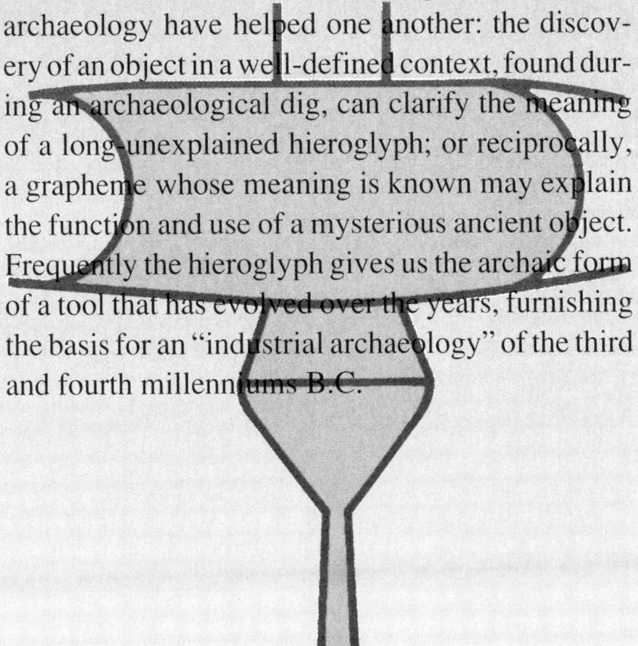

Ship

Determinative or ideogram in names of boats and ships, determinative in verbs designating navigation.

In the Egyptian graphic universe prior to writing, boats played an important and sometimes enigmatic role. As eloquent witnesses to the river civilization, they appear with obsessive frequency in crude desert graffiti and in the first experiments with painting, the decorated ceramics of Upper Egypt, the painted fabric of Gebelein now in Turin, and the wall paintings of tomb #100 at Hierakonpolis. The slim, fundamental form of these round-bottomed boats, with numerous long oars and one or two cabins, translates without stylization into the hieroglyph meaning boat.

A wealth of additional written and painted documentation shows other boat models in miniature or in scale. In addition, real boats found in the course of excavations illustrate different types of vessels and their evolution over time: from primitive little papyrus boats to wooden ships with oars, soon furnished with masts and often a cabin, and from the large barges able to carry heavy stone obelisks to the narrow war ships with high sides and a lion's head on the prow. These boats had a shallow draught, and until the New Kingdom had no keel. Deeper hulls distinguished sea-going ships from riverboats. In the second millennium the two steering oars at the bow, were replaced by a true rudder.

We know that these boats could reach respectable size: sixty meters and more in length, with crews of one hundred and twenty and even two hundred men. But the most common types were probably not more than twelve to fifteen meters, with crews averaging from twenty to twenty-five men.

Viceroy Huy's ship leaving for Nubia. Sheikh Abd el-Qurna, tomb of Huy (TT 40), Eighteenth Dynasty.

Fishing Boat

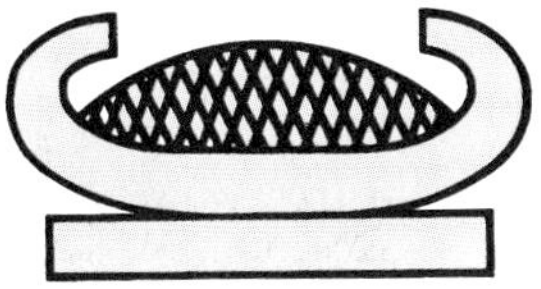

Ideogram in* wḥʿ*, "fisher," and connected words.

The half-moon shape of the stylized variants of this hieroglyph, which was common in classical times, derives from the high prow and stern typical in the sign of the Old Kingdom. The arc of the circle inside the half-moon represents the tangle of nets in the bottom of the boat. Sometimes, in a very pertinent graphic pun, a cat-fish (*wḥʿ*) is drawn in place of the net. The fishermen's boats were generally constructed of bunches of papyri tied together, an ingenious and simple method that provided light and flexible boats adapted to local navigation and fishing. Like the cane boats used today on Lake Titicaca, between Peru and Bolivia, the papyrus boats were made and used for centuries: Pliny the Elder (*Hist. nat.*, VII, 57) recounted that in his time, the Roman period, the Egyptians made boats of papyrus, rush, or cane. Numerous tomb scenes are dedicated to the construction of papyrus boats, but unfortunately do not give us information as to the intermediate phases of the technique: the boats are shown nearly complete, in the final stages of being tied with cords; these cords wrapped the whole width of the boat two or three times at regular intervals, thus locking together the walls constructed with the juxtaposition of the bands of papyrus. It is likely that the papyri were, in the preliminary phases, deprived of their flowers (except those meant for prow and stern) and placed together on some sort of framework of crossed branches. The stern of these boats is normally quite a bit higher than the bow.

Egyptian fishing methods were various: from the hook on a rudimentary cord, to the harpoon, to fishing with traps or nets. Many artifacts have been found in archaeological expeditions—from the oldest harpoons and Neolithic hooks of bone, ivory, and shell, to their metal descendants. Also discovered are nets of vegetable fibers—which were used in various methods that are well illustrated in the lively fishing scenes to be found in the tombs.

Hunting for hippopotamus from a typical papyrus boat. Saqqara, tomb of Ti, Fifth Dynasty.

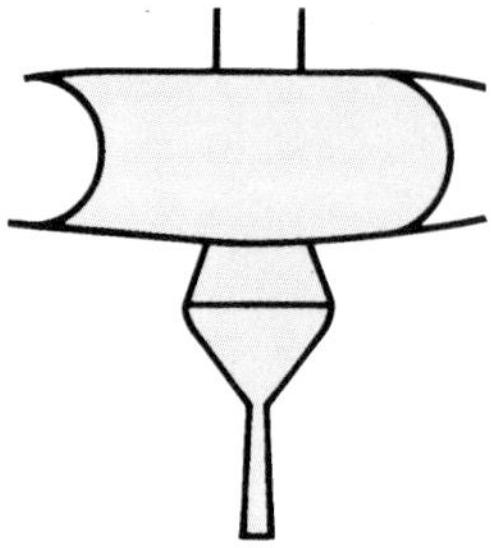

Sail

Ideogram or determinative in* ṯ3w, *"puff," "wind," and in* nfw/nfy, *"sailor." Determinative in names of the winds and in verbs designating navigation.

Even when the air over the land of the Nile Valley and desert is heavy and still, there is always a light breeze moving over the river. Thus the image of the white sail full of wind is a natural and solidly visible translation of the idea of air. The sail is rectangular, and in the Old Kingdom it was taller than it was broad; its anxious tenseness partly covers the mast, which is made of two oblique trunks joined at the top. One can spy the crossbars that, beginning at a certain height, join the two trunks like a staircase. At the top, a ring allows the lines to be tied to the mast. At first there was a single rope that ran from the top of the mast to the stern, however; only later was a second fixed to the prow, giving the mast greater stability. Since the sail was generally turned to take the wind from the stern, the first rope, intended to conterbalance the wind's pressure, was the more important one. Sailboats were primarily used for long voyages, whether by river or sea. Oars were common on both types of boats, and used more than one might imagine: the sails could be used only in a following wind; tacking was very difficult.
On the Nile this generally meant that one traveled south by sail, given the predominance of the cool northerlies, and on the return voyage united the power of the current to that of the oars. This was so common that it influenced hieroglyphic writing: the words used for "travel south" (go upstream by sail) and "travel north" (row downstream) were respectively the signs of the sailboat and the rowboat.

Menna's ship under full sail on the river. Thebes, Sheikh Abd el-Qurna, tomb of Ipuy (TT69), Eighteenth Dynasty.

Harpoon

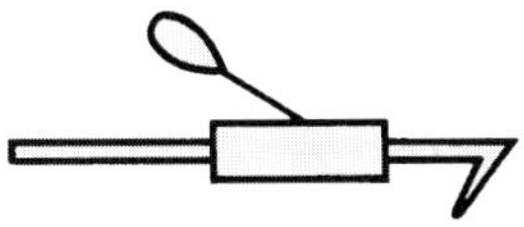

Ideogram in* wʿ *and its derivatives.

Once again the hieroglyphic code, like an old photograph, immortalizes reality as it was at the end of the fourth millennium. This sign represents a harpoon with only a single side barb, typical of the predynastic era. The hieroglyph also shows a cord fixed to the harpoon; once the prey is speared, the cord could be unrolled slowly, leaving the hook solidly anchored in the flesh of the animal so that it could be brought in.

The heads were of bone, ivory, horn, and later metal (first copper and then bronze). The harpoons found on predynastic sites have from one to three barbs aligned along a single side; heads with barbs on both sides are quite rare before the Middle Kingdom and really developed only after the beginning of the New Kingdom.

We are not certain whether the harpoon was used for fish alone, or also for the crocodiles and hippopotamuses that were abundant in the waters of the ancient Nile. The small size of most of the oldest harpoons (from 2.5 to 3 in. long) excludes large or thick-skinned game like the aquatic reptiles or the hippopotamuses: it is more likely that these were used for large fish like the *Perca nilotica*, which can weigh more than one hundred chilos.

However, larger points were presumably used for crocodiles and hippopotamuses. From scenes in tombs it appears that harpoons were typically thrown with rope when used to hunt these large animals, similar to its use for whales. When fishing, the fishermen never let go of the harpoon's shaft, but plunged it into the water and speared the fish.

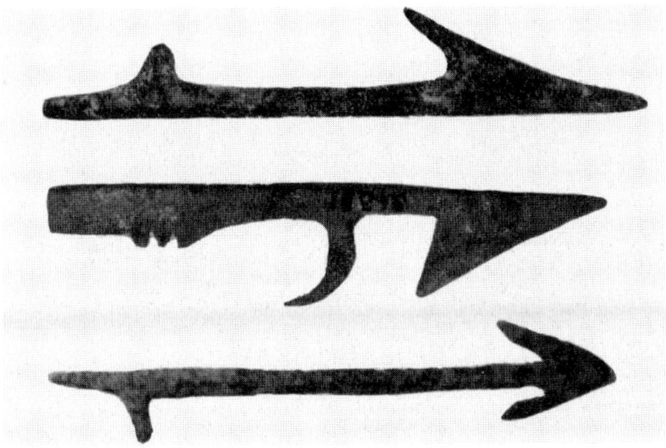

Copper harpoons.
Cairo, Egyptian Museum.

VARIANTS/COMBINATIONS

Harpoon head with double barb and cord. Ideogram or determinative in *ḳs*, "harpoon," "bone," whence its use as the phonogram *ḳs*. Determinative in names of objects of bone, ivory, etc. Phonogram *gn*.

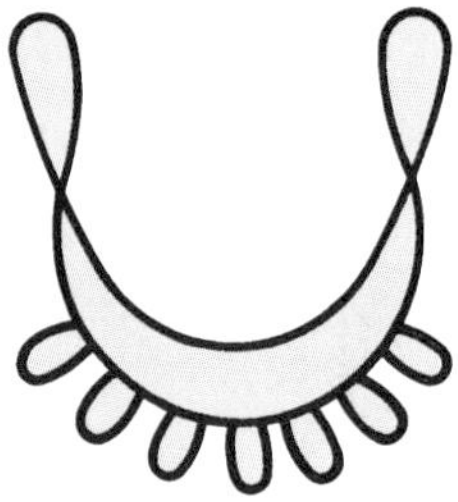

Fish net

Determinative in ʿḥ, ỉḥ, "net" for animals, whence the phonogram ʿḥ.

Almost every kind of net used in the ancient world has been found in Egypt, since fishing was always one of the fundamental factors of the Nile economy. The ancient Egyptians used all their ingenuity in finding ever more efficient ways of catching fish. The oldest example of a whole net which has been found in Egypt comes from one of the Neolithic levels of El-Omari in the Delta, while the first representations are not earlier than the Fourth Dynasty.

The net portrayed in the hieroglyph is a trawling net, a long rectangle requiring a group of men to manage it. The rectangular meshwork was made of vegetable fiber, and had long ropes at either end so that it could be dragged to shore. Along the upper edge there were generally floats; along the lower edge, there were weights to keep it down in the water, quite visible in the hieroglyph. These weights were usually of stone, sometimes of ceramic, and in later times, lead. The floats are not shown in the sign and often are not accurately depicted even in the most detailed fishing scenes in the tombs of the Old Kingdom. It seems, however, that they were probably triangular pieces of wood.

In order to bring the drag net to shore once it was heavy with fish, men frequently used shoulder belts: the animated gestures and the postures of the fishermen in the scenes clearly suggests that great physical effort was involved.

In scenes from the Old Kingdom the fishermen worked primarily from the shore. Only rarely (but more frequently in later eras) was fishing done from boats. Small models of papyrus boats lined up side by side, their crews pulling the net full of fish, were deposited in the tombs of ancient Egypt and are today on display in various museums around the world.

Fishermen in a boat haul in a net full of fish. Deir el-Medina, tomb of Ipouy (TT 217), Nineteenth Dynasty

Throw stick

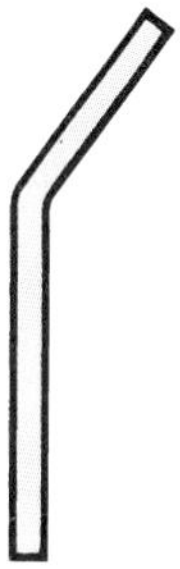

D ***eterminative in*** ʿmʿ3t, ***"throw stick," and in connected words such as*** ḳm3, ***"throw." Also used in the verb*** ḳm3, ***"to create," and derivatives. Ideogram in*** ṯḥnw, ***"Libya, Libyans"; and by extension, the determinative of all names of foreign peoples and lands.***

T he throw stick illustrated in the hieroglyph is very similar to the Australian boomerang, and it is also a very ancient weapon. The Museum at Turin has a predynastic one from Gebelein which is carved from a single piece of sycamore. It is about 35 inches long and weighs about 11 ounces. The weight and size meant that a notable strength was needed to manage it efficiently. Experimental reproduction of similar sticks has shown that, when properly thrown, it will return to the thrower in a slow but strong flight with considerable inertia.

The stick was used mostly for hunting swamp birds and can still be seen in this context in scenes from the New Kingdom. But in the historic era this weapon was identified as typical of the semi-nomadic peoples of Libya and the hieroglyph was associated with that group.

Lasso

P ***honogram*** w3, ***from a family of words designating cords and ropes (see*** w3t ***and*** w3w3t, ***"cord"), among which were, perhaps, a now lost*** *w3, ***"lasso," the sign of which was the ideogram.***

F rom prehistoric times, in graffiti and painting, the lasso appears as a hunting weapon used to capture antilopes, gazelles, ibexes, lions, ostriches, and other wildlife. The crude graffiti of the Neolithic hunters sometimes show them in the act of lassoing a giraffe, and then killing it with a club. Its Egyptian name, at least in the historic era, is *spḥw* : if the word *w3*, "lasso," ever did exist, written with the hieroglyph that represents it, it has been lost. In hunting scenes of the historic eras it is generally used by the various servants and helpers, and not by the nobleman himself, indicating that by this time it had become its secondary to other more prestigious weapons.

But a memory of its much more significant role in prehistoric hunting is shown in the ritual capture of the wild bull, the first act of an ancient offering ceremony which is illustrated on the walls of the temple of Seti I at Abydos.

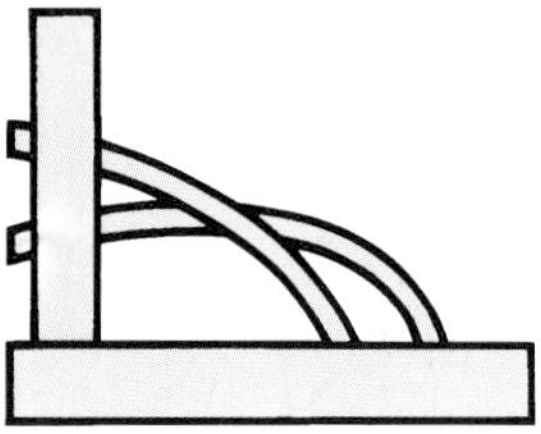

Bird Trap

Ideogram or determinative in sḫt, "trap," and derivatives.

Before the mechanism depicted in this hieroglyph was discovered during an excavation at Saqqara, it was difficult to understand how the item worked, though the meaning of the word *sḫt* and illustrations left no doubt that it was a trap for birds. The trap was composed of three basic pieces: two wooden sticks, an attached net (represented in the sign by the two superimposed curved elements), and a complicated type of stand (the right-angled piece in the hieroglyph). By an ingenious system of intertwined strings held in tension by small sticks (which an experimental reconstruction of excavated pieces has allowed us to understand), the two main sticks were held open in tension and in a horizontal position to form an oval. The position was precarious, and the least movement would cause the two sticks to snap together.

To insure that the prey would be a bird, a worm was placed as bait between the string and the sticks. As soon as the bird pecked at the worm and made the string slip, the two sticks snapped together and trapped the bird in the net.

Reconstruction of a bird trap, based on original pieces.

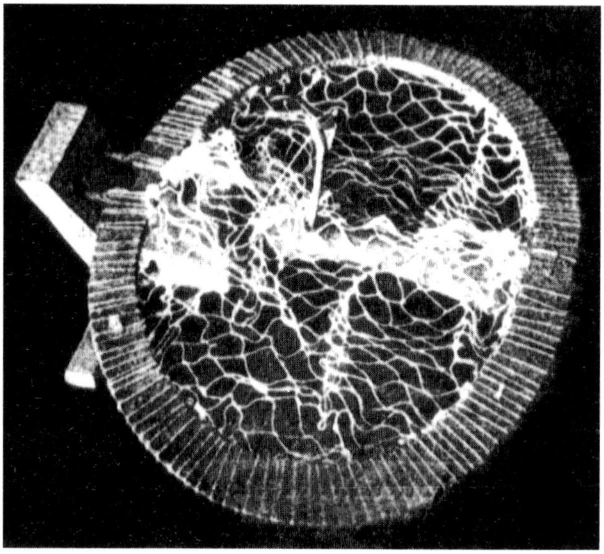

The system was probably not used for hunting (boomerangs, bows, and nets were preferred), but by gardeners who wanted to catch the hungry little gobblers of seeds and fruit, those inveterate winged enemies of gardens and orchards. The existence of variants is evidence of the trap's evolution over time.

VARIANTS/COMBINATIONS

Variant of the hieroglyph in the Old Kingdom.

Bow

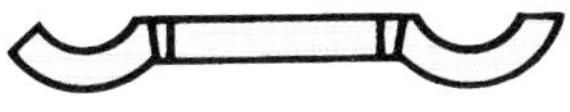

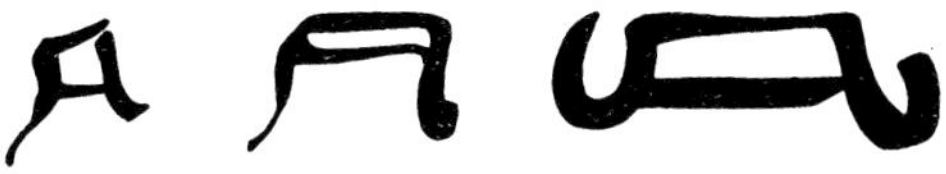

***Ideogram or determinative in* pḏt, *"bow," whence the phonetic value* pḏ.**

This was the most important of long range weapons, used since the beginning of time for hunting and warfare; the abundance of flint arrowheads found on prehistoric sites is eloquent documentation. The hieroglyph represents the archaic type of bow, found in graffiti as early as the end of the Paleolithic period, made of antilope horns held together by a central wooden piece. Later, and until the Second Intermediate Period, the wooden bow became common, characterized by a slight double convexity. It was made of a single piece of hardwood—almost always acacia, the most easily found in Egypt—and was usually about sixty-seven inches long. The string was made of animal fiber; the arrow's shaft was made of cane; and the head was made of bone for birds, or flint or bronze for warfare. The double curve in the bow was obtained by working the wood while wet and heated, and by using special tools. Numerous examples have been found among funeral provisions. Calculations estimate the power of the bow at 65 to 80 pounds, and the range at 55 to 65 yards in a direct shot, 175 yards in a parabolic arc—enough to pierce unprotected flesh.

With the beginning of the Hyksos Dynasties, the composite bow was introduced from Asia. It was made of thin overlaid strips of different materials and had more power and range. Many examples of this powerful weapon were found in the tomb of Tutankhamen. The materials used, more flexible and elastic than wood, made the bow straighten more rapidly when released, giving the arrow greater velocity. The composite bow was also much easier to manage.

VARIANTS/COMBINATIONS

Composite bow.

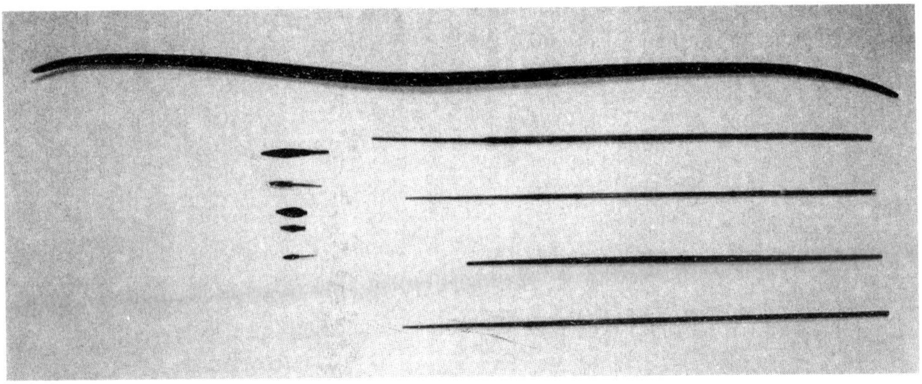

Double-curved wooden bow, with arrows and arrowheads. From Gebelein. Turin, Egyptian Museum.

Cone-headed Club

***Ideogram in* mnw*, name of this type of weapon, whence its phonetic value* mnw.**

The memory of a short-lived prehistoric weapon is preserved in this hieroglyph: a frightening club, with a wooden handle and head of conical or disc-shaped stone, flattened at the base or slightly rounded. It was common mostly in the south. The first examples come from Neolithic Sudan and date from near the end of the fifth millennium B.C.
Later the club appears at Hierakonpolis, in the larger tombs of the Amratian phase, in the first half of the fourth millennium. It was already an undoubted symbol of power, even though it would soon be abandoned.
The future conquerors of Lower Egypt, the founders of the First Dynasty, replaced it with the weapon of their northern enemies, a club with a pear-shaped head. The examples of clubs that have been found have small perforations, to keep the stone from breaking. This explains the need for strong cords tying the head to the handle, which sometimes run the whole length of the handle. This is well illustrated in older variants of the hieroglyph.

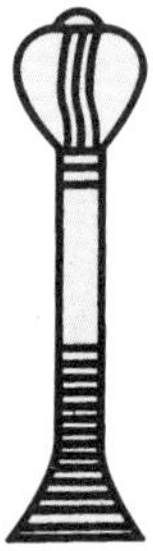

Pear-headed Club

***Ideogram in* ḥḏ*, name of the club, whence its phonetic value* ḥḏ.**

The pear-headed club, called *ḥḏ*, originated in the north. The earliest documentation is from the Neolithic village Merimde, fifth millenium B.C. In the second half of the fourth millennium, in ways and for reasons that are still a mystery, the pear-headed club replaced the traditional weapon of the south. It became the weapon of choice for all of Egypt, even in the remote Nubian villages, as is demonstrated by the splendid sample covered in gold leaf and worked in relief which was found in the tomb of a prince of Sayala.
The club became such a potent symbol of power that it survived intact for the whole pharaonic period. It is the weapon brandished by the pharaoh above enemies' heads, in an iconographic motif that is repeated up to the Roman era.

VARIANTS/COMBINATIONS

The *ḥḏ* club with the sign *ḏ* as phonetic complement.

War Chariot

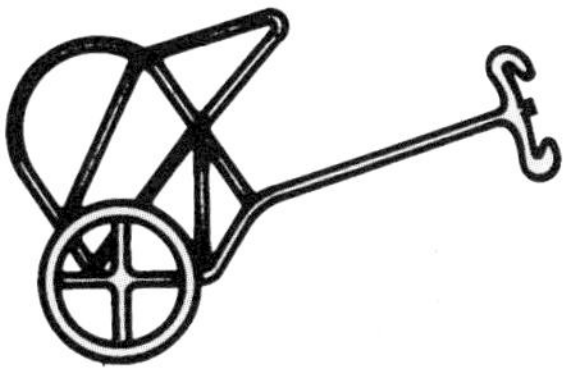

Ideogram or determinative in wrrt, "chariot."

This hieroglyph entered the Egyptian graphic code after the Second Intermediate Period, when the chariot was introduced into Egypt after the Hyksos domination. After that, it was used by the elite warrior class and became an important status symbol. It was a light vehicle with two wheels, each of which had four or six spokes, drawn by horses, made of wood but with some parts of metal or leather. The origin of the two-wheeled chariot drawn by two trained horses is usually considered to be Iranian, but with its transferral into the Near East it underwent improvements. It carried two people: the charioteer, and the warrior armed with bow, lance, and shield. The version modified by the Egyptians was much faster, more agile, and lighter than the heavy Asiatic types. Its use in battle, which revolutionized combat techniques, primarily took advantage of the element of surprise, which was made possible by its great mobility. In the disorderly flight of the retreating enemy, it was the best means of pursuing foot soldiers and sowing panic in enemy ranks. In the powerful armies of the New Kingdom the charioteer represented a potent weapon, and had more social prestige than infantrymen. Nonetheless, the scribes made satiric jibes, as is shown in the papyrus Anastasis I (Twentieth Dynasty): "Your road is full of rocks, the way is not passable, as it is full of canes, brambles, thorns. . . . The precipice is on one side of you, the mountain on the other. You bounce along, with the chariot all on its [the mountain's] side. . . ."

Tutankhamen standing in a chariot during a lion hunt. Detail from the lid of a chest in his tomb at Thebes, Eighteenth Dynasty. Cairo, Egyptian Museum.

Plow

***Determinative in terms connected to plowing. From* hb, *"plow," is derived the phonogram* hb.**

Herodotus (II, 14) claimed that the Egyptians did not plow the earth, but only spread seed, which pigs trod into the ground when they were led into the fields. Contradicting the Greek historian's report, there are hieroglyphs representing the plow and the hoe, numerous detailed scenes illustrating work in the fields, and discoveries of ancient agricultural tools or miniature reproductions in tombs.
The Egyptian plow remained constant for the entire dynastic period. It was forked, made entirely of wood. One longer, pointed part was tied to the handle with a rope, and served as the ploughshare to break the clods. Over the course of time considerable improvements were made, giving the handle a long rudder that passed between the animal's horns so that the tool could be more easily controlled.

Hoe

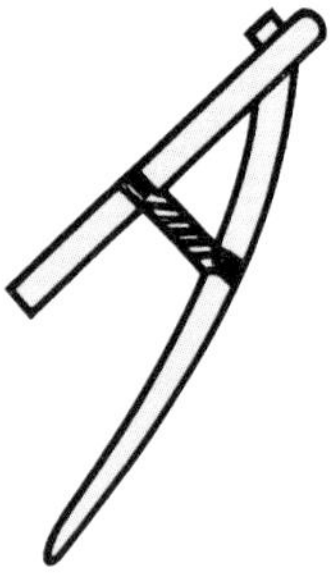

***Determinative in verbs relative to working the earth. Phonogram* mr.**

Originally the Egyptian hoe was a simple forked branch. One end functioned as a handle, and the other dug into the earth. The tool portrayed in the hieroglyph, like the real examples found in excavations, shows the forked shape. The handle was a slightly curved staff that was easy to hold; the blade itself made of wood, in a variety of flat and broad shapes. A rope passed through two holes in the blade and was tied around the handle to keep the two pieces together. The hoe was an adjunct to plowing, helping in the breaking up of the tougher clods, but was also used to loosen the earth between plants, especially in vegetable gardens. It was also used to mix the clay in brickmaking. In the ritual life of the

ancient Egyptians, the hoe had a very important role. It took part in all the groundbreaking ceremonies for sacred buildings, as numerous scenes from the era show. Even in the predynastic period, the iconography for this was already well elaborated.

Sickle

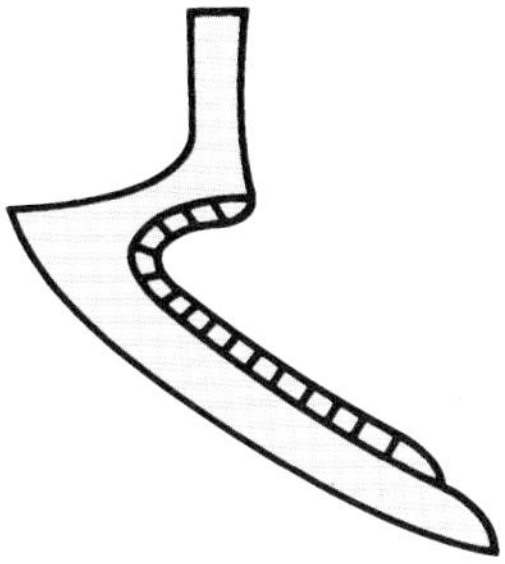

P ***honogram* m3; *determinative in* 3sẖ, *"to mow."***

The oldest versions of this hieroglyph clearly show the small honed flint blades that were set into grooves in the sickle's internal edge. Except for these blades, the whole tool was made of wood. Only in the Graeco-Roman period were the sharp flint teeth supplanted by steel blades. The angle of the graceful Egyptian sickle also changed over time, as examples found in archaeological digs demonstrate.
Reaping scenes show that the farmers armed with sickles cut the spikes of grain, letting them fall on the ground, while women followed and collected them into bundles.
These bundles were then placed on great stacks, where they stayed until they were moved to the threshing area.

VARIANTS/COMBINATIONS

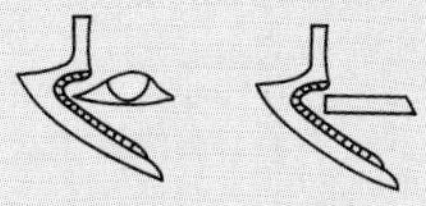

The sickle with the eye as determinative for *m3*, to see."
The sickle with the sign *m3*ʿ, in *m3*ʿ, "right, in agreement."

Axe in a Block of Wood

D ***eterminative in* stp, *"cut into pieces," whence the use as ideogram in* stp, *"choose, choice."***

The Egyptian axe was structurally quite similar to the hoe, with the blade more or less at right angles to the handle and tied to it by leather thongs.
In effect, both exercised a downward percussive action followed immediately by a backwards traction. This may have influenced the specialized adaptation of the primitive hoe form to carpentry uses. Carpenters used the axe to cut and shape rough boards, since the plane was not yet known in ancient Egypt.
From the woodworkers' language, the verb *stp* soon acquired another technical meaning when it was adopted by the butchers of sacrifical animals. Here it designates the dismembering of a bull or other animal that has had its throat cut. It was especially associated with the operation of cutting off the foreleg, which was the best and therefore most desired for sacrifice.

Knife

Determinative in* ds, *"knife"; in all terms that designate something sharp and in verbs of cutting.

There is a broad range of hieroglyphs showing the various types of Egyptian knives, from the ancient obsidian blades (like *ds*) to the metal types (more recent, but nonetheless known as far back as the First Dynasty) to the knives called *dw* made of cane (these were mostly for medicinal use: the knife used to evirate Bata, the protagonist in the *Tale of Two Brothers*, was of cane).
The name *ds* probably derives from the material used to make the first knives of that form: *ds* is in fact the designation of obsidian, the shiny black volcanic stone that the Egyptians imported as early as the predynastic periods: perhaps from the island of Melos in the Aegean, or perhaps from Anatolia or Abyssinia.
Herodotus speaks of it as the "sharp Ethiopian stone," the instrument that the Egyptian embalmers used on the corpses.

Chisel

Phonogram for* mr *and* 3b, *for unknown reasons in both cases.

This hieroglyph represents a chisel or a punch. In the canonic version of the sign, which appears after the Old Kingdom, the point is long and thin. Older variants show a handle which is quite broad and bell-shaped, with a small point.
The tool was used for various tasks. Carpenters used it to cut or carve wood; sculptors used it when the stone (like limestone) was soft enough to allow it; goldsmiths, metalworkers, and the carvers of semi-precious stone also used the chisel.
Often the tool was used in tandem with a broad-headed mallet, with which it was hammered. The point was generally of metal; first of copper, then bronze, and finally iron, founded in ceramic molds and beaten while hot.
The supervisors of the work gangs in the Valley of the Kings, the royal necropolis of the New Kingdom, were in the habit of weighing the chisels before giving them to the workers and again at the end of the day's work, so as to be sure that not even a gram of the precious metal had been subtracted for personal use.

Drill

Ideogram in* ḥmt*, name of the tool, as well as the term for "art," "artisan," and connected words.

This hieroglyph represents the hand drill used by stone workers. This type of drill was used essentially for making vases of semi-precious stone. It consisted of a wooden vertical part fixed in a sleeve, ending in a two-toothed fork. In the hieroglyph the fork is often crossed by a bar. The upper part of the tool was surmounted by an off-center handle that worked like a crank. The two round projections, which are quite visible in the older and less stylized variants, are weights—stones or sacks of sand—tied with strong cords, which gave heft to the instrument and helped to maintain even pressure and regulate the rotation speed.

At first glance, the fork and its bar at the bottom seem puzzling. The whole tool cannot be understood unless another piece is hypothesized: the cylindrical piece that did the perforating. Its existence cannot be deduced from the hieroglyph, but is documented in the concrete traces of its use in many monuments, up to the protodynastic era. A scene of stoneworking from the solar temple of Abusir (Fifth Dynasty) seems to show the instrument complete with its cylinder. The fork with its little bar was a sort of joint, whose purpose was to transmit the combined turning force of man and weights to the drilling cylinder.

With the foundation of the pharaonic civilization, the language of power chose carved semi-precious stone as its tangible manifestation. From then on, the craft became an art par excellence.

Making a stone vase with the drill. Bas relief from the temple of Sahura at Abusir, Fifth Dynasty

VARIANTS/COMBINATIONS

Form of the sign in the Old Kingdom.

Scale

I ***deogram or determinative in mḫ3t, "scale."***

T his eloquent hieroglyph illustrates the typical standing scale used in ancient Egypt. It consisted of a tall stand, with a base that permitted it to remain upright, and a horizontal yoke from which the plates were hung by cords. A plumbline attached to the top of the upright assured correct positioning. Scales of this sort must have been rare and restricted to use in government warehouses or to the temples and their laboratories.

Temple scenes almost always show the scales in scenes portraying gold being weighed, or in the spiritual "weighing of the soul." It was imagined that this weighing occurred in the otherworld before a divine tribunal, in order to establish the degree of lightness (that is, purity) of the heart of the deceased. The heart, placed on one of the plates, needed to be equal in weight to a feather symbolizing truth and justice, placed on the other plate.

Lighter and more manageable scales appear in scenes from tombs and have been found in archaeological digs. These too had double arms: lever scales with one arm did not come into use before the Roman era. In the Museum at Turin there is an elegant wooden case in which the architect Kha kept his scales; unfortunately it was found empty in his tomb. Until two other cases were found with the scales intact inside, the function of Kha's case and others like it had been a puzzle. It seems that scales were used in Egypt before 3,600 B.C., as the discovery of sample weights for gold in a tomb of this era shows. In any case, the oldest piece of a scale found in Egypt dates from the second half of the fourth millennium.

A goldsmith weighs gold ingots in one of the royal laboratories. Thebes, El Khokha, tomb of Nebamon and Ipuky (TT 181), Eighteenth Dynasty.

Sled

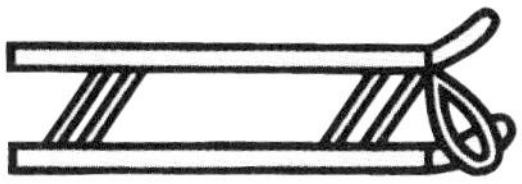

***Ideogram in* tmt, *"sled," whence its use as the phonogram* tm,**

Without the simple and ingenious tool shown in the hieroglyph *tm*, the construction of the pyramids would certainly have been more difficult.
In an era in which the wheel was not yet in use, the Egyptians exploited the natural characteristics of the desert in order to transport loads, even heavy ones. The two runners of the sled were connected by crossbars and curved upwards to reduce drag. Pulled by men or oxen, they slipped over the sand easily.
The large, heavy blocks of stone used to construct the pyramids were transported in this way. In addition, the system was commonly used to carry sarcophagi, statues, or sacred boats, like that of the god Sokar, whose sled remains part of his iconography.

Sled with Jackal Bust

Determinative in* wnš, *"sled with a jackal's head." Ideogram or determinative in* bỉ3, *"mineral, metal," "rare, marvelous object."

This special sled, decorated on the front with a jackal's head, was called *wnš*, the jackal-sled (from the Egyptian name for the jackal or similar canines). For motives not known to us, it was connected to the word family *bỉ3*, designating metal, and thereby connoted strange and marvelous things. The sled may have been used by the ancient desert explorers who searched for mines. It has been speculated that the block drawn on the sled in the related hieroglyph represents a load of metal.
Inscriptions in mines and quarries show that in fact the sled was widely used in quarries, evidently the most suitable mode of transport.
The jackal's bust is still unexplained. As a desert animal, it may have represented a protective deity for mines and miners.

Float, Small Plane

Ideogram in ḳd, "construct," and in connected words, whence its use as phonogram.

For many years the object pictured in this hieroglyph was not identifiable, even though the use of *ḳd* as ideogram in the verb "construct" suggested a connection with building. The discovery of some samples of a tool quite similar to that shown in the grapheme clarified its nature: it is a small plane, the kind of tool used today by housepainters to level and smooth fresh plaster. In ancient Egypt it must have had an important role: most urban and rural construction was of sun-dried mud covered by plaster, and the foundation for wall paintings in houses and in tombs was a plaster of mud and straw. In tombs that were cut in the rock, where the poor stone was unsuitable for the carving of reliefs and the expensive blocks of smoothed stone were unavailable, many layers of plaster provided a uniform, smooth base for the painters' traditional works.

Device for Making Fire

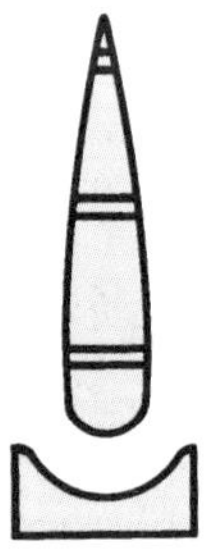

Ideogram in ḏ3, name of the tool; whence its use as phonogram.

This hieroglyph represents an ancient device for producing fire. As a grapheme, it certainly belongs to the oldest strata of the formation of script. The mechanism it illustrates is rather elementary and crude, composed of only two elements—a stick narrowed at the ends and a block. Holding the stick perpendicular to the block and turning it rapidly between the hands would create enough friction between the point and the block to make sparks, which would light straw or other flammable materials placed nearby.
In the Middle Kingdom, however, and perhaps even earlier, the device had been perfected, and became more complex. Examples from this era show the presence of a cap of stone or half of a doom palm nut adapted to the top of the stick, or a bow, both of which allowed the stick to be turned with greater speed.
The block was often covered with resin or tar to increase friction. A simple but essential tool, it followed even the young Pharaoh Tutankhamen into the tomb.

Potter's Kiln

***Ideogram in* t3, *"oven," whence its use as phonogram* t3.**

In the making of pots, the firing is the most crucial and delicate phase. Guaranteeing a correct and constant temperature was no small problem for the ancient potters, and yet much of the quality and durability of the product depended on it. From the very earliest times the Egyptians were successful in resolving this vital problem in a satisfactory way, making terracotta pots of great beauty and fine quality. The oldest identifiable kiln has been found at Hierakonpolis and dates from 3,650 B.C. However, the hieroglyph *t3* does not seem to depict one of these open-air uncovered structures, but rather the kiln that was typical of the Old Kingdom, as represented in the mastaba of Ti at Saqqara (Fifth Dynasty). It is a tall biconic structure, apparently with some kind of drop cover (which the man in front of it is shown lifting with one hand, as he protects his face from the heat with the other). It has been plausibly suggested that this was an expedient used to increase the draught and enliven the fire. The top of this kiln, just like the one shown in the hieroglyph, was covered, presumably with clay or potsherds. The cover was temporary rather than permanent, and was removable after every firing. This type of kiln had two internal spaces, one above the other: the pots to be fired were placed in the upper chamber, while the fire was lit in the lower. A partition with holes separated the two chambers.

Throwing and firing pots. Thebes, Sheikh Abd el-Qurna, tomb of Kenamon (TT 93), Eighteenth Dynasty.

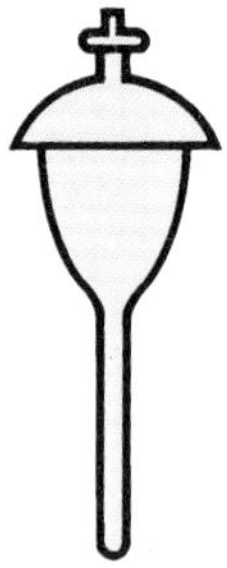

Spindle

Ideogram or determinative in* ḫsf, *"spindle," "spin"; phonogram in the verb* ḫsf, *"to turn away."

The ancient Egyptian spindle was a tapered stick ending in a disk or hemisphere of wood or stone, which functioned as the fly-wheel. The art of weaving has an extensive history in Egypt; fragments of linen fabric have been found in the Fayum in strata dating to about 5,000 B.C. From a millennium earlier there is a decorated plate, found in the tomb of a woman at Badari, which illustrates a horizontal loom with the warp threads strung. The tomb scenes are rich in details of the various techniques used, and archaeologists have found wooden models of cloth workshops that would delight modern children.

Depending on how the spindle was used, the thread could be more or less fine and even. The fibers could be twisted by holding them between the hands and letting the spindle turn on a thigh, or by turning the spindle between one's hands and running the thread from a support. The most refined technique, apt to produce threads of the highest quality, was running the fibers through a ring cut in the center of a terracotta vase, winding them around a hanging spindle which was kept in constant rotation thanks to the fly-wheel. Apparently these vases contained water to keep the fiber damp, increasing the quality of the thread. Spindles and vases of this type have been found in numerous sites, clarifying the splendid tomb scenes of the Middle Kingdom. The hanks of thread thus obtained were then woven on a horizontal loom (fixed to the ground by four sticks). Tomb scenes from the New Kingdom show the adoption of a vertical loom, which was better for creating decorated fabrics. But as far as clothing is concerned, the Egyptians' real passion was for simple white linen, often pleated or ruffled.

Wooden spindles from Deir el-Medina, New Kingdom. Turin, Egyptian Museum.

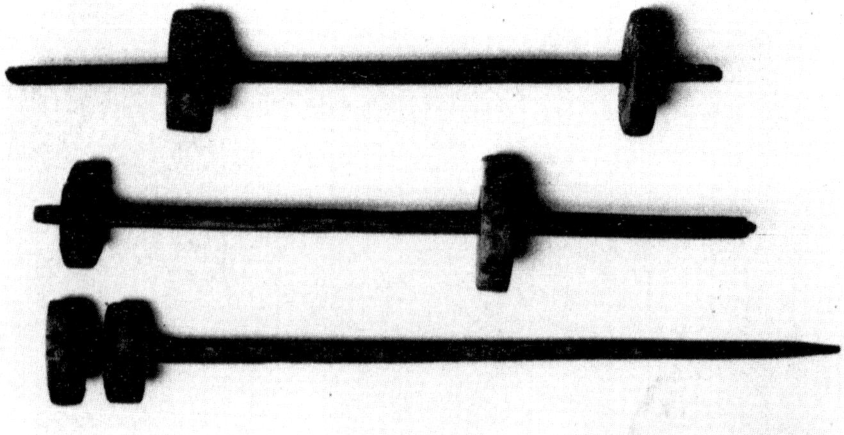

Papyrus

Ideogram in **md3t**, ***"roll of papyrus"; determinative in terms connected to writing or abstract concepts.***

In a culture as writing-conscious as that of ancient Egypt, thought and writing were identified to such a degree that a knotted and sealed roll of papyrus came to designate the notion of abstractness. Still, the first known hieroglyphs had been entrusted to other mediums: amphoras of terracotta, stelae of stone, palettes of ivory and bone, seals. Perhaps papyrus was in use simultaneously with those other ancient writing mediums, or perhaps hieroglyphic was not conceived for use on papyrus. The first examples of written papyrus are not older than the Fourth Dynasty. Once it was discovered that strips of fiber from the trunk of *Cyperus papyrus* L. could be dried, superimposed, and pressed together to create a flexible and resistant sheet, the bureaucratic minds of the Egyptians could not resist the tremendous temptation that this presented. Thousands and thousands of these pale yellowish sheets, glued into long rollable strips, were filled with the fluid cursive of the administration or by the more ornate hieratic of the literary script. The few remaining fragments of the thousand papyri from the Abusir archive (Fifth Dynasty), which recorded the economic activity of the temple over an eighty-year period, make us dizzyingly aware of the mountains of administrative documentation that must have been lost. But not only numbers and ration counts filled the

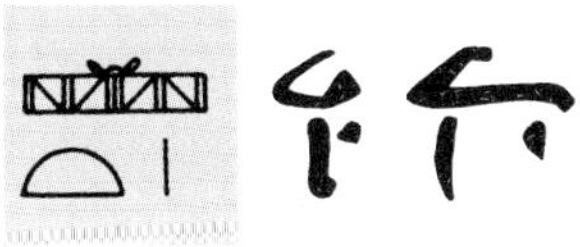

fragile sheets which have survived these millennia: there are also letters from husbands tormented by the ghosts of dead wives, stories of inheritances and contestations of wills, patient exercises by not always diligent students, obscure religious texts, satiric or erotic passages, and finally, the remains of an eclectic and often surprising literature, whose partial loss is to be much regretted.

The Chester Beatty I Papyrus with the tale of the dispute between the god Horus and Seth, still rolled, end of Twentieth Dynasty.

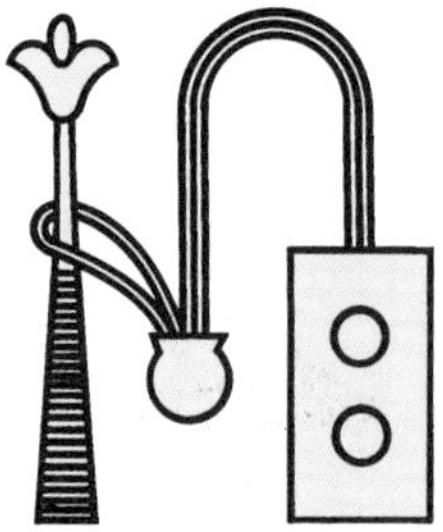

Scribe's Palette

Ideogram or determinative in* sš, *"to write," "scribe," and connected words; and in* mnhd, *name of the scribe's equipment.

The equipment of the Egyptian scribe is synthesized in the hieroglyph that espressed the act of writing and designated the scribe and the object of his technique, the written document, as well. The sign represents the scribe's palette, generally of wood, with two carved depressions for ink (black and red, the two canonic colors used in texts), and a brush holder made of cane from which the unraveled point of the cane brush emerges. The scribes habitually chewed the end of the brush to soften it and obtain the fringed, filamented point needed for drawing fluid cursive signs on the papyrus. The kit was completed with a bag containing the pigments necessary to the ink's preparation: black made from carbon black, red from natural ochre, both mixed with water and gum.

In the hieroglyph the three elements are represented separately, tied together by a leather thong. In fact, however, the brushes and palette were united in a single piece—a palette with a brush chamber and a sliding cover, numerous examples of which, from different ages, are held in museums around the world.

The equipment of a good scribe also contained small stone bowls in which to pound and mix the pigments, at least one container of water to dip the brush into, and the tools needed to make papyrus or at least cut the sheets. With a greater number of small basins for colored inks, the palette was useful to the painter as well.

Since cursive writing ran from right to left, writing technique required that the scribe hold his hand off the page, like a painter; if in fact he had touched the page, it would have smeared. Using this system, a scribe could write about a dozen signs before having to dip his brush into the ink again.

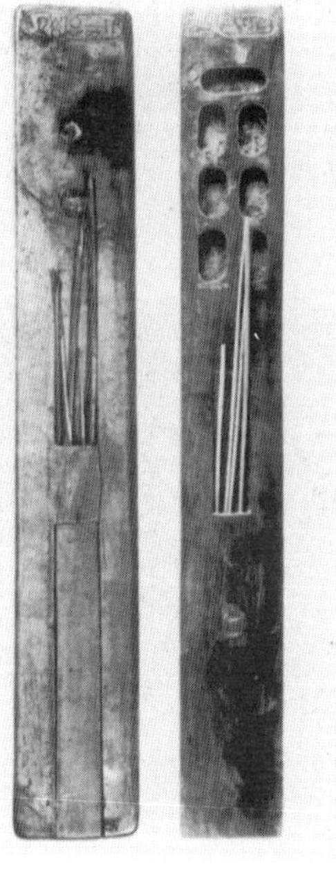

Left: *A scribe or painter's palette, probably from Thebes, New Kingdom. Paris, Louvre Museum .*

Far left: *Detail of the high functionary Hesire with his scribe's equipment on one shoulder. From his tomb at Saqqara, Third Dynasty. Cairo, Egyptian Museum.*

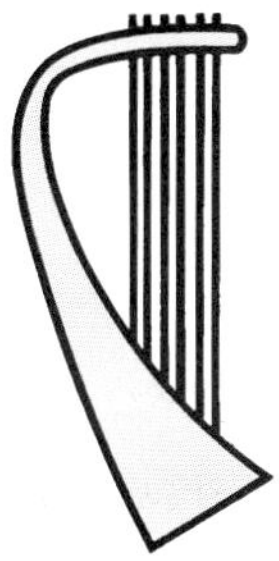

Harp

D ***eterminative in* bìnt,** *"harp"*

The harp, widely represented in Egyptian painting and known to us through numerous examples found in excavations, was ancient Egypt's favorite musical instrument. Diverse types are known, all of them vertical, with the sound box sitting on the ground and a long curved handle. Strings were attached to the handle with pegs—seven in the Old Kingdom, and up to eleven or twelve in the New Kingdom. The hieroglyph, in the common variant shown here, indicates only three strings: it may be an intentional stylization. Alternatively, it may portray a type that was relatively common in the New Kingdom, the so-called "shoulder harp," similar in form but fairly light, and manageable enough to be held on the player's shoulder. The harp made its first appearance during the Old Kingdom. It was made from a single piece of wood, often precious. It was a valuable instrument, and frequently texts speak of harps inlaid with gold and silver that were part of a temple's treasure. Up until the New Kingdom the social status of musicians, men or women, was rather high; it seems that there were real dynasties of musicians which transmitted the valued talent from father to son. Music was omnipresent and much loved in ancient Egypt; of all the ancient civilizations, the Egyptian has given us the greatest wealth of documentation of its role and its importance in daily and religious life. Strangely enough, this people that was so obsessed with writing did not elaborate a system of musical notation (as the Babylonians did). However, by studying the instruments and making models of them, Egyptologists and musicologists have succeeded in gaining some idea of this ancient music which charmed Greek visitors to Egypt, impressing with the serenity and harmony of their melodies.

It seems that many instruments of modern Africa, like a part of the folk music of modern Egypt, derive from that of ancient Egypt. Almost all modern musical instruments have ancestors in ancient Egypt: the lute, lyre, and harp for stringed instruments; the flute, oboe, clarinet, and trumpet for the winds; and drums, tambourines, and castanets for percussion.

Left: *A blind harpist. Saqqara, tomb of Paatonemheb, Eighteenth Dynasty. Leiden, Rijksmuseum van Oudheden.*

Far left: *Mereruka's wife plays the harp for him on a bed. Tomb of Mereruka at Saqqara, Reign of Teti.*

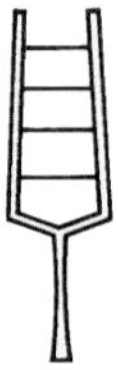

Main mast
Ideogram in *ʿḥʿ*, "mast," and connected terms (like *ʿḥʿ*, "stand erect").

Oar
Determinative in *wsr*, "oar." Phonogram *ẖrw*.

Rudder
Determinative in *ḥmw*, "rudder," and connected words.

Mooring post
Determinative in *mnỉt*, "mooring post," and connected words.

Axe
Determinative in *mibt*, *minb*, "axe." Ideogram in *mḏḥw*, "carpenter."

Dagger
Determinative in *mtpnt*. Ideogram in *tp*, perhaps the archaic name.

Arrow
Determinative in the names for arrow (*ʿḥ3*, *šsr*) and connected terms. Phonetic value *swn*.

Bowstring
Ideogram or determinative in *rwḏ*, "bowstring," and connected words.

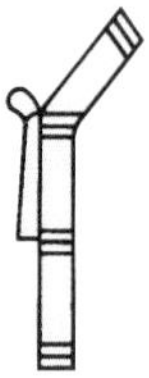

Part of the archer's equipment
Possibly a quiver. Phonogram *rs*.

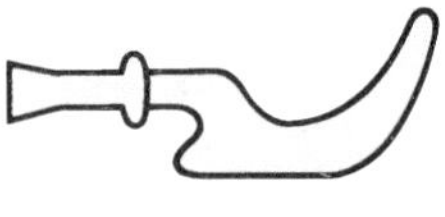

Scimitar
Determinative in *ḫpš*, "scimitar."

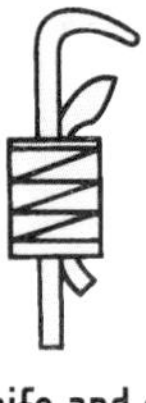

Staff with knife and other tools tied to it
Ideogram in *šms*, "follow," perhaps from the term designating the attendant.

Double-barbed arrowhead
Ideogram in *snw*, "two," and connected words.

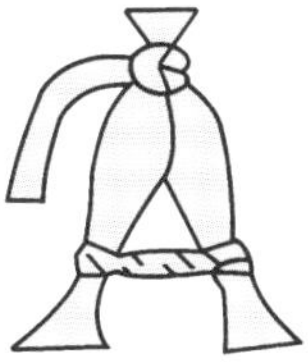

Float
Ideogram in *ḏb3* and connected words.

Butcher's block
Ideogram in *ẖr*, "that which is underneath."

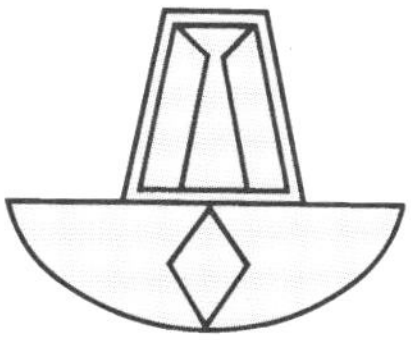

Block on a basin
In *ẖry-ḥbt*, "he who carries the book of the festival." Title of the lector-priest, ritualist.

Honing stone
Ideogram in *sšm*, "butcher."

Butcher's knife
Phonogram *nm*.

Pick
Ideogram or determinative in *grg*, "break through," and connected words.

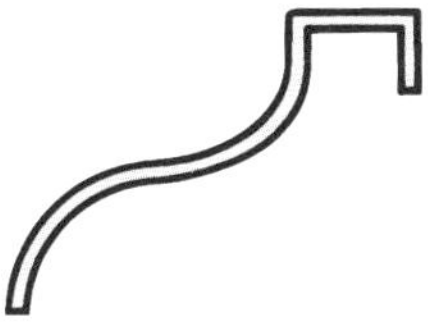

Hatchet
Ideogram or determinative in *nwt*, "hatchet." Phonogram *nw*.

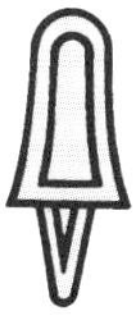

Chisel/scalpel
Determinative in *mnḫ*, "cut, give shape." Ideogram in *mnḫ*, "to be excellent."

Drill for pearls
Ideogram or determinative in *wb3*, "open, penetrate."

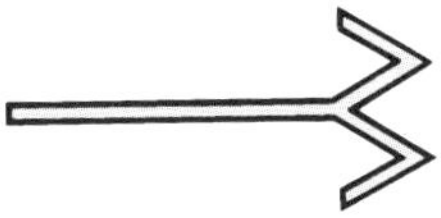

Tool for putting bread in the oven
Ideogram or determinative in *rtḥty*, "baker of bread," and connected words. Ideogram or determinative in *ẖnr*, "to be closed in, imprisoned," and connected words.

Washer's stick
Ideogram in *ḥmw*, "washer," and *ḥm*, "slave." Phonogram *ḥm*.

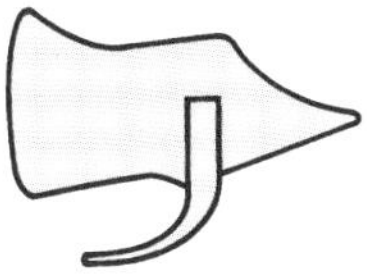

Razor
Determinative in *ẖ'ḳ*, "to shave."

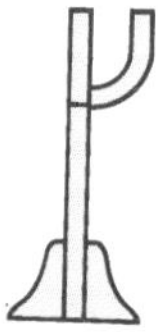

Stand for scales
Determinative in *wṯst*, name of this part of the scale and connected words (such as *wṯs*, "lift").

Rope for cattle
Phonogram *ṯ*.

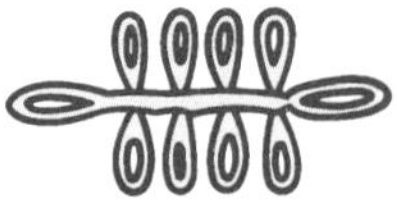

Fetter
Ideogram in *s3*, "fetter."

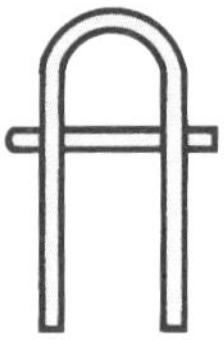

Fetter
Ideogram or determinative in *mḏt*, "stall"; *tm3*, "rush mat"

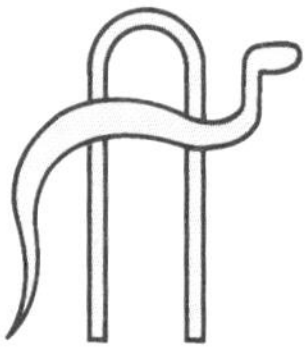

Fetter with cobra
Combination of the fetter sign with the phonogram *ḏ*, with phonetic value *mḏt*.

Lifesaver
Ideogram in *s3*, "protection."

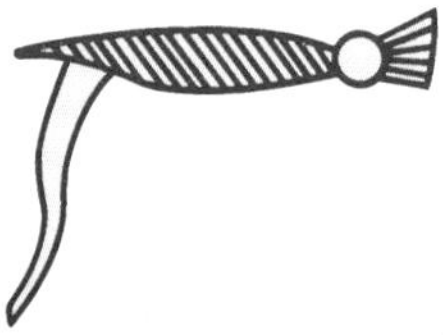

Whip
Phonogram *mḥ*.

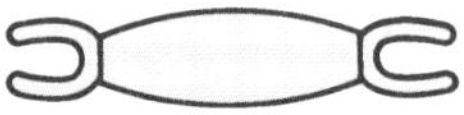

Weaver's shuttle
Ideogram in *ʿḏ*, "shuttle."
Phonogram *ʿnḏ*.

Fish trap
Determinative in *msnw*, "harpooner." Ideogram or determinative in *g3w*, "bundles, groups of vegetation tied together."

Part of the rudder
Ideogram or determinative in *ḥpt*, "rudder."

Cover
Phonogram *s3*.

Cover
More recent variant of the former.

Glossary

Animation (Ritual of) A group of rituals whose end was to give life to inanimate things, whether these were cult or funerary statues, or a mummified cadaver. They were carried out by the lector-priests and were comprised of various phases, of which the "Opening of the Mouth" was essential. (See "Statue of a Nobleman.")

ba Improperly translated as "soul," the Egyptian term *ba* designated one of the aspects of the personality which belonged to both men and the gods. For the gods, it was associated with the idea of power and could manifest itself in many ways (for example, the Apis bull at Memphis was called the ba of Ptah). For men, it was rather a personification of the vital energies, physical and psychic, which with appropriate rituals would permit another mode of existence for the deceased in the afterworld (See "Bird-*ba*.")

Book of the Dead A collection of formulas, generally written on papyrus and placed beside the dead in the tomb. The various chapters of which it is composed (about two hundred) derive from the formulas in the *Coffin Texts* and *Pyramid Texts* but had a complete, though variable, edition beginning in the New Kingdom. Their use is documented up to the Graeco-Roman era.

cartonnage This name designates the materials with which many mummies are covered. It is composed of many layers of fabric—mostly linen or pressed papyrus—glued together and covered with plaster.

coffin texts Collections of formulas and charms inscribed on the insides of sarcophagi in the Middle Kingdom, intended to help the deceased in his voyage to the afterworld. They derived from the formulas of the *Pyramid Texts*, broadening them, however, for private use.

cosmogonies Various versions of the creation story were developed in the more important centers of ancient Egypt. Three are most common and important: the Heliopolitan cosmogony, which considered Atum the creator, and thought that the first pair of cosmic elements were the fruit of his masturbation or spitting; the Memphite version, which attributed Ptah with the role of demiurge and considered the "heart" and the "tongue" to be the instruments of creation; and lastly, the Hermopolis version, which asserted an aquatic chaos from which four couples of primordial beings emerged (the males in frog form, the females in serpent form), together making the Egg from which the cosmos was born. (See Ogdoade.)

cuneiform Mesopotamian writing with letters composed of small hooked marks, made by pressing a stylus into a tablet of clay. Used to write many languages in the ancient Near East, this technique was very common in the second millennium B.C., as it was tied to the diffusion of Accadic, which was the diplomatic language of the period. Cuneiform tablets have also found in Egypt at Tell el-Amarna.

Ennead A group of nine gods. The number nine in Egyptian was indicative of a plurality of pluralities: the number three was the generic designation of multiplicity and nine (three times three) emphasizes that aspect. Of the various Enneads present in the greater cult centers, the one at Heliopolis was the most famous: it was composed of the demiurge Ra-Atum and Shu, Tefnut, Geb, Nut, Osiris, Isis, Seth, and Nephthys.

flood A regular phenomenon that affected the Nile Valley, caused by the summer monsoon rains on the Ethiopian highlands. The increase of water in the Nile's tributaries caused the river to flood. The inundation lasted from July to October, and covered the flood plain. Controls allowed the water to be evenly distributed, satisfying agricultural needs. Floods no longer occur today because a broad system of dams and dikes has been constructed, the most imposing of which is the Great Dam at Aswan.

guides to the afterworld These were texts illustrated by images intended to guide the dead—originally the king—through the insidious geography of the afterworld, describing the passage of the Sun God in the nocturnal regions. They covered the walls of royal tombs from the New Kingdom, though preliminary forms of the guides appear on sarcophagi from the second millennium. Only in the late period did common people appropriate these guides and use them to decorate their own tombs. Egyptologists have diverse names for the various known texts: *Book of That Which is in the Afterworld, Book of Gates, Book of Caverns,* and *Book of Day and Night.* (See "The Otherworld.")

Horapollon The author (about whom nothing is known) of a treatise on hieroglyphs which was probably composed in the late Roman era. The first copy of the work, brought to Italy from Greece in 1422, indicates that Horapollon was born in the Egyptian city of Nilopoli. It affirms that the text was "written in the Egyptian tongue," and was then "translated into the Greek tongue" by a certain Philip. The treatise is a good example of the allegorical interpretation of hieroglyphs.

Hyksos The name of groups of people (probably Canaanite) who settled in the Egyptian Delta during the First Intermediate Period, near what is now called Tell el-Dab'a (ancient Avaris). The name derives from the Greek form of the Egyptian words meaning "sovereign of foreign lands." Towards 1640 B.C. they became powerful and united. Thus dominating most of Egypt, they created the Fifteenth and Sixteenth Dynasties, according to Manetho's division of Egyptian history.

ithyphallic The erect penis (from the Greek) is a characteristic attribute of male gods associated with fertility—principally Min, but also Amon at Luxor, and Osiris in his role as a resurrected god.

ka Like the *ba,* the word designates an aspect of personality. It is a vital force which belongs to both men and the gods, and can be transmitted from father to son or from god to man. Probably it was originally related to sexual potency and fertility. At first considered a sort of "double" of the person, it became an independent entity after death. Thanks to funeral offerings, the *ka* guaranteed the survival of the deceased. (See "Arms.")

Manetho Priest of Heliopolis, he was given the task of writing a history of Egypt by Ptolemy II Philadelphus in the third century B.C. Only a few passages of it are extant, incorporated in later works. The traditional division of Egyptian history into dynasties is based on his work and is still used, with slight modifications, by Egyptologists today.

mastaba The name (derived from the Arab "bench") designates a type of tomb which was not cut in the rock, common in the protodynastic era and in the Old Kingdom. The upper part of the structure, which covered the entrance to the subterranean funerary chamber, was usually rectangular, with a flat roof and rough, slightly inclined, brick walls. Many splendid scenes of daily life come from the internal decorations of these mastaba.

mummification Method of artificially conserving the bodies of dead animals and people, documented in various civilizations, but developed with particular refinement and precision by the ancient Egyptians. Probably already conceived of as early as the protodynastic era, it reached its apex at the end of the New Kingdom. The method perfected in this period required, among other operations, dehydrating of the body by means of natron, removing the internal organs, and filling the body with aromatic resins and natron. The body was then tightly bound in cloth.

Nine Bows Thus the Egyptians called the nine traditional enemies of their land (using the metaphoric sense of the most powerful weapon to indicate "enemy"). The list of the nine peoples, which was accompanied by the respective images and decorated the bases of statues, thrones, and sandals, was made in quite ancient times, when those populaces which were later admitted into the Egyptian political entity were still considered hostile. The usual Egyptian tendency to conservatism continued to use the term with little modification over millennia.

nomos A Greek term for an ancient Egyptian administrative division; the Egyptian term was *sepat.* The number and distribution of the various names of these divisions, probably existing even in the predynastic era, changed over time, reaching its final arrangement only in Ptolemaic times.

Ogdoade Group of eight gods. In ancient Egypt it was tied to the cosmogony developed in the cult center of Hermopolis, in Middle Egypt. Here it represented the four male (frog) and female (serpent) couples, symbolizing matter as yet unmodelled by creation: Nun and Naunet, the primordial waters; Huh and Hauhet, unlimited space; Kuk and Kauket, darkness; Amon and Amaunet, that which is hidden. (See also "cosmogonies.")

oracle A god's answer to a mortal's question about unknown events in the present, past, or future, or about the correct manner of acting in a given circumstance. In Egypt, starting with the New Kingdom, it became common for the movement of sacred boats in the course of a procession to be interpreted as oracles. A particular development in the Late Period was the technique of "oracular letters," in which two small sheets of papyrus with requests written on them were placed in an urn and then extracted, probably by one of the priests of the god to whom the request was made.

ostrakon A fragment of a vase or a limestone chip used to write on the vase (from the Greek for "pottery"). Used as an everyday writing material, these shards were a poor cousin to papyrus, which was restricted to official and "good copy" use. Ostraka (the plural of "ostrakon") have provided a wealth of documentation—including accounts, letters, exercises, drawings, and sketches—mostly in hieratic and demotic script.

pyramid texts A miscellany of texts of various types (including extracts of rituals, charms, and spells) inscribed for the exclusive benefit of the king on the walls of his burial chamber inside the pyramid, beginning in the Fifth Dynasty.

The custom continued until the Eighth Dynasty, after which the texts were partially reworked and passed also into private use. They became part of the collections of funerary formulas known as the *Coffin Texts* and *The Book of the Dead*.

royal jubilee (*sed*-festival) A very ancient ceremony of the regeneration of the king, usually celebrated every thirty years (although jubilees could come at lesser intervals after the initial one). It was central to the protodyanstic royal cult, and thereafter maintained great importance. It is a frequent theme in temple decoration, especially in funerary temples. (See "festival pavilion.")

royal protocol The complete name of a king was made up of five principal names. The first three, which were the oldest, referred to the king as manifestation of a god (the name of Horus; the name of the Two Ladies; and the golden name of Horus). The fourth and fifth names were written inside the name-ring called a cartouche: the first, known as the *nesut-biti*, qualified the king's relation to the sun god Ra; the second, introduced by the appellative "son of Ra," corresponded to the name received at birth.

serekh The Egyptian name given to the conventional reproduction of the brick façade of a predynastic palace or wall, closed in a rectangle and surmounted by the head of the falcon Horus. On the inside was inscribed the Pharaoh's "name of Horus." (See "Horus," "palace," and "walled rectangular settlement.")

syncretism Association of one or more gods to another god (generally a more important one), whose name and character they assume in addition to their own identity. The most frequent association was with the sun god Ra, given his universal characteristics and the importance of his religion. Syncretism was a powerful instrument in the hands of Egyptian theologians, who used it to limit local cults and unify the state religion.

solar cycle The sun's revolution around the Earth was the origin of much of Egypt's theology. They associated the sun's course through the sky with man's destiny: morning/infancy; midday/maturity; afternoon/old age; night/death and regeneration). The continual rebirth of the sun at each new dawn was focus of the Egyptian faith in life after death. In myth, the astronomical aspect of the circumnavigation was visualized as the sun's birth at dawn from the womb of the celestial Mother Nut; at sunset it was swallowed by the same mother. Sun and stars traveled through her body during the night. (See "Ra," "sky," "sun," "star," and "otherworld.")

temple Building or complex of buildings dedicated to religion, around which much of the Egyptian economy gravitated. Besides the temples for the daily cults of the gods, there were also the important temples dedicated to the funeral cults of the sovereigns. The temples, even though marked by functionality, were constructed according to a precise symbolism which saw them as microcosms of the universe.

vizier The highest administrative functionary, second only to Pharaoh. The post existed even in protodynastic times and, with varying importance, lasted until the Late Period. In the New Kingdom, the position was divided, creating an office in Memphis for the administration of northern Egypt and another in Thebes for southern Egypt.

Bibliography

Arnett, W. S. *The Predynastic Origin of Egyptian Hieroglyphs*. Washington, 1982.

Caminos, R., and H. G. Fischer *Ancient Egyptian Epigraphy and Paleography*. New York, 1976.

Cenival. J.-L. *La naissance de l'écriture*, catalogue Paris: Galeries nationales du Grand Palais, May–Aug. 1982: 61-62.

Davies N. M. *Picture Writing in Ancient Egypt*. London, 1958.

Davies, W. V. *Egyptian Hieroglyphs*. London-Berkeley, 1987.

Fischer, H. G. *Ancient Egyptian Calligraphy*. New York: The Metropolitan Museum of Art, 1979.

———. *Egyptian Studies I: Varia*. New York, 1976.

———. *Egyptian Studies II: The Orientation of Hieroglyphs*. New York, 1977.

———. "Hieroglyphen." *Lexikon der Ägyptologie II*. Wiesbaden, 1977: 1189-90.

Gardiner, A. H. *Egyptian Grammar*, 3rd revised edition. London, 1969.

Griffith, F. Le. *A Collection of Hieroglyphs: A Contribution to the History of Egyptian Writing*. London, 1898.

Iversen, E. *Papyrus Carlsberg Nr. VII. Fragments of a Hieroglyphic Dictionary*. Kobenhavn, 1958.

Kaplony, P. *Die Inschriften der ägyptischen Frühzeit*, vol. 3. Wiesbaden, 1963.

———. "Die Prinzipien der Hieroglyphernschrift." *Textes et Languages de l'Egypte pharaonique I*, Cairo, 1972: 3-4

———. *Kleine Beiträge zu den Inschriften der ägyptischen Frühzeit*. Wiesbaden, 1966.

———. "Strukturprobleme der Hieroglyphenschrift." *Chronique d'Egypte* 41. 1966: 60-99.

Kees, H. et al. *Ägyptische Schrift und Sprache*. Leiden, 1973.

Petrie, W. M. F. *The Formation of the Alphabet*. London: Quaritch, 1912.

Ray, D. J. "The Emergence of Writing in Egypt," *World Archaeology* 17: 3. 1986: 307-16.

Scharff, A. "Archäologische Beiträge zur Frage der Entstehung der Hieroglyphenschrift," *Sitzungsberichte der bayerischen Akademie der Wissenschaften, Phil.-Hist. Abteilung*. Munich, 1942.

Schenkel, W. "Schrift," *Lexicon der Ägyptologie V*. Wiesbaden, 1984: 713-35.

———. "Zur Struktur der Hieroglyphenschrift," *Mitteilungen des Deutschen Archäologischen Instituts, Abteilung Kairo* 27. 1971: 85-98.

———. "The Structure of Hieroglyphic Script," *Royal Anthropological News* 15. 1976: 4-7.

Schott, S. "Hieroglyphen," *Abhandlungen der Akademie der Wissenschaften und der Literatur in Mainz*. Wiesbaden, 1950.

Sethe, K. *Das hieroglyphische Schriftsystem*. Glückstadt-Hamburg, 1935.

———. *Vom Bilde zum Buchstaben. Die Entstehungsgeschichte der Schrift*. With an essay by Siegfrid Schott, "Untersuchungen zur Geschichte und Altertumskunde Ägyptens" 12, Leipzig-Berlin, 1939.

Quotes from ancient Egyptian literary texts are taken from E. Bresciani, *Letteratura e poesia dell'Antico Egitto*, 2nd ed., revised,Turin: Einaudi, 1990.

Index